# Mediated Ideologies

Nordic Views on the History of the Press and Media Cultures

Edited by

**Jukka Kortti**
University of Helsinki, Finland

**Heidi Kurvinen**
University of Turku, Finland

**Series in Critical Media Studies**

 VERNON PRESS

www.vernonpress.com

*In the Americas:*
Vernon Press
1000 N West Street, Suite 1200
Wilmington, Delaware, 19801
United States

*In the rest of the world:*
Vernon Press
C/Sancti Espiritu 17,
Malaga, 29006
Spain

Series in Critical Media Studies

Library of Congress Control Number: 2024930699

ISBN: 978-1-64889-851-8

Design by Vernon Press with resources from Freepik.

# Table of contents

# List of tables

# List of figures

# Introduction:
# Ideologies in Nordic media history

Jukka Kortti

*University of Helsinki, Finland*

Heidi Kurvinen

*University of Turku, Finland*

Ideologies interested communication scholars, especially in the 1970s and 1980s, but they have not been a focus of interest in the field of humanities and social sciences in recent decades. Such phenomena as ubiquitous capitalism—especially concerning the ideological formation of neoliberalism[1]—and the comeback of propaganda have, however, meant rethinking the power of ideologies in the media sphere. According to one of the most influential scholars in the field, Marxist structuralist Louis Althusser, media are one of the "ideological state apparatuses" and, according to cultural theoretician Stuart Hall, the mass media are crucial in producing, reproducing and molding ideologies, not just something that reflects them.[2] Both scholars were engaged with the Marxian tradition in which ideology was characterized as the ruling class's ideas, the hegemonic tool of class domination.[3]

Besides economics and politics, the importance of culture has become an essential component in the critiques of ideology in Western Marxism since the 1920s. Most importantly, the Frankfurt School developed the critical theory of ideology as they aimed to analyze how dominant ideologies served to maintain social structures and control individuals. Theodor Adorno and associates were particularly interested in understanding how ideology could perpetuate oppression and alienation. The media was a part of the "culture industry." The philosophers of the Frankfurt School argued that mass media, culture, and entertainment industries were producing standardized, mass-produced cultural

---

[1] See e.g., Jan Rehmann, *Theories of Ideology: The Powers of Alienation and Subjection* (Leiden: Brill, 2013), 271–300.
[2] Louis Althusser, *Positions, 1964–1975* (Paris: Éditions sociales, 1976; Stuart Hall, "Ideology and Communication Theory," in *Rethinking Communication. Volume 1: Paradigm Issues*, ed. Brenda Dervin (Newbury Park: Sage, 1989).
[3] Karl Marx, Friedrich Engels, *The German Ideology* (Moscow: Progress, 1976).

products that reinforced conformity and a passive, consumerist society. This analysis helped reveal how ideology could be propagated through popular culture.[4]

British cultural studies in particular adapted ideology studies as the central concept in their studies on culture and society, and particularly media.[5] According to cultural studies, mass media are important in shaping our perceptions of the world, interpreting things on our behalf, and helping us classify the world into different categories. Media discourse is often based on "common sense," and for this reason, it is very ideological in nature. For example, they present a capitalist society and its consumerist values as natural.[6]

Cultural studies also revitalized the ideas of hegemony introduced by Italian Marxist philosopher Antonio Gramsci in the 1940s. The concept of hegemony refers to the dominance or control that a ruling class or group exercises over a society. Ideology plays a crucial role in maintaining hegemony. In the same way as the media, hegemony is a continuous historical process that is constantly changing and is not static or systematic in its forms. The mass media also help to shape the dominant consensus in society at any given time.[7] Concerning the concept of hegemony, Hall emphasizes that it is wrong to assume that the media simply reflects the consensus prevailing in society. Instead, media institutions actually create consensus.[8]

In the forming of the *worldview* of an individual, ideology is located in its reflected, active dimension, namely in the first place *a philosophy of life*. In media, this is most apparent when individuals or a group of people establish a cultural periodical, or further their political agenda on different platforms of social media, for instance. However, *ideology* is different from a philosophy of life as it is always intended for several individuals, whereas a philosophy of life can also be understood on an individual level. On the other hand, media also operate on the "passive," subconscious side of a worldview, namely the *mentality*, when they present and represent ideologically loaded formations of

---

[4] See e.g., Andrew Edgar and Peter Sedgwick, eds. *Cultural Theory: The Key Concepts* (London and New York: Routledge, 2004), 150–55.

[5] Douglas Kellner, *Media Culture: Cultural Studies, Identity and Politics between the Modern and the Postmodern* (London and New York: Routledge, 1995), 57.

[6] Norman Fairclough, *Language and Power* (London and New York: Longman, 1989), 66–67.

[7] Chantal Mouffe, "Hegemony and Ideology in Gramsci," in *Culture, Ideology and Social Process: A Reader*, eds. Tony Bennet, Graham Martin, Colin Mercer and Janet Woollacott (London: The Open University Press, 1985), 219–34; Nick Stevenson, Understanding Media Cultures: Social Theory and Mass Communication (London: Sage, 1995), 17.

[8] Stuart Hall, "The rediscovery of 'Ideology': Return of the Repressed in Media Studies," in *Culture, Society and the Media*, 56–90, eds. Michael Gurevich, Tony Bennet, James Curran and Janet Woollacot (London: Methuen, 1982), 87.

everyday life as "natural." Signifying "hidden" encoded meanings through "common sense" makes ideologies powerful when represented in media, both through facts and fiction.[9]

Of all ideologies, democracy is perhaps the most intrinsically linked to media, "like a couple walking hand in hand."[10] One of the most influential accounts of democracy, Alexis de Tocqueville's *Democracy in America* (1835, 1840), saw democratic media systems as providing information to the public in order for people to make wise decisions. They did not simply function as a marketplace for ideas.[11] The definition of democracy depends on the perspective of the tradition from which it is viewed. *Liberalism* emphasizes the sovereignty of the individual, which guarantees freedom of choice. Other people or the community are not necessary for freedom to be achieved. *Republicanism*, on the other hand, emphasizes the sovereignty of the community, where equality between individuals means freedom and an opportunity to participate in public affairs and decision-making. Freedom is achieved according to the way in which the community finds a correct solution through *deliberation*, the interactive exchange of opinions seeking a reasonable consensus.[12] In Nordic media systems, the opportunity to participate in both the local and the national public sphere has been possible because of the early spread of literacy to the lower social groups and the Protestant religion. Protestantism facilitated questioning and the (rational) weighing of options.

Both the media and ideology are very much the creations of the modern age. The two centuries following the American (1776) and the French (1789) Revolutions have been called "the age of ideology." The rise of modern societies along with industrialization and class conflicts gave rise to many kinds of questions and problems to which new ideologies provided answers. Liberalism, socialism, nationalism, even conservatism are profoundly modern ideologies. Ideology as a general concept has been built on the idea of the transformation of society as a whole.[13] The "discourse of modernity" meant,

---

[9] Jukka Kortti, "Generations and Media History," in *Broadband Society and Generational Changes Series: Participation in Broadband Society – Volume 5*, eds. Leopoldina Fortunati and Fausto Colombo (Frankfurt am Main: Peter Lang, 2011), 69–93.
[10] Josef Trappel and Hannu Nieminen, "Media and Democracy: A Couple Walking Hand in Hand?" in *Comparative Media Policy, Regulation and Governance in Europe*, eds. Leen d'Haenens, Helena Sousa and Josef Trappel (Bristol: Intellect, 2018).
[11] John Nerone, *The Media and Public Life: A History* (Cambridge and Malden: Polity, 2015), 11.
[12] Clifford G. Christians, Theodore L. Glasser, Denis McQuail, Kaarle Nordenstreng and Robert A. White, *Normative Theories of the Media: Journalism in Democratic Societies* (Urbana and Chicago, IL: University of Illinois Press, 2009), 105–11.
[13] See e.g., John Schwarzmantel, *The Age of Ideology: Political Ideologies from the American Revolution to Post-Modern Times* (Basingstoke: Palgrave Macmillan, 1998).

besides the triumphal progress of the market economy, democracy, civil society, progress and emancipation.[14] Professional journalism played a central part in such changes when newspapers circulated national texts that inspired their readers with these new ideologies.[15]

The media and modernity have always lived in symbiosis. This was noted by Daniel Lerner's classic study on post-war societies in the Middle East: "No modern society functions efficiently without a developed system of mass media."[16] Or, as another influential book, John B. Thompson's *Media and Modernity* puts it: "Media play a crucial role in the cultural transformations associated with the rise of modern societies."[17] In this process, mass communication is particularly crucial in mediating "symbolic forms" of ideology in modern societies. This "mediated worldliness" also shapes people's experiences of their place in a given society and in the world at large.[18] Consequently, analyzing the role of different ideologies in media history provides wider perspectives in understanding past and present media landscapes and people's mediated experiences that are fostered by them. In this book, the role of media—comprising both popular media and news journalism—as a forum for ideologies and their circulation will be analyzed by focusing on the Nordic region

### Ideologies in news and popular media

Ideologies are an inherent part of modern communication, and they are actualized in various ways in everyday news work. On the one hand, the media can be used consciously to spread the ideological message to wider groups of people. A prominent example of this is the Nordic party press that consisted of journalists who often—but not always—shared the ideological premises of the

---

[14] Jürgen Habermas, *The Philosophical Discourse of Modernity: Twelve Lectures* (Cambridge: Polity Press, 1987).

[15] Hannu Salmi, Jukka Sarjala and Heli Rantala, "Embryonic Modernity: Infectious Dynamics in Early Nineteenth-Century Finnish Culture," *International Journal for History, Culture and Modernity* 8 (2020): 105–27.

[16] Daniel Lerner, *The Passing of Traditional Society: Modernizing the Middle East* (New York: The Free Press, 1958), 55.

[17] John B. Thompson, *The Media and Modernity: A Social Theory of the Media* (Cambridge: Polity Press, 1995), 190.

[18] John B. Thompson, *Ideology and Modern Culture: Critical Social Theory in the Era of Mass Communication* (Cambridge: Polity Press, 1990), 123; Thompson, *The Media and Modernity*, 33–5.

party in question.[19] A more current example is Russian state propaganda. Both news and social media have been used to spread the ideological understanding of the country's place in the world throughout the 2000s. Besides the Russian people, the target audience consists mainly of the former Soviet satellites but disinformation has also reached Global North countries, including the Nordic region.[20] On the other hand, by reporting on topics that are in the air in the wider societal discussion, such as contemporary social movements, all media outlets represent ideological dimensions of the public discussion to the media consumers. In this case, the journalists are more or less committed to producing an objective image of the topic at hand, but their work is shaped by the composition of the journalism workforce, for example. An illustrative example is the share of women journalists that has developed at a slightly different pace within the Nordic region since the late nineteenth century and has had an effect on the content of journalism.[21] Journalists' worldmaking is, however, confined by the practices of the craft that alongside ideals of journalistic objectivity consist of fundamentals such as balance fairness and accuracy. Professional journalists have viewed them as essential virtues for the free press in democratic societies but they have been complemented with the urge for sellable news since the nineteenth-century Penny Press.[22] Agenda

---

[19] E.g., Jesper Strömbäck, Lars Nord and Adam Shehata, "Swedish Journalists: Between Professionalization and Commercialization," in *The Global Journalist in the 21st Century*, eds. David H. Weaver and Lars Willnat (New York and Abingdon: Routledge, 2012), 307; Morten Skovsgaard, Erik Albæk, Peter Bro and Claes de Vreese, "Media Professionals or Organizational Marionettes? Professional Values and Constraints of Danish Journalists," in *The Global Journalist in the 21st Century*, eds. David H. Weaver and Lars Willnat (New York and Abingdon: Routledge, 2012), 156.

[20] Svetlana Pasti, Mikhail Chernysh and Luiza Svitich, "Russian Journalist and Their Profession," in *The Global Journalist in the 21st Century*, eds. David H. Weaver and Lars Willnat (New York and Abingdon: Routledge, 2012), 267–68; Sarah Oates, "Russian Media in the Digital Age: Propaganda Rewired," *Russian Politics* 1, no. 4 (2016): 398–417; Todd C. Helmut et al., *Russian Social Media Influence: Understanding Russian Propaganda in Eastern Europe* (Santa Monica, California: Rand Corporation, 2018).

[21] Heidi Kurvinen, "Nordic Women Journalists." *The International Encyclopedia of Gender, Media, and Communication*, ed. Karen Ross et al. (Hoboken: Wiley Blackwell, 2020), https://doi.org/10.1002/9781119429128.iegmc226.

[22] Patricia Bradley, *Mass Media and the Shaping of American Feminism, 1963–1975* (Mississippi: University of Mississippi Press, 2003), 77–9.

setting and framing theories have been widely used to analyze these editorial processes that underlie the ideological dimensions of the news media.[23]

News work is also influenced by the relation between the local and the global, the most illustrative example of which is the Cold War era, which influenced the work of journalists in various ways in different countries.[24] Within the Nordic context, the discussion of the Finlandization of the media, i.e. self-censorship that prevented Finnish journalists from openly criticizing the Soviet Union, is a prominent example of this.[25] An opposite example is the reporting of *glasnost* and *perestroika* by Moscow correspondents, which gradually changed the image of the Soviet Union in the West in the late 1980s.[26] It was not only the news media that dealt with the power politics of this era but magazines, too, brought the ideological struggle into the homes of people in Nordic countries and around the world.[27] While the mainstream public discussion always reflects the prevailing hegemony of the wider society, counter publics emerge that question dominant ideas and circulate their own ideological messages to like-minded citizens.[28]

---

[23] See e.g., Maxwell McCombs, *Setting the Agenda: The Mass Media and Public Opinion* (Cambridge: Polity, 2004); Sigurd Allern, "When Journalists Frame the News," in *Media and Revolt: Strategies and Performances from the 1960s to the Present*, eds. Kathrin Fahlenbrach, Erling Sivertsen and Rolf Werenskjold (Oxford: Berghahn Books, 2014), 91–106; Baldwin Van Gorp, "Culture and Protest in Media Frames," in *Media and Revolt: Strategies and Performances from the 1960s to the Present*, eds. Kathrin Fahlenbrach, Erling Sivertsen and Rolf Werenskjold (Oxford: Berghahn Books, 2014), 75–90.

[24] E.g. Laura Saarenmaa, "Interviewing the Enemy and Other Cold War Players: US Foreign Policy as Seen Through Playboy During the Reagan Years," in *Media and the Cold War in the 1980s: Between Star Wars and Glasnost*, eds. Henrik G. Bastiansen et al. (Cham: Palgrave Macmillan, 2019), 43–62; Jan Fredrik Hovden and Rolf Werenskjold, "The Cold War Reporters: The Norwegian Foreign-News Journalists and Foreign-News Correspondents, 1945–1995," in *Media and the Cold War in the 1980s: Between Star Wars and Glasnost*, eds. Henrik G. Bastiansen et al. (Cham: Palgrave Macmillan, 2019), 189–221.

[25] Henrik G. Bastiansen and Rolf Werenskjold, eds. *Nordic Media and the Cold War* (Gothenburg; Nordicom, 2015); Raimo Salokangas, "The Shadow of the Bear: Finnish Broadcasting, National Interest and Self-censorship during the Cold War," in *Nordic Media and the Cold War*, eds. Henrik G. Bastiansen and Rolf Werenksjold (Gothenburg: Nordicom, 2015), 67–82.

[26] Henrik G. Bastiansen, "Reporting Glasnost: The Changing Soviet News in a Norwegian Daily, 1985–1988," in *Media and the Cold War in the 1980s: Between Star Wars and Glasnost*, eds. Henrik G. Bastiansen et al. (Cham: Palgrave Macmillan, 2019), 235–61.

[27] E.g., Laura Saarenmaa, "Political Nonconformity in Finnish Men's Magazines during the Cold War," in *The Nordic Media and the Cold War*, eds. Henrik G. Bastiansen and Rolf Werenskjold (Gothenburg: Nordicom, 2015), 101–13.

[28] About counter publics e.g. Nancy Fraser, "Rethinking the Public Sphere: A Contribution to the Critique of Actually Existing Democracy," *Social Texts* 25/26 (1990): 56–80.

Prominent examples of this are the cultural magazines published by various social movements and publications of party political organizations.[29]

Alongside professional journalism, popular media, such as mainstream and alternative movies, have contributed by circulating ideas and ideologies. Most obviously, this has been manifested in totalitarian systems such as the Soviet Union and Nazi Germany, which have produced landmarks of film art.[30] Likewise, the fear of nuclear disaster resulted in several Hollywood movies in which the end of the world was the main theme during the Cold War.[31] The Star Wars saga, too, was originally influenced by the Cold War climate, as were *Rocky* and *Rambo* films—all propagating the conservative patriotism of the Reagan era. The popular media was also used to brand political campaigns such as the US Strategic Defense Initiative in the early 1980s.[32] However, ideologies were often embedded in the products of popular culture in more subtle ways, an example of which is the circulation of the image of a particular Nordicness that included aspects such as gender equality and sexual freedom.[33] Similarly, the worldwide success of Moomin comics and books has created a positive image of the entire Nordic region from the 1950s onwards, even though they were solely created by a Finnish-Swedish author, Tove Jansson.[34]

### Nordic region as a point of contact

Fred Siebert, Theodore Peterson and Wilbur Schramm's *Four Theories of the Press* introduced the first influential classification of press theories for media

---

[29] E.g. Heidi Kurvinen, "Adopting Public Relations-Like Strategies to Promote Labour Feminism in Finland, 1965–1975," *European History Quarterly* 53, no. 4 (2023): 668, 673–74.

[30] E.g. *October* (1928) by Sergei Eisenstein and *Triumph of the Will* (1934) by Leni Riefenstal.

[31] E.g. *On the Beach* (Stanley Kramer, 1959), *Fail Safe* (Sidney Lumet 1964), *Dr. Strangelove* or: *How I Learned to Stop Worrying and Love the Bomb* (Stanley Kubrick, 1964), *WarGames* (John Badham, 1983).

[32] William M. Knoblauch, "Selling 'Star Wars' in American Mass Media," in *Media and the Cold War in the 1980s: Between Star Wars and Glasnost*, eds. Henrik G. Bastiansen et al. (Cham: Palgrave Macmillan, 2019); Jon Raundalen, "The End of the World Revisited: Nuclear War Films and their Reception in Norwegian Media," in *The Nordic Media and the Cold War*, eds. Henrik G. Bastiansen et al. (Gothenburg: Nordicom 2015); Kellner, *Media Culture*, 69–75; Tony *Shaw, Hollywood's Cold War* (Edinburgh: Edinburgh University Press, 2007).

[33] Elena Lindholm-Narváez, "The Valkyrie in a Bikini: The Nordic Woman as Progressive Media Icon in Spain, 1891–1975," in *Communicating the North: Media Structures and Images in the Making of the Nordic Region*, eds. Jonas Harvard and Peter Stadius (London and New York: Routledge, 2016).

[34] Hideko Mitsui, "Uses of Finland in Japan's Social Imaginary," in *Reflections on Imagination: Human Capacity and Ethnographic Method*, eds. Mark Harris and Nigel Rapport (Farnham and Burlington: Ashgate, 2015).

and communication scholars in the 1950s. According to them, the functioning of the world's presses could be divided into theories of *authoritarian, libertarian, social responsibility* and *Soviet communism*.[35] Later communication theorists have updated the theories, the latest version of which are: *corporatist, libertarian, social responsibility* and *citizen participation*.[36] Of these, the Nordic press and broadcasting systems have mostly belonged to the theory of *social responsibility*, but have also included elements of *corporatist, libertarian* and *citizen participation* theories in recent years. Indeed, in *Comparing Media Systems*, Daniel C. Hallin and Paolo Mancini famously classified the Nordic countries as belonging to the *democratic-corporatist model*, which is characterized by high newspaper circulation, a historically strong party press, strong professionalization, institutionalized self-regulation and strong public service broadcasting.[37]

One aspect of the democratic-corporatist model is the strong intervention of the state in media systems. This is emphasized when scholars use the concept of Nordic "media welfare states" to pinpoint the interconnectedness of the state and the mass media. One prominent example of state intervention is press subsidies that have been used to various degrees in all Nordic countries.[38] Another example of the strong connection between the state and the media are the media literacy programs that have been increasingly adopted in the Nordic countries during the post-war era.[39] The strong role of the state in supporting and regulating the media is most evident in broadcasting, which has followed the ideas of public service in all Nordic countries. This so-called BBC model has been seen as a significant social institution for which the state has responsibility, and hence parliamentary or other civic institutions are somehow involved in public

---

[35] Fred Siebert, Theodore Peterson and Wilbur Schramm, *Four Theories of the Press: The Authoritarian, Libertarian, Social Responsibility and Soviet Communist Concepts of What the Press Should Be and Do* (Urbana: University of Illinois Press, 1956).

[36] See Christians et al., *Normative Theories of the Media*, 3–34.

[37] Daniel C. Hallin and Paolo Mancini, *Comparing Media Systems: Three Models of Media and Politics* (Cambridge: Cambridge University Press, 2004).

[38] Gunn Enli, Trine Syvertsen and Ole J. Mjøs, "The Welfare State and the Media System," *Scandinavian Journal of History* 43, no. 5 (2018): 601–2; Trine Syvertsen, Gunn Enli, Ole J. Mjøs and Hallvard Moe, *The Media Welfare State: Nordic Media in the Digital Era* (Michigan: University of Michigan Press, 2014); Eli Skogerbø, "The Press Subsidy System in Norway: Controversial Past – Unpredictable Future?," *European Journal of Communication* 12, no. 1 (1999): 99–118; Lars Nord, "Comparing Nordic Media Systems: North between West and East?" *Central European Journal of Communication* 1, no. 1 (2008): 95–110; Aske Kammer, "A Welfare Perspective on Nordic Media Subsidies," *Journal of Media Business Studies* 13, no. 3 (2016): 140–52.

[39] Michael Forsman, "Media Literacy and the Emerging Media Citizen in the Nordic Media Welfare State," *Nordic Journal of Media Studies* no. 2 (2020): 59–70.

broadcasting. State-owned broadcasting companies have also reflected institutional media ideologies, such as the education of citizens and the reduction of social inequalities.[40] Likewise, the tendency towards consensus has characterized public service broadcasting in the Nordic region. However, it is important to note that consensus-making affects both state-owned and commercial media institutions in these countries.[41]

The changes in ownership structures after the fall of the party press are yet another media development that integrates Nordic countries. The relatively extensive local press in Sweden, Norway and Finland has diminished in the 2000s, and many of the local papers that are left are part of major publishing companies with partly common content. In addition, ownership structures, especially in broadcasting, are no longer limited by national borders but are exercised across the borders of the Nordic countries. An important aspect in the understanding of the Nordic media system are also the changes in journalistic self-understanding in the editorially controlled media. Especially the social media have dramatically changed such fundamental questions as that of media's social responsibility, since social media often lack the gatekeepers of information.

The perceived similarities in the media systems of the Nordic countries constitute a perfect extent for a regional media history against not only a European but also a global backdrop. This does not mean that there have not been many national differences. These include aspects, such as different histories of censorship, but also variances in political development, such as the forming of the political left, the feminist movement, or the relationship between the East and the West during the Cold War. On a global scale, the similarities have been, however, significant enough to foster collaboration and a sense of belonging to a shared regional community. As an example, the Nordic region has served as an important arena for collaboration among communication studies researchers since the early 1970s, when Nordicom, a center for Nordic media research, was established in 1972 and the first Nordic conference on

---

[40] Gunn Enli, Trine Syvertsen and Ole J. Mjøs, "The Welfare State," 601–2, 609–12; Trine Syvertsen, Gunn Enli, Ole J. Mjøs and Hallvard Moe, *The Media Welfare State*; Heidi Kurvinen, "Children and the Mediated Experiences of the Welfare State: The International Year of the Child (1979) in the Finnish Public Sphere," in *Experiencing Society and the Lived Welfare State*, eds. Pertti Haapala, Minna Harjula and Heikki Kokko (Cham: Palgrave Macmillan, 2023), 237.
[41] Hall, "The rediscovery of 'Ideology,'" 87.

xviii                                                        *Introduction*

media and communication research was organized in 1973.[42] At that time, media historical research focused mainly on nationally framed case studies when institutional histories of media organizations, in particular, were written. The cultural turn in media history has, from the late 1990s onwards, questioned this methodological nationalism, and currently interest in comparative research as well as studies on transnational entanglements of Nordic media is increasing.[43]

The Nordic Media History Network (NOMEH) was established in 2018 to promote collaboration in this area and this compilation of chapters is one example of such a collaboration. Even though most chapters in this collection focus on national case studies, the book as a whole is based on an understanding of the entangled nature of media in the Nordic region. Contrary to a recent book on media's role in constructing "Nordicness," i.e., a specific image of the region, outside and within the Nordic countries,[44] this book will focus on the mediation of ideologies within the region. Originally, the Nordic region consisted of Scandinavian countries alongside with Finland and Iceland. Currently, the widest definition can include the Baltic countries.[45] In this book, the chapters cover only the Scandinavian countries of Norway and Sweden with the addition of Finland. However, with their many similarities, as well as differences, the three countries discussed in this book provide a rich environment for our approach. Moreover, concentrating on these three countries also reflects where media historical research in the Nordics currently stands strong.

### Previous research on ideologies in Nordic media history

Media history is an emerging field of study although studies on the history of media, particularly newspaper histories, have been written since the nineteenth century. The early media historical scholarship conducted by historians consisted of media institution histories and studies that used media

---

[42] Ullamaija Kivikuru, and Kaarle Nordenstreng, "National, global, regional – Where is the core of the Nordic communication research?" in *Norden och världen: Perspektiv från forskningen om medier och kommunikation (The Nordic Countries and the World: Perspectives from Research on Media and Communication): en bok tillägnad Ulla Carlsson*, ed. Thorbjörn Broddason (Gothenburg: Gothenburg University, 2010).

[43] About the so-called entangled media histories, see e.g., Marie Cronqvist and Christoph Hilgert, "Entangled Media Histories: The Value of Transnational and Transmedial Approaches in Media Historiography," *Media History 23*, no. 1 (2017).

[44] Jonas Harvard and Peter Stadius, "A Communicative Perspective on the Formation of the North: Contexts, Channels and Concepts," in *Communicating the North: Media Structures and Images in the Making of the Nordic Region*, eds. Jonas Harvard and Peter Stadius (London and New York: Routledge, 2016), 1.

[45] Ibid., 2.

methodologically through the prism of source criticism. In social sciences, the positivist sociological approaches of the post-war decades followed by Marxist theories and the rise of cultural studies from the 1960s to the 1980s were not very favorable for retrospective views on media, although there were some remarkable exceptions.[46]

As in many other fields of humanities and social sciences, media historical research has witnessed various scientific turns in the past. Until the 1950s, historians studying communication participated in nation building with studies that had an interest in the history of ideas or a literary historical emphasis. The next phase, however, emphasized ideologies, and scholars used the party-political stances of each publication as a motivation for their research.[47] This was also manifested in journalism scholarship on news ideologies. Contrary to news values, such as proximity, unexpectedness or magnitude, that are rather static and refer to the quality of a news story,[48] news ideologies were viewed as changing over time and as being influenced by other ideologies, such as political ideologies, media ideologies and the overall climate of opinion.[49] Simultaneously, a move towards a more media-centered approach took place. During the 1970s and 1980s, all Nordic countries had their own major projects on the history of the media. This produced a nationally focused series of books on the history of various media organizations as well as longitudinal studies on the history of newspapers in their country. This first generation of media histories was gradually accompanied by a variety of approaches to the mediated past.[50]

---

[46] Michael Bailey, "Editor's Introduction," in *Narrating Media History*, ed. Michael Bailey (London and New York: Routledge, 2009); Vincent Mosco, "The Two Marxes: Bridging the Political Economy/Technology and Culture Divide," in *The International Encyclopaedia of Media Studies, Volume I: Media History and the Foundations of Media Studies*, ed. John Nerone. General Editor Angharad N. Valdivia (Malden, MA: Wiley-Blackwell, 2013).

[47] See e.g. *Suomen lehdistön historia, 1–10*, ed. Päiviö Tommila (Helsinki: Kustannuskiila, 1988); Jette Söllinge and Niels Thomsen, *De Danske Aviser 1634–1911, 1918–1991 1–3* (Odense: Dagspressens Fond, 1991); Svennik Høyer, Pressen mellom teknologi og samfunn (Oslo: Universitetsforlaget, 1995); *Den svenska pressens historia 1–5* (Stockholm: Ekerlid, 2000–2003).

[48] About news values and their change over time, see e.g. Tony Harcup and Deirdre O'Neill, "What is News?," *Journalism Studies 18*, no. 12 (2017): 1470–488.

[49] Jörgen Westerståhl and Folke Johansson, "News Ideologies as Moulders of Domestic News," *European Journal of Communication* 1, no. 2 (1986): 134–36; Orvar Löfgren, "Medierna i nationsbygget: Hur press, radio och TV gjorde Sverige svenskt," in *Medier och kulturer*, ed. Ulf Hannerz (Stockholm: Carlssons, 1990) 85–120.

[50] Raimo Salokangas, "Tekstit, kontekstit ja poikittaiskatse mediahistorian kohtauspaikalla," in *Media historiassa*, eds. Erkka Railo and Paavo Oinonen (Turku: Turun historiallinen yhdistys ry., 2012).

Accordingly, media history as a specific research field emerged. In the early 1990s in particular, media scholars and historians started to formulate what media history was and should be. For instance, in 1994 the Norwegian historian and journalist Hans Fredrik Dahl looked into the essence and identity of media history.[51] This resulted in the gradual development of proper "media history" that combined analytical standpoints from media studies with contextual analyses of historical sources.[52]

Since the 1990s, an increasing number of Nordic media scholars have developed an interest in history, and the cultural turn that took place at that time has provided historians with new tools and concepts to understand the media.[53] One manifestation of the popularity of media history is the increase in media history overviews that focus on more than one medium. These kinds of overviews were first produced in Denmark in the 1990s,[54] and were soon followed by Norwegian studies in the early 2000s.[55] Finland and Sweden lacked the same kinds of overviews, although Swedish and Finnish media and history scholars have published cultural historical compilations on the history of national media in recent years.[56] Chapters on Finnish media history have also been included in a Finnish textbook on media history.[57] In the recent scholarship, the concept of the media has been widened beyond mass communication to include material aspects of communication, such as copy machines, office furniture and the history of the A4 paper format, to mention just a few examples.[58]

---

[51] Hans Fredrik Dahl, "The Pursuit of Media History," *Media, Culture & Society* 16, no. 4 (1994): 551–63.

[52] Ib Bondebjerg, "Scandinavian Media Histories: A Comparative Study. Institutions, Genres and Culture in a National and Global Perspective," *Nordicom Review* 23, no. 1–2 (2002); Raimo Salokangas, "Mediahistorian tutkimuskohdetta etsimässä: Aatehistorian materiaalista kohti viestintähistoriaa," *Historiallinen Aikakauskirja* 103, no. 4 (2005).

[53] Salokangas, "Tekstit, kontekstit ja poikittaiskatse mediahistorian kohtauspaikalla."

[54] Klaus Bruhn Jensen, *Dansk mediehistorie, 1–4* (Fredriksberg: Samfundslitteratur, 1996–1998, 2016).

[55] Henrik G. Bastiansen and Hans Fredrik Dahl, *Norsk mediehistorie* (Oslo: Universitetsforlaget, 2003).

[56] See e.g. Marie Cronqvist, Patrik Lundell and Pelle Snickars, eds., *Återkoplingar* Mediehistoriskt arkiv nr. 28 (Lund: Lund University, 2014); Erkka Railo and Paavo Oinonen, eds., *Media historiassa* (Turku: Turun Historiallinen Yhdistys ry., 2012).

[57] Jukka Kortti, *Mediahistoria: Viestinnän merkityksiä puheesta bitteihin* (Helsinki: SKS, 2016).

[58] E.g. Charlie Järpvall, *Pappersarbete: Formandet av och föreställningar om kontorspapper som medium* (Lund: Mediehistoriskt arkiv, 2016); Matts Lindström, *Drömmar om det minsta: Mikrofilm, överflöd och brist 1900–1970* (Lund: Mediehistoriskt arkiv, 2017); Johan Jarlbrink and Charlie Järpvall, eds., *Deskbound Cultures: Media and Materialities at Work* (Lund: Föreningen Mediehistoriskt arkiv, 2021). See also Sune Bechmann Pedersen,

Ideologies have also returned to the center stage among researchers who have been interested in the Cold War era in the Nordic media. These researchers have asked how Nordic newsrooms were influenced by the ideological divide of the world and how they portrayed the two superpowers and their allies.[59] Researchers have shown that this period, which was a highly ideological battle over hearts and minds in Europe and worldwide, had a major impact on the media beyond the hotspots of this battle. During recent years, the history of propaganda has also awakened interest among Nordic scholars along with the rise of "info wars," "cyber-attacks," "trolling," "disinformation," and "post-truth politics." The newly found interest in propaganda has meant that the concept itself has been under scrutiny.[60]

The widening scholarship on ideological aspects in media histories not only derives from an interest in the topic itself, it also reflects the technological development that has had a great impact on media history since the 1990s. Old newspapers have been a relatively easy source group for mass digitization projects throughout the world, and the digitization of newspapers—and to a lesser extent magazines—has exponentially increased the number of historical studies that rely on Nordic media material.[61] Although only a few of these scholars identify themselves as media historians, relatively easy digital access to past print media enables scholarly discussions relating to media material and its analysis. The digital turn has made past media available for scholars in a completely new way, but to be able to make solid interpretations, historians need to understand how media have worked as a system and what kind of role journalists and newsroom cultures have had on publication decisions at different periods of time. Our book will contribute to this field of enquiry by focusing on media as a forum for ideologies and their negotiations.

---

Marie Cronqvist and Ulrika Holgersson, "Introduction: Expanding media, expanding histories," in *Expanding media histories: Cultural and material perspectives*, eds. Sune Bechmann Pedersen et al. (Lund: Kriterium, 2023), 9–14.

[59] See e.g., Bastiansen and Werenskjold, eds., *The Nordic Media and the Cold War.*

[60] See Fredrik Norén, Emil Stjernholm and Claire Thomas, ed., *Nordic Media Histories of Propaganda and Persuasion* (Cham Palgrave Macmillan, 2022).

[61] E.g., Hannu Salmi, *What is Digital History?* (Cambridge and Medford: Polity Press, 2020); Paul Gooding, *Historic Newspapers in the Digital Age: Search All About It!* (London and New York: Routledge, 2016); Henrik Grue Bastiansen, "Nettarkivenes digitale objekter som intellektuell utfordring: Mediehistorie 2.0 og behovet for en ny filologi," *Mediehistorisk Tidsskrift* 33, no. 1 (2020); Patrik Lundell, Hannu Salmi, Erik Edoff, Jani Marjanen, Petri Paju and Heli Rantala, eds., *Information Flows across the Baltic Sea: Towards a Computational Approach to Media History* (Lund: Föreningen Mediehistoriskt arkiv, 2023); Henrik Grue Bastiansen, *Når fortiden blir digital: Kilder, medier og historie i digitaliseringens tid* (Oslo: Universitetsforlaget, 2023).

## The themes and the structure of the book

This compilation is by no means a comprehensive overview, nor is it an extensive study of ideologies in the history of Nordic media. Rather, the chapters provide selected, yet justified approaches to the mediated ideologies from several historical periods, from the mid-nineteenth century through the interwar period until the 1980s. Media history, more than many other fields of history, is highly dependent on changing techno-cultural contexts. The content of this book shows the multidimensional role that media have had in transmitting ideologies to their audiences and public. Accordingly, we focus on three themes concerning the ideological dimensions of media.

In the first section, the book concentrates on interpreting "ideological conflict and consensus." The media is historically layered so that often old media forms and especially their uses at least resonate if not be repeated by later media historical forms and applications.[62] Moreover, the plurality of media- historical time makes the understanding of such vague and contextualized concepts as ideologies fruitful for analyses. Often the media play a central role in the development of an ideology, such as nationalism.

The influential classic of nationalism studies, Benedict Anderson's *Imagined Communities*,[63] emphasizes the role the mass press played in the nineteenth century in creating a nation out of people who did not know each other and in bringing together communities that were too large for individuals to meet one another face to face. The key notion in Anderson's idea is that the birth of imagined communities is not about the spontaneous awakening of the self-consciousness of a nation but rather about the deliberate formulation of such a notion. Media often turn the concept of a nation into something fictional and ritualistic. Ernest Gellner, another well-known theorist of modern nationalism, has also emphasized that media not only communicates the idea of nationalism but actively creates it.[64] Finally, one of the most influential studies concerning media in the field of nationalism studies is Michael Billig's *Banal Nationalism*,[65] which studies everyday representations of the nation in different forms of "flagging" in cultural events and the media. Nationhood provides a continual background for mainstream political discourses and for cultural products and especially affects the structuring of media.

---

[62] See, Jukka Kortti, "Temporalities and Theory in Media History," *Media History* 28, no. 3 (2022).

[63] Benedict Anderson, *Imagined Communities: Reflections on the Origin and Spread of Nationalism* (London: Verso, 1983).

[64] Ernest Gellner, *Nations and Nationalism. Second Edition. Introduction by John Breuilly* (Ithaca, NY: Cornell University Press, 2006), 121–22.

[65] Michael Billig, *Banal Nationalism* (London: Sage, 1995).

Nationalism was one of the influential ideologies of the nineteenth century, together with other major ideologies such as socialism, liberalism and conservatism. They were all also the creations of a bourgeois elite. As Heikki Kokko shows in his chapter, nationalism was not only the ideology of a national elite in the beginning, but a transnational ideology that had difficulties to fit with the vernacular culture. Analyzing local letters published in the Finnish newspapers of the mid-nineteenth century, Kokko shows that the way ordinary Finns wrote in newspapers was largely ignored because the writing of the common people did not fit the idea of a Finnish nation according to a European standard. In that sense, the attitudes of the elite remind one of national branding.

The search for a consensus has been the characteristic of Nordic media systems. On the other hand, Nordic countries have traditionally considered that partisan communication, namely a party press, has an important role to play. In order for decisions made in public affairs to be beneficial for everyone, parties have been ready to compromise. However, this does not mean that there have not been conflicts in the Nordic public sphere, quite the contrary. Moreover, although media institutions may create a consensus, they do not necessarily reflect the consensus in society at large.[66] Multiparty political systems with ideological heterogeneity have often been at odds with the deliberative consensus. Cultural journals, in particular, have offered avenues for influence that are free from institutions. In the 1960s in particular, a diverse and extensive alternative press was born that questioned media institutions. As John McMillian stated in his study on the American alternative press of the 1960s "typewriters were smoking." That was also the case in the Nordic countries.[67]

Cultural and alternative journals have mostly constituted the media of the activist elite, which they have used to develop their philosophies of life.[68] The rise of the internet and social media has changed the situation both regarding media as a former of worldviews, as well as with regard to the public sphere. With social media, anyone can participate in discussions. Instead of providing a utopia of freedom of speech and democracy, social media have encouraged biased, manipulative, propagandist, disinformational, distorted, cynical, and xenophobic communication. This is nothing new, the media have been used to

---

[66] Hall, "The Rediscovery of 'Ideology.'"

[67] John McMillian, *Smoking Typewriters: The Sixties Underground Press and the Rise of Alternative Media in America* (New York: Oxford University Press, 2011); Juho Saksholm, *Reform, Revolution, Riot? Transnational Nordic Sixties in the Radical Press. c. 1958–1968* (Jyväskylä: University of Jyväskylä, 2020).

[68] Kortti, "Generations and Media History."

mock ideological opponents and dehumanize peoples and social groups by means of "hate speech" long before the arrival of modern media.[69]

In their chapter on the hate speech of the radical right in Finnish history, Markku Mattila and Ari Haasio show how constant many forms of hate speech are in media history. Although recent social media have provided faster tools and platforms virtually without monitoring or controlling editors, the same kind of rhetoric, techniques, and "topoi" for attacking an ideological adversary can be found in newspaper articles in the 1930s. In their diachronic comparative analysis of two Finnish right-wing newspapers, they show that although the targets of hate speech vary due to different historical circumstances, some of the features are unchanged.

Ideologies are very much associated with concepts. In the chapter about the way in which the Swedish Social Democratic press used the term "solidarity" during the 1980s, Karin Jonsson shows that the concept was, first and foremost, used to convince and enthuse potential supporters. Although solidarity was not a central ideological concept during the formative years of socialism and early social democracy, it became a key social democratic concept later in the 1970s. Indeed, ideologies depend on the temporal changes of (modern) history—its past, present and future—as Reinhard Koselleck has famously theorized.[70]

Media do not only reflect topical concerns of a particular historical context, they also serve as an arena for negotiations of their meanings. This is particularly clear in terms of various social movements, and the relation between the mass media and collective agency for social change has generated an extensive body of research.[71] Scholars have demonstrated that social movements try to use the media strategically to spread their ideological message but, in the end, the power to set the agenda for public discussion is in newsrooms. Resulting of this, movements' own publications have served as important counter-publics in which ideologies have been formulated and, in some cases, also contested.[72]

---

[69] Jukka Kortti, *Media in History: An Introduction to the Meanings and Transformations of Communication over Time* (London: Macmillan Red Globe Press, 2019).

[70] Reinhart Koselleck, *Futures Past: On the Semantics of Historical Time* (New York: Columbia University Press, 2004).

[71] E.g., Alice Mattoni, *Media Practices and Protest Politics: How Precarious Workers Mobilise* (London: Routledge, 2016); Bradley, *Mass Media and the Shaping of American Feminism.*

[72] E.g. Heather A. Haveman, *Magazines and the Making of America: Modernization, Community, and Print Culture, 1741–1860* (Princeton: Princeton University Press, 2016); Victoria Bazin, "Miss-Represented? Mediating Miss World in Shrew Magazine," *Women: A Cultural Review* 27, no. 4 (2016).

In the section titled "Promoting and discussing feminism," the interplay between social movement and the media is approached from the point of view of the women's movement. Tiina Kinnunen focuses on the first wave of the feminist movement when analyzing the publication plans of a magazine that never started. In this case, the magazine itself was about to become an ideological tool when the movement's aims were negotiated within the movement. This case study illustrates the interconnections between the women's movement within the Nordic region, which is complemented by Hannah Yoken's chapter, which focuses on second-wave feminism. Yoken demonstrates how ideas relating to feminist publications circulated transnationally within the Nordic region during the 1970s and 1980s. She points out, moreover, the role of agency in these processes. Women's emancipation is also of interest to Arja Turunen, who analyzes women's magazines and their role in circulating ideas that questioned prevailing gender contracts. She uses modern women of the 1920s and 1930s as her analytical starting point and shows the connections between the ideas presented in feminist magazines and in commercial women's magazines. All these chapters focus on genres aimed specifically at women and illustrate that the gendered practices of news journalism have excluded women's concerns from news journalism throughout the twentieth century.[73]

The final section of the book interprets transnational conflicts by focusing on 1980s news journalism and television advertising of the post-World War II era. As the Cold War defined the experiences of people around the world at this time,[74] it forms the background for two of the chapters that share an interest in journalism history. In her chapter, Birgitte Kjos Fonn illustrates that the interpretations of the gradual end of the Cold War kept changing in Norwegian newspapers at the turn of the 1980s and 1990s. Almost from the beginning, the political process was accompanied by economic interests, and business framing gradually became important means through which this historically meaningful period was explicated. However, papers differed in their manner of framing the fall of the Berlin Wall, which reminds one of the importance of contextualization in media historical analysis. This applies also to Heidi Kurvinen's chapter, which discusses the early 1980s peace movement. Kurvinen compares the representation of the movement in two neighbouring countries,

---

[73] E.g. Laurel Brake, "Gendered Space and the British Press," *Studies in Newspaper and Periodical History* 3, no. 1–2 (1995).

[74] Henrik G. Bastiansen, Martin Klimke and Rolf Werenskjold, "Introduction: Mapping the Role of the Media in the Late Cold War," in *Media and the Cold War in the 1980s: Between Star Wars and Glasnost*, eds. Henrik G. Bastiansen et al. (Cham: Palgrave Macmillan, 2019), 4–5.

Finland and Sweden, and shows how differences in the journalism cultures as well as in the geopolitical positions of the countries affected the ways in which people's transnational organizing for world peace was portrayed. Thus, the gatekeeping role of journalists was influenced by wider developments in professional journalism at the local and regional level, as well as by the ideological tendencies that were shaped by global developments, such as the awakening of neoliberalism.

The Nordic countries have obviously not developed in a vacuum but have been exposed to international and transnational influences throughout their histories. When it comes to culture and media, one of the most effective ideological campaigns in modern history was the Americanization process of Western Europe in the post-war decades. Jukka Kortti approaches this phenomenon through the advertising of cigarettes on Finnish television, the chapter being the only one in our book concentrating on a topic other than press history. In Finland, advertisers, including the tobacco industry, had better opportunities for modern advertising than in other Nordic countries, which did not begin television advertising until the 1980s. The very American-influenced tobacco industry particularly used connotations of "modern life" in their advertising. In other words, these cigarette commercials did not only advertise tobacco, they also promoted the notion of modern ideology. Kortti shows how these American modernization ideologies were interconnected with the ethos of the Scandinavian welfare state.

# Ideological conflict
# and consensus

Chapter 1

# Village gossip or voice of the people? The culture of letters to the press in the grasp of transnational ideologies in mid-1800s Finland

Heikki Kokko

*Tampere University, Finland*

**Abstract:** A nationwide culture of readers' letters to newspapers developed in Finland during the first phase of modernization from the 1850s onwards. A characteristic of this culture was that the letters were written in the name of local communities. In the tens of thousands of "local letters" to newspapers, thousands of ordinary people documented their everyday experiences of the societal transformation. However, the culture was largely ignored and underrated by the Finnish-language journalists of the era who were also members of the nationalistic elite. The vernacular character of the culture was contradictory to the new transnational ideologies of nationalism, which emphasized the forms of cultural life that were considered to represent higher culture, such as prose fiction, poetry, and theatre. The chapter opens a new perspective to the transnationality of nationalism and the ideological struggle regarding it in the nineteenth century press.

**Keywords:** nationalism, newspapers, letters to the press, translocal, 19th century

***

The book *Seitsemän veljestä* (English title: *Seven brothers*) written by Aleksis Kivi in 1870 describes vernacular country life in mid-1800s Finland. The book reaches its climax when one of its main characters, Eero, starts to read and write the readers' letters that were sent from all around Finland and published in the newspapers. According to Kivi, by reading and writing these letters, Eero began to realize what Finland is and its position in the world.[1] Kivi is considered the

---

[1] Aleksis Kivi, *Seitsemän veljestä* (Helsinki: SKS, 1870), 328.

national writer of Finland mainly because of this classic novel, the first to be written in Finnish.

Kivi was a contemporary witness to a nationwide culture of readers' letters to newspapers that was largely ignored by the Finnish-language elite of the era and by the later Finnish historiography.[2] The culture developed in Finland during the first phase of modernization from the 1850s onwards. A characteristic of this culture was that the letters were often written in the name of local communities. In the tens of thousands of "local letters" to newspapers, thousands of ordinary people documented their everyday experiences of the societal transformation occurring in the second half of the nineteenth century.[3]

The nationwide culture of local letters was a particular Finnish phenomenon that developed due to the social circumstances of this Grand duchy of the Russian Empire. In the Western world, the press generally developed as an urban and regional phenomenon during the seventeenth and eighteenth centuries before the advent of steam power and advanced printing technology. Newspapers in those times were commercial enterprises, which could be made to show a profit with a small amount of capital and a circulation of a few hundred copies. This tied the early newspapers efficiently to their local and usually urban environment, which had the easily accessible market for printing products. Although the publishing of readers' letters was in general a common practice in the early press, the newspapers did not usually develop into a broad-based and integrated national or societal forum of discussion but as an extension of the urban face-to-face oral cultures.[4] The Finnish-language press,

---

[2] Heikki Kokko, "Kotomaamme katveinen kuva: Suomenkielisen lehdistön paikalliskirjekulttuurin marginalisoituminen," in *Kaanon ja marginaali: Kulttuuriperinnön vaiennetut äänet*, ed. Niina Hämäläinen and Lotte Tarkka (Helsinki: SKS, 2022), 263–65.

[3] See Laura Stark, *The Limits of Patriarchy: How Female Networks of Pilfering and Gossip Sparked the First Debates on Rural Gender Rights in the 19th-Century Finnish-Language Press* (Helsinki: SKS, 2011), 48–77; Heikki Kokko, "From Local to Translocal: The Nationwide Culture of Letters to the Press in Mid-1800s Finland," *Media History* 28, no. 2 (2022): 181–198.

[4] See Hannah Barker and Simon Burrows, "Introduction," in *Press, Politics and the Public Sphere in Europe and North America, 1760–1820*, ed. Hannah Barker and Simon Burrows (Cambridge: Cambridge University Press, 2004), 5–6, 15–6; Hannah Barker, "England, 1760–1815," in *Press, Politics and the Public Sphere in Europe and North America, 1760–1820*, ed. Hannah Barker and Simon Burrows (Cambridge: Cambridge University Press, 2004), 104–5; David Copeland, "America, 1750–1820," in *Press, Politics and the Public Sphere in Europe and North America, 1760–1820*, ed. Hannah Barker and Simon Burrows (Cambridge: Cambridge University Press, 2004), 142–3; Nicolaas Van Sas, "The Netherlands, 1750–1813," in *Press, Politics and the Public Sphere in Europe and North America, 1760–1820*, ed. Hannah Barker and Simon Burrows (Cambridge: Cambridge University Press, 2004), 48–68.

which main readership was in the rural areas, is an exception in this development. This is due to the late emergence of the Finnish-language press. As it initially arose in the 1850s, it could benefit from the contemporary technological progress in printing and transportation and develop instantly nationwide. Due to the societal circumstances and rapid advances in printing technology, telecommunications links, and transportation connections, the way for a nationwide culture of local letters was opened.[5]

Furthermore, the peculiar language situation of Finland paved the way for the culture of local letters in the Finnish-language press. In the mid-1800s, the entire central administration functioned in Swedish, although 85% of the population were Finnish-speaking and only 14% Swedish-speaking.[6] Swedish, which is linguistically unrelated to Finnish, was the language of the educated classes. Only a minority of common people spoke Swedish. There were no state schools in Finnish and Finnish-language literary culture was still thin. The only institution that worked in Finnish was the Lutheran church, which oversaw the local administration in the agrarian parishes and worked as a linkage between the state administration and the Finnish-speaking majority.[7] Briefly, Finnish was the language of the common people, who lived their self-sufficient lives in the numerous local rural communities. The language situation was the main source for the ideological struggle that was related to nationalism in late nineteenth-century Finland. This was also a transnational struggle in which the belonging of Finnish people to the Nordic countries and to the Western world was defined.[8]

In this chapter, I analyze the public attitudes towards the culture of letters to the press in mid-1800s Finland. I ask why the culture was marginalized by newspaper editors in the 1850s and 1860s. I begin my analysis by exploring the first discovery of the existence of this culture in the 1850s. After that, I analyze the attitudes of newspaper editors towards this culture and the transnational ideologies that were behind the public stance on the phenomenon. I argue that the main reason why the culture of letters to newspapers was ignored in the Finnish-language public sphere was that the culture was contradictory to the

---

[5] Kokko, "From Local to Translocal," 181–83, 193–94; Heikki Kokko, "Suomenkielisen julkisuuden nousu 1850-luvulla ja sen yhteiskunnallinen merkitys," *Historiallinen Aikakauskirja* 117, no 1 (2019): 5–21.

[6] SVT VI 1865,1.

[7] See Heikki Kokko, *Kuviteltu minuus: Ihmiskäsityksen murros suomenkielisen kansanosan kulttuurissa 1800-luvun puolivälissä* (Tampere: Tampere University Press, 2016), 67–74.

[8] See e. g. Meri Arni-Kauttu, *Itäistä kelvottomuutta vastaan: Suomen ruotsinkielisten diskursiiviset mielikuvat suomalaisista 1896–1924* (Joensuu: Itä-Suomen yliopisto, 2020), 59–130.

transnational ideologies of the era that legitimized nationalism. On a more general level, my analysis opens a new perspective to the transnationality of nationalism and the ideological struggle regarding it in the middle of the nineteenth century.

My theoretical framework is an application of the sociology of knowledge promoted by Peter Berger and Thomas Luckmann.[9] According to Berger and Luckmann, human reality is socially constructed, and based on their thinking, I see ideology as the definition of reality that relates to concrete power interests. Usually, ideology is related to the struggle between the competing traditions in the particular social world. These traditions are all-embracing frames of reference that constitute the reality of the individuals that have absorbed it, because all their experience takes place within it.[10] In this chapter, I use the concept of ideology in this wide sense, which emphasizes that in addition to political ideology, a religion or a science could be an ideology if used in the struggle against other worldviews.

My research material consists of the writings published in the Finnish-language press in 1850–1870 regarding the Finnish phenomenon of letters to newspapers. I especially focus on the writings of David Emanuel Daniel Europaeus (1820–1884)—who was a folklorist, linguist, and the main promoter of the culture of local letters—and the notices and programmatic articles published by the editors of newspapers.

### The emergence of culture of letters to the press

Although the revolutions of 1848 in Europe did not reach Finland, the beginning of the culture of local letters was connected to these upheavals. To avoid social unrest, the administration of the Russian empire began to increase censorship of the Finnish-language press. The restrictions were aimed especially at the newspaper *Suometar*, which had intensively followed the revolutions in its foreign news section. Thus, in 1849–1850 the authorities

---

[9] See Heikki Kokko and Minna Harjula, "Social History of Experiences: A Theoretical-Methodological Approach," in *Experiencing Society and the Lived Welfare State*, eds. Pertti Haapala, Minna Harjula and Heikki Kokko (Cham: Palgrave Macmillan, 2023), 17–40.

[10] Peter Berger and Thomas Luckmann, *The Social Construction of Reality* (London: Penguin, 1991 [1966]), 33–42, 113–14, 141, 201–4, 233. On the role of Berger and Luckmann as the representatives of sociology of knowledge, see Peter Hamilton, *Knowledge and Social Structure: An Introduction to the Classical Argument in the Sociology of Knowledge* (London: Routledge & Kegan Paul, 1974), 137–46. On the relationship between the sociology of knowledge and ideology, see Karl Mannheim, *Ideology and Utopia: An Introduction to the Sociology of Knowledge* (London: Routledge & Kegan Paul, 1936), 67–74.

forbade *Suometar* from publishing any international news and permitted only such writings to be published in Finnish that aimed to advance the common economic development or Christian devoutness.[11] In answer to these measures, the editors of *Suometar* created a new publishing strategy. Instead of foreign news, they concentrated on local domestic news, which did not suffer so much from censorship. In practice, they created a network of correspondents among the members Finnish nationalist movement and started to publish the letters they sent from their local communities. These correspondents were usually priests, civil servants and teachers who lived around the country. The new publishing strategy of *Suometar* was an instant success. The circulation of the newspaper doubled between 1851 and 1852.[12]

After this, D. E. D. Europaeus became interested in the local letters. In January 1853, he wrote an article in which he requested readers around the country to send all kinds of contributions to every Finnish-language newspaper. He especially wanted articles about local incidents, accounts about attempts to find schools and libraries, and reports about the local church's meetings for *Suometar*. In addition, he requested information about literacy and the industrial plants around the country. Europaeus wanted to know how these things had influenced local life. Europaeus was the former editor of *Suometar* but had no official role in the newspaper at that time. However, the newspaper was involved in this request, because in the same article, it promised a modest payment for longer contributions.[13] In 1854, Europaeus wrote an article to *Suometar* where he renewed his plea for the common people to write local letters from their communities. Furthermore, he gave advice on how to make a subscription to *Suometar* and how to write a letter to the newspaper.[14]

Following Europaeus' request, both the number of local letters published and the number of places from which they came increased about threefold between 1852 and 1855. Among the writers, there were dozens of people outside the original network of correspondents created after the publication of foreign news was banned. This meant that the organized top-down activity turned into civic activity from below. Indeed, the local letters were clearly something that people wanted to read. When the number of letters increased in the columns of *Suometar*, the circulation of the newspaper increased exponentially. In 1852, the

---

[11] O. W. Louhivuori, *Suometar: Perustaminen ja ensimmäiset vaiheet 1847–1852* (Helsinki: Oy Uusi Suomi 1940), 255–70, 343–60.

[12] Ibid., 427–29; Kokko, "From Local to Translocal," 185–87; Päiviö Tommila, "Yhdestä lehdestä sanomalehdistöksi 1809–1859," in *Suomen lehdistön historia 1: Sanomalehdistön vaiheet vuoteen 1905*, eds. Päiviö tommila, Lars Landgren and Pirkko Leino-Kaukiainen (Kuopio: Kustannuskiila, 1988), 200–4.

[13] D. E. D. Europaeus "Kehoitus maamiehille lähettämään kirjoituksia maamme sanomalehtiin," *Suometar*, January 14, 1853.

[14] D. E. D. Europaeus, "Suomalaisten sanomalehtien levittämisestä," *Suometar*, May 26, 1854.

circulation figure was 249, but by 1856 it had risen to 4,600.[15] Europaeus' request in the name of the editors of *Suometar* was the catalyst for this development.[16]

The culture of local letters grew markedly during the 1850s and 1860s, because after the success of *Suometar*, all the other Finnish-language newspapers followed in its stead. Figure 1.1 presents the local letters published in Finnish-language newspapers between 1850 and 1870. In 1860, over 1,000 local letters were published in the Finnish-language press. This was more than 22 times the number in 1850. In 1870, about 500 more letters were published than in 1860.[17] At the same time, the circulation of the entire Finnish-language press increased significantly. There is a lack of systematic information about this, but, for example, the total circulation of the Finnish-language press climbed from 1,000 to 8,000 between 1851 and 1856.[18] The culture of local letters was a significant factor in this first rise of the Finnish-language press.[19]

**Figure 1.1.** Local letters in the Finnish-language press.

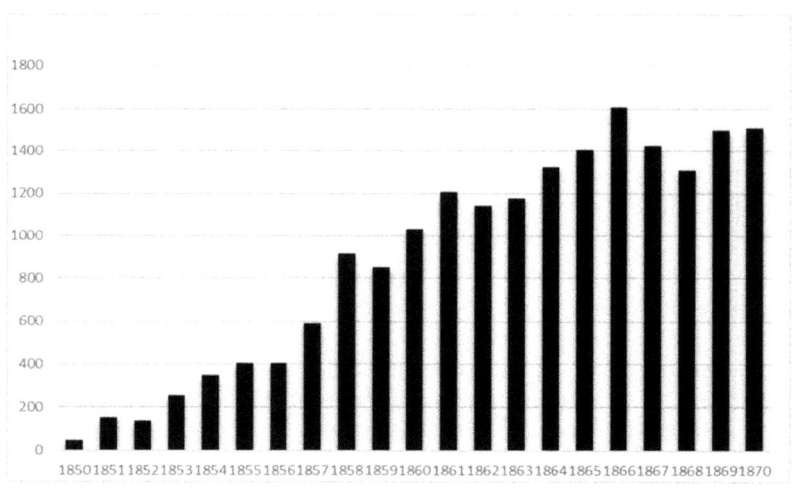

---

[15] Päiviö Tommila, *Suomen lehdistön levikki ennen vuotta 1860* (Helsinki: WSOY 1963), 332–35. The popularity of the press rose also because of the Crimean War 1853–1856, which reached Finland when the British and French navies engaged in operations on the Baltic Sea. The nearby warfare fueled the hunger for news in Finland. Tommila, "Yhdestä lehdestä sanomalehdistöksi," 175–78. Indeed, the events of the Crimean War and local efforts in Finland were reported in the local letters. Kokko, "From Local to Translocal," 186.
[16] Kokko, "Kotomaamme katveinen kuva," 270–5.
[17] Translocalis Database.
[18] Tommila, *Suomen lehdistön levikki*, 332–35.
[19] Kokko, "Suomenkielisen julkisuuden nousu 1850-luvulla," 12–6.

The popularity of local letters attracted the attention of the authorities in imperial Russia. Instead of advocating censorship, the officials saw the advantages of the developing press and increasing participation around the country. In 1857, the authorities launched an official newspaper, *Suomen Julkisia Sanomia*, which achieved immediate popularity.[20] It began to publish local letters and the authorities even encouraged people to send their contributions by exempting them from postage fees.[21] This administrative measure by the authorities institutionalized the culture of local letters.

The culture of local letters spread across the sparsely populated country (Figure 1.2). In 1858, local letters were received from over half of all towns and parishes in Finland. In 1866, the number was over two-thirds of the towns and parishes.[22]

**Figure 1.2.** Geographical distribution of local letters in the Finnish-language press 1850–1870.

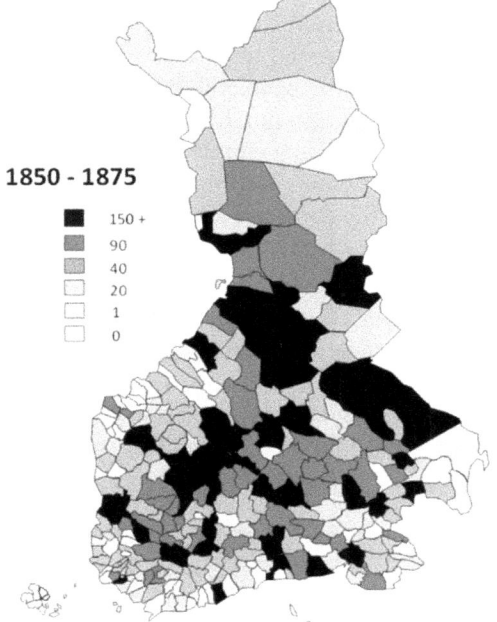

[20] Tommila, "Yhdestä lehdestä sanomalehdistöksi," 179–81.
[21] Heikki Kokko, "Suomenkielisen lehdistön paikalliskirjekulttuuria tallentava digitaalinen Translocalis-tietokanta," *Ennen ja nyt. Historian tietosanomat*, no. 2 (2019).
[22] Translocalis Database.

The societal significance of the culture of local letters was in the circulation of knowledge. As a result of these societal, administrative, and linguistic factors, Finland consisted of numerous different local communities in which the interaction was based mainly on local oral cultures. In the local letters, various local experiences in the sparsely populated country could be shared in the public sphere for the first time. The culture connected the local communities and created a public sphere that enabled the societal circulation of knowledge for most of the population in Finland. Furthermore, the culture marked the starting point for the first civic nationwide activity of most of the population in Finland.[23]

## Europaeus as a promoter of the culture

Europaeus, who gave the development of the culture its start, was also the one who first understood the significance of the phenomenon. In 1861, he pointed out that there was no similar phenomenon in Sweden. According to him, the same applied to the Swedish-speaking ordinary people in Finland. There were hardly any letters written by Swedish-speaking freeholder peasants in Sweden or Finland.[24] In 1862, he extended this observation to the whole of Europe. According to him, the Finnish people should be happy about their letter-writing, which had become a common habit, because elsewhere the press was under the supremacy of individual editors.[25] Indeed, later historical research has confirmed the assumptions of Europaeus about the uniqueness of the culture of local letters to the press in Finland. A comparable nationwide and population-wide phenomenon could not be found elsewhere.[26]

Europaeus understood the specific character of the Finnish phenomenon and did his best to promote the culture of local letters in the 1850s and 1860s. In 1856, he wrote an article in which he raised the local letters to the category of Finnish national literature.[27] In another article, published in the same year, he suggested that a new newspaper "Nation's Newspaper" (*Kansakunnan Lehti*) should be founded that concentrated on publishing the letters that people sent to the editorial offices.[28] He finally succeeded in establishing the

---

[23] Kokko, "From Local to Translocal," 193–94. More broadly, see Kokko, *Kuviteltu minuus*, 67–74.

[24] D. E. D. Europaeus, "Flaamilaisten kansallisista liikkeistä," *Suometar*, May 17, 1861.

[25] D. E. D. Europaeus, *Kirjoituksia Suomen kansan tärkeimmistä asioista suurimmaksi osaksi syrjä-sensuureista paenneita, 1 nidos: Onko Suomen kansa voimihinsa päästettävä vain eikö?* (Helsinki 1862), 30–4.

[26] Kokko, "From Local to Translocal," 181–83, 193–94.

[27] D. E. D. Europaeus "Suomalaisten velollisuuksista sanomalehdellistä ja muuta kirjallisuuttansa kohtaan," *Sanan-Lennätin*, March 29, 1856.

[28] D. E. D. Europaeus, "Kansakunnan Lehdestä," *Suomen Julkisia Sanomia*, April 30, 1857.

newspaper himself in 1863. However, he could only publish a couple of issues of *Kansakunnan Lehti* at his own expense before having to quit the newspaper.[29] Furthermore, Europaeus made other efforts to promote the culture of local letters to newspapers. In 1862, he published a book that focused on the letter-writing culture and the need for a special newspaper for it.[30] In the same year, Europaeus planned to publish a handbook that would teach the common people to become better writers.[31]

First and foremost, Europaeus was a scholar, not a journalist. The reason why he resigned as an editor of *Suometar* in 1848 was that in his opinion the newspaper did not concentrate enough on readers who came from the lower strata.[32] This attitude was also visible in his other work. At the turn of the 1850s, he was known and recognized for his significant work in collecting Finnish folk poetry. His work in the 1840s significantly influenced the world-famous work of the epic poem, *Kalevala* (1849), which was compiled by Elias Lönnrot from Karelian and Finnish oral folklore and mythology.[33] However, after *Kalevala* was published, Europaeus started to criticize it, because as a collector of folklore he noticed immediately that Lönnrot had edited the poetry in order to make it meet Western ideals of the epic and that it did not describe real historical events, even though this was commonly both explicitly and implicitly indicated among the Finnish-language elite.[34]

In his own scientific work, Europaeus was driven by the desire to publish the folklore as it was, without editing.[35] The same applies to the local letters, in which Europaeus became interested at the beginning of the 1850s. It seems that

---

[29] Lars Landgren, "Kieli ja aate – politisoituva sanomalehdistö 1860–1889," in *Suomen lehdistön historia 1: Sanomalehdistön vaiheet vuoteen 1905*, eds. Päiviö Tommila, Lars Landgren and Pirkko Leino-Kaukiainen (Kuopio: Kustannuskiila, 1988), 314. The plan of Europaeus was finally implemented by the district doctor of Central Finland Wolmar Schildt, who published a newspaper titled "Newspaper of the People" (*Kansan Lehti*) in 1867–1870, which columns were filled with the readers' letters that were not edited almost at all. Stark, *The Limits of Patriarchy*, 49–55, 178.

[30] D. E. D. Europaeus, *Kirjoituksia Suomen kansan tärkeimmistä asioista.*

[31] Kokko, "Kotomaamme katveinen kuva," 273.

[32] Jouko Teperi, *Vanhan Suomen suomalaisuusliike I: kehityspiirteitä ja edustajia 1830-luvulta 1850-luvun alkuun* (Helsinki: SHS, 1965), 96–7.

[33] Matti Kuusi and Senni Timonen, "Suurmies? Kummajainen? Uhrilammas? Keskustelua Europaeuksen elämästä ja työstä," in *D. E. D Europaeus. Suurmies vai kummajainen*, eds. Matti Kuusi, Pekka Laaksonen and Senni Timonen (Helsinki: SKS, 1988), 25–4.

[34] Väinö Kaukonen, "Europaeuksen osa Kalevalan laadinnassa," in *D. E. D Europaeus. Suurmies vai kummajainen*, eds. Matti Kuusi, Pekka Laaksonen and Senni Timonen (Helsinki: SKS, 1988), 76–81.

[35] Kuusi and Timonen, "Suurmies?," 35.

Europaeus saw the local letters as a possibility to hear the authentic voice of the people, something *Kalevala* was unable to do. This is why he wrote numerous pieces in the 1850s and 1860s criticizing editors of newspapers who did not publish local letters or edited them before they were printed.[36]

## The dilemma of journalism

The relationship between the individuals who worked as press editors and local letters was complex.[37] The editors of the Finnish-language press were usually volunteers or worked only part-time, because newspaper publishing in Finnish was not a lucrative business.[38] For example, Fredrik Polén, who was the editor of *Suometar* in the 1850s, worked at the same time as a teacher and as a translator for government agencies.[39] This led to the situation in which the letters from readers were usually happily accepted as material that could fill the empty columns of the newspapers.[40]

On the other hand, publishing the letters diminished journalism's room for maneuver, because the letters took space from content that the editors may have considered more important. However, the letters became too important to be neglected because the readers wanted to read them. Indeed, the letters to the newspapers became so important for the Finnish-language press that at the end of the 1850s, it became common to ask the readers to send writings in the papers' subscription announcements. In these announcements, the tone was respectful. By calling the readers "fellow countrymen" or "fellow citizens," the newspapers highlighted their respect for their readers. In return for the letters, some newspapers even promised exemption from postage fees and free

---

[36] E.g. *D. E. D. Europaeus, Kirjoituksia Suomen kansan tärkeimmistä asioista,* 49–54.
[37] About the relationship between the writers and editors, see Laura Stark, "Toimittajien ja itseoppineiden maaseutukirjeenvaihtajien suhde osana suomenkielisen lehdistön nousua 1847–1865," *Historiallinen Aikakauskirja* 117, no. 1 (2019): 28–42; Laura Stark, "Sanomalehtien maaseutukirjeet: Itseilmaisun into ja lehdistön portinvartijat," in *Kynällä kyntäjät: Kansan kirjallistuminen 1800-luvun Suomessa,* eds. Lea Laitinen and Kati Mikkola (Helsinki: SKS, 2013); Stark, *The Limits of Patriarchy,* 49–55. About the early professionalization of journalism in Finland, see Pirjo Munck, *Valistajista ammattimiehiksi: Toimittajien ammattilaistumisen pitkä tie 1771–1921* (Helsinki: Helsingin yliopisto, 2016), 27–50.
[38] Kokko, "Suomenkielisen lehdistön paikalliskirjekulttuuria tallentava"; Tommila, "Yhdestä lehdestä sanomalehdistöksi," 196–97.
[39] Kai Laitinen, "Polén, Rietrikki," *Kansallisbiografia-verkkojulkaisu* (Helsinki: SKS, 1997).
[40] Kokko, "From local to translocal," 185.

volumes for frequent writers.[41] The editors usually legitimized the publishing of letters by the assumption that the writings described everyday life and the common state of the ordinary people.[42] Another common explanation was that the readers' letters simply prevented bias, which was a problem when all the articles of a newspaper were written by one individual editor.[43] In 1854, *Suometar* legitimized the publishing of the letters by stating that it accustoms the common people to publicity and connects the inhabitants of the country with each other.[44] The following year, *Suometar* referred to the great number of letters by stating that "in a manner of speaking, not any single person but the whole Finnish people has edited *Suometar*."[45]

However, the polite tone of the writings directed towards the readers was gone when the newspapers commented on each other's content. Already in 1854, *Sanomia Turusta* criticized *Suometar* for publishing long letters that described only information about deaths, crops, or weather conditions from all around the country, which tested the readers' patience.[46] In its reply, *Suometar* pitied the small size of *Sanomia Turusta* and wrote how it was a shame for the city of Turku that no better Finnish-language newspaper was published there.[47] The following year, *Sanomia Turusta* continued to mock *Suometar* by stating that: "The greatest part of *Suometar* is a totally empty speech from all around the country." According to it, "*Sanomia Turusta* does not sell pieces of paper as *Suometar* does."[48]

*Sanomia Turusta* was edited by Gustaf Eurén, who alone fought against the new culture and published relatively few letters in his newspaper in 1853–1857. However, when Eurén established a new newspaper (*Hämäläinen*) in Hämeenlinna in 1858, the paper began to publish an increasing number of readers' letters.[49] The tables were turned when the new editors of *Sanomia Turusta* began to concentrate increasingly on the publishing of the readers' letters. Indeed, in 1862, *Suometar* criticized *Sanomia Turusta* for publishing the

---

[41] E.g. Fredrik Polén, "Kuopion Sanomia," *Suometar*, December 19, 1856; Konstantin Schroeder, "Suomen Julkisia Sanomia," *Suomen Julkisia Sanomia*, November 10, 1856; Henrik Konstantin Corander, "Vuosi 1856," *Sanan-Lennätin*, November 1, 1855; Johan Bäckvall, "Oulusta 6 päivänä Tammikuuta," *Oulun Wiikko-sanomia*, January 6, 1854.

[42] E.g. Johan Bäckvall, "Vuoden lopuksi," *Oulun Wiikko-Sanomia*, December 27, 1856.

[43] Antti Manninen, "Tapion mietteitä vuoden lopuksi," *Tapio*, December 27, 1862.

[44] Fredrik Polén, "Sanomain Turusta lukijat," *Suometar*, November 24, 1854.

[45] Paavo Tikkanen, "Suometar," *Suometar*, January 5, 1855.

[46] Gustaf Erik Eurén, "Suomettaret lukiat," *Sanomia Turusta*, November 7, 1854.

[47] Gustaf Erik Eurén, "Sanomain Turusta lukijat." *Suometar*, November 24, 1854.

[48] Gustaf Erik Eurén, "Näillä Sanomilla," *Sanomia Turusta*, January 23, 1855.

[49] Translocalis Database.

letters and news at the expense of the articles of more general issues.[50] The next year, *Helsingin Uutiset* claimed that *Sanomia Turusta* had wanted to become so vernacular that its columns had been transformed into the "narrow alley of the village."[51] In 1862, *Suometar* bemoaned that there were some newspapers, which published the letters without editing them only to fill their empty columns. According to *Suometar*, by doing this they published local rumors and ramblings, which led to long and boring arguments between the writers. *Suometar* pointed the finger especially at its main rival, *Suomen Julkisia Sanomia*. According to *Suometar*, the editing of this kind of newspaper was easy, but it was against the vocation of the newspaper editor.[52] Later in 1869, *Suometar* mocked *Kansan Lehti*, that had begun to publish all the letters it received. According to *Suometar*, it was "trash that *Kansan Lehti* presents to its readers."[53]

The main question of the era was whether it was the task of the editor to control public opinion by writing his own articles or simply to make public debate possible. The publishing of letters threatened the editors' identity as journalists, because in the case of letters, the main task of the editors was only to proofread and shorten submissions sent by uneducated writers. The professionalization of journalism from the 1860s onwards escalated this contraction. Still, in the 1850s, the newspapers sought to publish all readers' letters sent to the editorial offices. In the 1860s, the editors assumed more of a gatekeeper function vis-à-vis the public because the number of readers' letters grew so large that they could reject some submissions.[54]

Furthermore, it seems that the different backgrounds of the editors who belonged to the cultural elite and the ordinary rural letter-writers caused problems. For the ordinary people, who generally lived an almost subsistent life, the weather, crops, and cases of death were knowledge needed for surviving in their world, but to the editors, it was idle talk that they had to publish if they wanted their newspaper to survive. However, a great number of letters were published because newspaper editors had to tread a fine line between pleasing the paying public and meeting their own ideals of journalism.

Europaeus himself was a victim of this journalistic dilemma. For him, the press was all about the public debate without maneuvering done by journalists. At the same time, he publicly promoted the culture of local letters, he was continually marginalized among the editors of the Finnish-language press. At

---

[50] Paavo Tikkanen, "Uusia Suomenkielisiä sanomalehtiä," *Suometar*, December 16, 1862.

[51] Jaakko Forsman, "Vähän keskustelemusta hra E-s´en kanssa," *Helsingin Uutiset*, January 8, 1863.

[52] Tikkanen, "Uusia Suomenkielisiä."

[53] Anton Fredrik Almberg, "Marraskuun 25 p:nä," *Uusi Suometar*, November 25, 1869.

[54] Stark, *The Limits of Patriarchy*, 49–55, 178.

the end of the 1850s, the newspapers began to block his writings. In the 1860s, he was publicly stigmatized as an insane and illiterate person by the members of the Finnish nationalistic elite.[55] The main reason for this was his critique of Lönnrot's *Kalevala*. Its status as the original epic of the people had become an invincible dogma of Finnish nationalism—to put it simply, its criticism was not acceptable for a member of the Finnish-language elite. Furthermore, Europaeus broke many social norms in his personal life. He usually had no permanent place of residence and was ignorant of the normative dress codes.[56] His position worsened in the 1860s when he could no longer get financial support for his scientific actions from Finland. Due to this, Europaeus turned to Russian academic societies, which funded his ethnographic expeditions. This created the suspicion among the Finnish elite that Europaeus lacked commitment to Finnish nationalism, which isolated Europaeus further.[57] The fact that he publicly promoted the local letters that were a threat to the identity of journalism did not improve his position either.

In a sense, the culture of local letters became marginalized along with the social status of Europaeus. If the importance of the letters to the press had been recognized by the editors, the significance of Europaeus on its development would have also had to be acknowledged. However, the phenomenon of local letters was so widespread that it could not be completely ignored, at least when the history of the Finnish-language press was written in ceremonial speeches. In 1866, when *Suometar* published its last issue, the closing words stated that because of the great number of letters sent to the paper, a new idea of the newspaper was noticed for the first time. Besides telling the news, the new task of the newspaper was to serve as an organ of the people, to defend its interests and make the will, needs, hopes, and opinions of the people known while also directing public opinion. According to *Suometar*, all this was understood for the first time in the 1850s, when letters from readers flooded in from all around the country.[58] However, the editors of *Suometar* did not mention the role of Europaeus in the emergence of the culture of letters to the press.

## The shadows of transnational ideologies

The controversial character of Europaeus and the idea that the local letters were a threat to the developing professional identity of Finnish-language journalism could not completely explain the fate of the letter-writing culture in

---

[55] See for example Ernst Linder, "Helmik. 5 p," *Päivätär*, February 6 1864.
[56] Irma Sulkunen, *Suomalaisen Kirjallisuuden seura 1831–1892* (Helsinki: SKS, 2004), 83–4, 109–15; Kuusi and Timonen, "Suurmies?," 23–6, 39–50.
[57] Kuusi and Timonen, "Suurmies?," 25–6, 40.
[58] Fredrik Polén, "Loppulause," *Suometar*, December 31, 1866.

the middle of the nineteenth century. To understand the general attitude towards the phenomenon more deeply, attention must be directed more closely towards the social status of the editors of the Finnish-language press and the transnational ideologies of the era.

In general, the editors of the Finnish-language press were not journalists in a modern sense. Almost all the editors of the era were members of the sparse Finnish-language elite. This applies especially to the most important Helsinki-based newspapers, whose editors were major figures of the elite. *Suometar*, the most important newspaper of the era, was edited by Rietrikki Polén (1851–1856) and Paavo Tikkanen (1823–1872). Its most important contributor was Georg Zacharias Forsman (later Yrjö Sakari Yrjö-Koskinen), who in 1863 also edited *Helsingin Uutisia*. These three were also the first three individuals to write a doctoral thesis in Finnish (in 1858–1859). Gustaf Erik Eurén, who was the editor of *Sanomia Turusta* (1853–1857) and *Hämäläinen* (1858–1860 and 1862–1872) was a well-known linguist who had published one of the first Finnish dictionaries and grammars.[59]

The main ideological incentive of these members of the Finnish-language elite was Finnish nationalism, whose main task was to improve the position of the Finnish language. The nationalism of the era was not just a cultural identity, but a closely transnational phenomenon that was at the general level connected with the relationship between the national elites and ordinary people. In the Romantic period at the beginning of the nineteenth century, the culture of the common people was idealized.[60] The epic of *Kalevala*, which contained the folk poetry of the Finnish people, was a good example of this. The idea was that the natural conditions defined the characteristics of both individuals and the people as a nation. Thus, the individual character of the ordinary people legitimized nationalism, which was seen as an ingredient of humanity.[61]

Europaeus, who was interested in and promoted the culture of local letters, was a typical representative of this kind of Romantic nationalism. He hunted for the authentic experience of the common people both from oral folklore and the local letters. However, in the 1850s Europaeus was a representative of the old world. After the Revolutions of 1848 in Europe, the transnational ideals of the nationalistic elites changed. The elite in general no longer saw the common

---

[59] Lauri Hakulinen, "Euren, Gustaf Erik," in *Kansallinen elämäkerrasto 1*, eds. Kaarlo Blomstedt et al. (Porvoo: WSOY, 1927), 601–3.
[60] See e.g. Joseph Theodoor Leerssen, *National Thought in Europe. A Cultural History* (Amsterdam: Amsterdam University Press, 2006), 93–118.
[61] See Gunnar Suolahti, *Y. S. Yrjö-Koskisen elämä: 1, Nuori Yrjö Koskinen* (Otava: Helsinki, 1974), 209–16.

people in an idealized light. On the contrary, the mass power of the ordinary people was seen as a threat to the social status of the elite.[62]

In the post-1848 world, nationalism became an increasingly political issue. Georg Zacharias Forsman explained this in 1861 in a letter he sent from Paris that was published in *Suometar*. By referring to the post-1848 world, he stated: "In these years a new power and authority has emerged among the fundamental principles of the world, namely *nationality*. To this point it has not meant anything; the state or correctly the government and its advantages have been all there is."[63] This meant that after 1848, the issue was no more about the plain originality of the national culture, which, for example, *Kalevala* had allegedly manifested. Now the attention was on the current vitality of nations. The topical questions were: at what point of development was the particular nation and culture? Which nation and culture had the right to live, and which were doomed to fade away?

Nationalism was also at the core of the scientific discussions of the era. The great cultural theories were constructed by combining the discoveries of history, linguistics, archaeology, craniometry, and the racial theories of the era. In general, these cultural theories divided European nationalities into two groups based on their imagined origins: the Aryans and Turanians. The problem for the Finnish-language elite was that according to these cultural theories, the Finnish-language people were Turanians, who were thought to be inferior to the Aryans. At the same time, the Swedish people in the neighboring country represented the elite section of the Aryan race that had not been mixed with Turanians. The Swedish-speaking people of Finland were thought to be a part of the elite people.[64] This was a heavy blow for the Finnish-speaking elite, whose worst domestic enemy was the Swedish-language elite, who defended the privileged position of Swedish in Finland.

This interpretation, which was based on contemporary science, seemed to be credible to many people because of the current societal situation in Finland, where Finnish was mainly the language of the common people, who lived their self-sufficient lives in the numerous local rural communities without a proper literary culture. To put it simply, from the point of view of the legitimate science of the era, Finnish-language culture seemed to be underdeveloped or even primitive. Therefore, the Finnish-language elite was in an awkward position in the transnational debate of the era considering which nation had the right to live and create culture.

---

[62] See Suolahti, *Y. S. Yrjö-Koskisen elämä*, 209–27.
[63] Y. K. [Forsman, Zacharias], "Pariisista 18 p:nä Jouluk. 1860," *Suometar*, January 1, 1861.
[64] See Heikki Kokko, "Sivistyksen surkea tila," in *Kansa kaikkivaltias: Suurlakko Suomessa 1905*, eds. Pertti Haapala, Olli Löytty, Kukku Melkas and Marko Tikka (Helsinki: Teos, 2008), 307–12.

The situation escalated further during the 1850s. In 1853–1855, J. A. Gobineau published his well-known study on the inequality of the human race. According to him, there were three races in the world: white, yellow, and black. For Gobineau, the white race had created all human culture. It was the elite race that had to lead and avoid miscegenation with the inferior races. In Gobineau's categorization, the Finnish people were representatives of the yellow race of Asia.[65] In 1855, a Swedish author, August Sohlman, published a book that was widely read in Finland. According to Sohlman, the Swedish people were the conquerors who had brought all the culture and civilization to Finland. All the culture that the Finnish people had was borrowed from the Swedish people. The Finnish people had no ability to create any culture of its own. According to Sohlman, hardly any group had played such an insignificant role in the historical development of Europe as the Finnish people had.[66]

The rise of the culture of local letters in Finland coincided with this change of direction of the elite's transnational ideologies. This is the root cause why the editors who represented the Finnish-language elite did not become excited by the culture of letters to newspapers in the 1850s. The other reason was that there were no transnational examples of this kind of phenomenon. As Europaeus had noticed, the legitimation of the culture of letters to the press was difficult due to the lack of examples from other countries. There was no more room for an original form of folk culture in the transnational field of nationalism—at least its status was no higher than prior to the revolutions of 1848.[67]

The editors and the main figures of the most significant Finnish-language newspapers lived in this transnational space, in which nationalism was legitimized by the science of the era. The ideologies of the time forced them to prove the ability of the Finnish language and culture to create forms of higher European culture. The first doctoral theses that Polén, Forsman, and Tikkanen wrote at the turn of the 1860s were a significant part of this defense of Finnish nationalism. The dissertations proved that Finnish could be a language of science, which had been questioned in the public debate between the members of the Swedish- and Finnish-language elites.[68] In the 1860s, the Finnish-

---

[65] Anna-Maija Virtanen, "Gobineaun rotuoppi ja germaanien ihannointi," in *Mongoleja vai germaaneja? – rotuteorioiden suomalaiset*, eds. Marjatta Hietala, Aira Kemiläinen and Pekka Suvanto (Helsinki: SHS, 1985), 53–7.

[66] August Sohlman, *Det unga Finland: En kulturhistorisk betraktelse* (Stockholm: C. M. Thimgren, 1855), 33–5; See also Arni-Kauttu, *Itäistä kelvottomuutta vastaan*, 59–70.

[67] See Kokko, "Kotomaamme katveinen kuva," 275–8.

[68] See e.g. Matti Klinge, *Keisarin Suomi*, trans. Marketta Klinge (Helsinki: Schildts, 1997), 230–37; Ilkka Liikanen, *Fennomania ja kansa: Joukkojärjestäytymisen läpimurto ja Suomalaisen puolueen synty* (Helsinki: SHS, 1995), 111–16.

language elite emphasized the forms of cultural life that were considered to represent higher culture. They put their effort into the arts, like prose fiction, poetry, and theatre.[69] Furthermore, the history of the Finnish nation was invented. In 1857–1859, Georg Zacharias Forsman published the history of the Cudgel War, the peasant uprising in Finland in 1596–1597. In his book, Forsman argued that the Finnish peasants had fought for their freedom and justice, and that the Cudgel War was a spark for the wars in the seventeenth century, in which Sweden rose to become a major power in northern Europe. According to Forsman, Finnish culture was founded in this era, when Finnish soldiers fought in Europe and brought glory to the Swedish crown, whose name hid the heroic deeds of Finnish men.[70] These were attempts to prove the ability to create a higher culture in Finnish under the pressure of the transnational atmosphere.

From the perspective of ideologies, the whole situation could be seen as a struggle between the two forms of transnational ideology—pre-1848 and post-1848 nationalism—that in Finland collided with the national-level nationalism that was based on the ideological competition between the Finnish and Swedish language. This national struggle was overshadowed by the transnational struggle, because the social world of the elite actors reached beyond the national level where the ideological science of the era legitimized the new kind of nationalism.[71] Paradoxically, this happened while the social world of the vernacular letter-writers was just beginning to extend from the local to trans-local level, which made it possible for them to see the nation as an "imagined community."[72]

## Conclusion

The culture of local letters to the press was marginalized by newspaper editors in the 1850s and 1860s because of the new transnational ideologies that were connected to nationalism after the 1848 revolutions. After the upheavals, the ideologies that defined nationalism as a transnational phenomenon no longer emphasized the originality of vernacular culture, but instead the stage of

---

[69] See Kokko, "Kotomaamme katveinen kuva," 277–78.

[70] Yrjö Yrjö-Koskinen, *Nuijasota. Sen syyt ja tapaukset. Jälkimmäinen osa* (Turku, 1859), 327–28.

[71] See Berger and Luckmann, *The Social Construction of Reality*, 33–42, 110–6, 201–4, 233.

[72] Benedict Anderson, *Imagined Communities: Reflections on the Origin and Spread of Nationalism* (London: Verso, 2016), 6, 22–5, 35; About the "imagined community" and the culture of local letters, see Kokko, "From Local to Translocal," 193–94; Heikki Kokko, "Temporalization of Experiencing: First-Hand Experience of the Nation in Mid-Nineteenth Century Finland," in *Lived Nation as the History of Experiences and Emotions in Finland, 1800–2000*, eds. Ville Kivimäki, Sami Suodenjoki and Tanja Vahtkari (London: Palgrave, 2021), 109–33.

development of the national culture in the present was compared with those of other nations. Emphasis was placed on higher culture, like literature and theatre, which was defined by the standards of the Western world. The culture of letters to newspapers that emerged in 1850s Finland did not fit with the new standards of transnational nationalism. Theatre, literature, and history all had their Western models and standards, but the emergence of the nationwide culture of letters to the press was something that did not have models anywhere else. Explaining it as a higher form of culture that could legitimize Finnish nationalism seemed to be an impossible task in the transnational atmosphere.

The local letters contained things that were significant to the agrarian letter-writers, but they were insignificant to the nationalistic elite, who had assigned themselves the task of promoting Finnish nationalism on the international stage. D. E. D. Europaeus was the only one who publicly addressed the uniqueness of the culture of letters to the press. However, he was excluded from the Finnish-language nationalist elite due to his controversial character and untypical behavior. The Finnish-language editors of the era were not essentially journalists but members of the Finnish-language nationalist elite. Thus, the ideology of nationalism was preferred at the expense of journalistic ideals.

In the wider sense, the Finnish case of the culture of letters to newspapers highlights the transnationality of nineteenth-century nationalism. Furthermore, it shows how any societally important phenomenon could be a blind spot for contemporaries due to the ideologies of the era. This is because the dominant ideology that outlines the reality for example in the name of science is not inevitably chosen because of its explanatory potential but simply because of the fact it happens to be available and dominant.[73]

In the Finnish case, the culture of letters to the press was not the only thing that was forgotten. The scientific achievements of Europaeus were acknowledged only after his death in 1884.[74] The same applies to Aleksis Kivi, who started this chapter as a contemporary witness to the culture of letters to the press. The Finnish-language elite pinned their hopes on this novelist, but marginalized him when his book *Seitsemän Veljestä* was criticized for not reaching the ideals of Western prose fiction. Kivi was promoted to the status of the national writer of Finland only after his death in 1872. However, the culture of letters to the press disappeared into obscurity for a significantly longer period. It became visible only after the digitalization of newspaper sources in the twenty-first century.

---

[73] See Berger and Luckmann, *The Social Construction of Reality*, 141–43.
[74] Kaukonen, "Europaeuksen osa," 76–81.

# Chapter 2

# Hate speech of the radical right in Finnish media during the 1930s and 2010s: The case of *Ajan Suunta* and *Suomen Uutiset*

Markku Mattila

*Migration Institute of Finland*

Ari Haasio

*Seinäjoki University of Applied Sciences, Finland*

**Abstract:** This chapter discusses the hate speech of two Finnish newspapers, *Ajan Suunta* and *Suomen Uutiset* (online newspaper). The former is an extreme right newspaper published in the 1930s, and the latter is the main supporter of Finnish right wing party True Finns. We compare the existing differences and similarities between the topoi of Finnish radical-right hate speech of the 1930s and 2010s. The research questions can be summarized as follows:

1) What topoi did Finnish radical-right hate speech use in the 1930s and 2010s, and how?

2) What mutual similarities and differences in hate speech can be observed in the 1930s and 2010s?

3) What is the significance of indirect hate speech as a part of hate speech rhetoric?

Our hypothesis is that both the Finnish radical right in the 1930s and the Finnish radical right of the 2010s used similar topoi in their hate speech.

**Keywords:** hate speech; extreme right; literary topos; Finland

***

Today hate speech is a hotly discussed topic, but actually, it is an old phenomenon. By speaking out, people have incited anger long before the current term was born or before Nazi Germany's Jewish propaganda and its consequences defined the matter in a way quite familiar to Europeans. Thus, it is clear that the subjects of hate speech have varied over time. However, it seems that the forms, techniques and themes of hate speech are relatively permanent. This is noticeable by looking at the hate speech of times past and present.[1]

Hate speech always needs an object or target. However, the targets change. For example, in 1930s Europe the target was very often Jews. After the Soviet Union and the "Eastern Bloc" collapsed, jihadist Islamism very quickly emerged as a new political enemy of the Western World. The hate speech directed against Arabs, Islam and Muslims intensified after the terrorist attack of 11 September 2001.[2] The attack was followed by a "war on terrorism" and several European terrorist attacks, beginning with the Madrid (2004) and London (2005) attacks. Combined with mass immigration to Europe from Islamic countries, this development has increasingly directed political hate speech towards Muslims. The terror attacks in Scandinavia (2017) have also increased hate speech and affected people's attitudes.[3]

In this chapter, we compare the hate speech of a newspaper published by a Finnish radical-right party in the 1930s with the hate speech of an online digital media site published by a Finnish radical-right political party in the 2010s. We use the term *radical right* to describe the two political parties. According to Bjørgo and Ravndal, the radical right is characterized by two central premises: in the opinion of those on the radical right, democracy should be maintained and liberal elites must be replaced.[4] Both parties are parliamentary parties, and their ideology fulfills both the first and second conditions.[5]

---

[1] See, e.g. Ari Haasio, Anu Ojaranta and Markku Mattila, *Valheen jäljillä* (Helsinki: Avain, 2018), 41–4; Markku Mattila, Ari Haasio and Anu Ojaranta, "Vihapuhetta valemediassa," *Tiede ja Edistys* 44, no. 1 (2019): 32–3.

[2] E.g. El-Sayed El-Aswad, "Images of Muslims in Western Scholarship and Media after 9/11," *Digest of Middle East Studies* 22, no. 1 (2013): 39–56.

[3] See, e.g. Moa Eriksson, "Pizza, beer and kittens: Negotiating cultural trauma discourses on Twitter in the wake of the 2017 Stockholmattack," *New Media & Society* 20, no. 11 (2018): 3980–96; Ari Haasio, Markku Mattila, Anu Ojaranta and Elisa Kannasto, "Terrori-isku tiedontarpeiden virittäjänä: Turun puukotusten aiheuttamat tiedontarpeet," *Informaatiotutkimus* 37, no. 2 (2018): 5–36.

[4] Tore Bjørgo and Jacob Aasland Ravndal, *Extreme-Right Violence and Terrorism: Concepts, Patterns, and Responses* (The Hague: International Centre for Counter-Terrorism, 2019), 3; see also Andreas Fagerholm, "The radical right and the radical left in contemporary Europe: Two min–max definitions," *Journal of Contemporary European Studies* 26, no. 4 (2018): 413–15.

[5] Isänmaallisen kansanliikkeen yleiset ohjelmaperusteet (Perusohjelma hyväksytty perustavassa kokouksessa Hämeenlinnassa 5.6.1932), https://www.fsd.tuni.fi/pohtivaohjelm alistat/IKL/291 (accessed 13.10.2021); Perussuomalaiset rp., *Periaateohjelma*, 19 October 2018, https://www.fsd.tuni.fi/pohtiva/ohjelmalistat/PS/ (accessed 13 October 2021).

According to our research hypothesis, a single key archetype can be assigned to the form and content of hate speech. This archetype is a book called *The Protocols of the Learned Elders of Zion* (hereinafter *Protocols*), which has circulated around the world since the early twentieth century. The *Protocols* is considered the most important anti-Semitic publication of the twentieth century.[6] We analyze hate speech from the 1930s and 2010s separately using literary topology as a method and the *Protocols* as a starting point. We synthesize the main findings followed by a more general discussion. The chapter is based on the idea that ideology and media are intertwined, because here one's own media is used to convey one's own ideology.

### Research problem, data and method

In literary studies, a common theme or motif or a rhetorical convention or formula is called topos (pl. topoi). The theory of topos dates to Aristotle and classical rhetoric, but the definition used in literary studies stems from a study published by Ernst Robert Curtius in 1948, which was soon translated into English.[7] Relying on Curtius and his tradition,[8] we argue that both historic and current Finnish radical-right political hate speech share common literary themes or conventions, i.e. distinguishable topoi that recur again and again.

Our hypothesis is that both the Finnish radical right in the 1930s and the Finnish radical right of the 2010s used similar topoi in their hate speech, and further, that these topoi were presented as a coherent set of talking points in the *Protocols*, making the book a "template" for the hate speech of the 1930s and 2010s. According to our hypothesis, the topoi of hate speech remain essentially the same over time, but the subject of the speech changes: whereas in the 1930s the target was "Jews" and "Jewry," in the 2010s "Muslims" and humanitarian migrants, above all "asylum seekers," are the targets. We have chosen the Jews as the target of our analysis of the 1930s, even though the main target of Finnish radical-right hate speech at that time was the Russians and Bolshevism, not the

---

[6] Richard Landes and Steven T. Katz, "Introduction: The Protocols in the Dawn of the 21st Century," in *The Paranoid Apocalypse: A Hundred-Year Retrospective on The Protocols of the Elders of Zion*, eds. Richard Landes and Steven T. Katz (New York: New York University Press, 2012), 1–2.

[7] Ernst Robert Curtius, *European Literature and the Latin Middle Ages*, trans. Willard R. Trask (London: Routledge & Kegan Paul, 1953).

[8] E.g. Alexander Gelley "Ernst Robert Curtius: Topology and Critical Method," *MLN* 81, no. 5 (1966): 579–94; Jeanne Fahnestock and Marie Secor, "The rhetoric of literary criticism," in *Textual Dynamics of the Professions: Historical and Contemporary Studies of Writing in Professional Communities*, eds. Charles Bazerman and James Paradis (Madison: University of Wisconsin Press, 1991), 77–96; Michelle R. Warren, "Introduction: Relating philology, practicing humanism," *PMLA/Publications of the Modern Language Association of America* 125, no. 2 (2010): 283–88.

Jews.[9] With this choice, we wanted to connect our 1930s data firmly to the *Protocols* and distance the data from the policy regarding Finland's eastern border and the Soviet Union, and only test our hypothesis with the 2010s data.

This chapter analyzes the differences and similarities between the topoi of Finnish radical-right hate speech of the 1930s and 2010s. The goal is to test our hypothesis, and the research problem can be summarized as follows:

1) What topoi did Finnish radical-right hate speech use in the 1930s and 2010s, and how?

2) What mutual similarities and differences in hate speech can be observed in the 1930s and 2010s?

3) What is the significance of indirect hate speech as a part of hate speech rhetoric?

Several methods could have been applied in the analysis, but our choice has been to use grounded theory[10] and content analysis[11]. That is because our primary starting point is a work of fiction (or pamphlet), not media. We could also have done framing analysis of the ways in which hate speech was used to structure individual's perception of society.[12] For example, Van Gorp uses inductive framing analysis in a case study on the decision to open a refugee center in a local community. As a result, he produces a table very similar to what we have obtained in this study. However, his inductive framing analysis is based on content analysis of all expressions of communication. As material, he uses newspaper articles, TV broadcasts, such primary data as the minutes of the gatherings and meetings, pamphlets of both supporters and opponents, petitions, and open and circular letters by political parties and pressure groups. He also uses his own observations of public happenings (meetings, information

---

[9] E.g. Kari Immonen, *Ryssästä saa puhua...: Neuvostoliitto suomalaisessa julkisuudessa ja kirjat julkisuuden muotona 1918–39* (Helsinki: Otava, 1987); Outi Karemaa, *Vihollisia, vainoojia, syöpäläisiä: Venäläisviha Suomessa 1917–1923* (Helsinki: SHS, 1998); Jari Hanski, *Juutalaisviha Suomessa 1918–1944* (Helsinki: Ajatus Kirjat, 2006).

[10] E.g. Barney Glaser and Anselm Strauss, *The Discovery of Grounded Theory: Strategies for Qualitative Research* (Chicago: Aldine, 1967); Juliet M. Corbin and Anselm L. Strauss, *Basics of Qualitative Research: Techniques and Procedures for Developing Grounded Theory, 4th edition* (Los Angeles: Sage, 2015).

[11] E.g. Klaus Krippendorf, *Content Analysis: An Introduction to Its Methodology*, 2nd edition (Thousand Oaks, London, and New Delhi: Sage Publications, 2004).

[12] Erving Goffman, *Frame Analysis: An Essay on the Organization of Experience* (Cambridge, Mass.: Harvard University Press, 1974).

sessions, protests marches, etc.).[13] Contrary to him, our aim was not to focus on the impact and power of the message,[14] due to which grounded theory and content analysis were more suitable for our purposes.

In practice, we have thematized and abstracted the topoi of hate speech in the first Finnish edition of *Protocols*, published in 1919.[15] Altogether, we identified 13 topos in the work (Table 2.1). For example, the conspiracy topos is represented in *Protocols* by such claims as Jews are seizing all the power, freemasons are the same as Jews and real power is hidden. Another example: the disorder topos is presented in such claims as the Jews are deliberately spreading discord among people, families, political parties and peoples. They spread disinformation, cause party disputes, incite religious and racial hatred, and break up traditional families. As the last example: the wrong ideals topos is represented in the *Protocols* by the claim that Jews are disseminating such "destructive ideas" as Darwinism, Marxism, Nietzsche's philosophy and anarchism. They are hijacking teaching in higher education institutions by removing the traditional curriculum and replacing it with a more suitable one.

**Table 2.1.** Common themes in *The Protocols of the Learned Elders of Zion* and the abstracted topoi based on such themes.

|   | *Protocols – themes* | *Topos* |
|---|---|---|
| 1 | Jews seize all power; freemasons = Jews; their real power is hidden | **Conspiracy** |
| 2 | globalism; global big capitalism | **Nation is at risk** |
| 3 | Jews own the press | **Media** |
| 4 | sowing discord | **Disorder** |

13 Baldwin Van Gorp, "Culture and Protest in Media Frames," in *Media and Revolt: Strategies and Performances from the 1960s to the Present*, eds. Kathrin Fahlenbrach, Erling Sivertsen and Rolf Werenskjold (New York, Oxford: Berghahn Books 2022), 75–90. We are much obliged to the referee to bring the work of Van Gorp to our attention.

14 Dhavan V. Shah, Douglas M. McLeod, Melissa R. Gotlieb and Nam-Jin Lee, "Framing and Agenda Setting," in *The Sage Handbook of Media Processes and Effects*, eds. Robin L. Nabi and Mary Beth Oliver (London: Sage, 2009), 83–98.

15 S.[ergei] Nilus, *Förlåten faller... Det tillkommande världssjälvhärskardömet enligt "Sions vises hemliga protokoll."* Översättning från det ryska originalets fjärde upplaga av S. (Helsingfors: Enskilt förlag, 1919). On the early history of the *Protocols* in Finland, see Markku Mattila, "'Förlåten faller...' Nimimerkki S. ja Siionin viisaitten pöytäkirjojen tulo Suomeen" (Master's thesis, University of Tampere, 1991).

| 5  | dissemination of destructive ideas | **Wrong ideals** |
|----|-----------------------------------|------------------|
| 6  | destroying of (Christian) religion | **Religion is in danger** |
| 7  | Jews as their own "race" | **Ethnic "other"** |
| 8  | politics of power | **By any means necessary** |
| 9  | They sacrifice themselves as victims to further their own cause | **Own people are expendable** |
| 10 | dissemination of vices and immoral lifestyle | **Criminality** |
| 11 | the judiciary of the world to come | **Judiciary** |
| 12 | economics and tax policy | **Citizen always pays** |
| 13 | government: Jewish kingship | **New World Order** |

Two media outlets have been used as research data in the study, the 1930s newspaper *Ajan Suunta* (Direction of Time) and the 2010s online media site *Suomen Uutiset* (News of Finland). *Ajan Suunta* has been fully digitized by the National Library of Finland and its digital interface has been used to analyze the content. *Suomen Uutiset* is a newspaper published only on the internet freely. The data has been gathered using the paper's own search engine, which shows the 50 most recent hits for each search. The material used represents the opinion of the paper, not the opinion of an individual writer. Therefore, the footnotes give only the date and page number (*Ajan Suunta*) or the date (*Suomen Uutiset*) of the material used.

The Finnish radical-right Patriotic People's Movement (Isänmaallinen kansanliike) party was established in 1932.[16] In December of the same year, the daily paper *Ajan Suunta* was published as the principal mouthpiece of the party. It was issued until the fall of 1944. The paper defined itself as a "struggle paper" promoting the worldview of the party.[17] The goal of the party was a "nationally strong" and politically radical right Finland, where a "patriotic way

---

[16] For more on the history of the Finnish radical right between the world wars, see, e.g. Juha Siltala, *Lapuan liike ja kyyditykset 1930* (Helsingissä: Otava,1985); Henrik Ekberg, *Führerns trogna följeslagare: Den finländska nazismen 1932–1944* (Helsingfors: Schildts, 1991); Oula Silvennoinen, Marko Tikka and Aapo Roselius, *Suomalaiset fasistit: Mustan sarastuksen airuet* (Helsinki: WSOY, 2016).

[17] Raimo Salokangas, "Puoluepolitiikkaa ja uutisjournalismia muuttuvilla lehtimarkkinoilla," in *Sanomalehdistö suurlakosta talvisotaan: Suomen lehdistön historia, 2*, ed. Päiviö Tommila (Kuopio: Kustannuskiila, 1987), 305–6.

of thinking," a strong "national spirit" and (Lutheran) religion are valued. It pursued the goal through a carefully crafted program that included the following objectives: 1) creating a strong and politically "white" (i.e. radical right) front in the country, 2) fighting "relentlessly" against communism and socialism, 3) supporting "uncompromisingly" the country's army and civil guard, 4) securing the "white" worker's right to work, i.e. resisting (left-wing) strikes and strikers, 5) increasing government power and sharing power between government and parliament in a new and "better" way, and 6) improving farmers' livelihoods in particular, which had been weakened by the current Great Depression.[18] As can be seen from the program, the party identified leftism as its enemy. On the other hand, the party's program did not include a racial agenda. However, *Ajan Suunta* strongly opposed the idea of Jewish refugees and their entry into Finland in the late 1930s.[19] Such "metabolic waste" was "not desired on the necks of Finns."[20]

The organizational development of the more recent radical right in Finland has to some extent followed the example of Sweden i.e. the Nordic country that has received the most support for the radical right both before and after the Second World War.[21] The rise of today's radical right in Sweden began at the turn of the 1970s and 1980s, and it was rooted in the economic recession and the simultaneous change in the ethnic structure of immigrants—the newcomers were no longer Nordic or European.[22] The organization Keep Sweden Swedish (*Bevara Sverige Svenskt*) was established in 1979, following the model of the British National Front. Today, the political activities of the radical right are mainly channeled through the Sweden Democrats (*Sverigedemokraterna*), which has its roots in the Keep Sweden Swedish movement.[23] The Finnish radical right has had connections with the Swedish organizations since the early 2000s. For

---

[18] Isänmaallisen kansanliikkeen yleiset ohjelmaperusteet, 5 June 1932.
[19] Sirpa Karhu, "Ajan Suunnan juutalaiskuva 1932–1944" (Master's thesis University of Jyväskylä, 2014), 37–45.
[20] *Ajan Suunta*, March 29, 1938, 6. Hereafter *Ajan Suunta* is shortened to AS in the footnotes.
[21] E.g. Holger Carlsson, *Nazismen i Sverige: Ett varningsord* (Stockholm: Federativs, 1942); Eric Wärenstam, *Fascismen och nazismen i Sverige* (Stockholm: Almqvist & Wiksell, 1972); Heléne Lööw, *Hakkorset och Wasakärven: En studie av nationalsocialismen i Sverige 1924–1950* (Göteborg: Historiska institutionen i Göteborg Universitet, 1990).
[22] Bengt Owe Birgersson, Stig Hadenius, Björn Molin and Hans Wieslander, *Sverige efter 1900: En modern politisk historia*. 10th edition (Stockholm: Bonnier Fakta, 1984), 308; *Statistik årsbok för Sverige, år 2000* (Stockholm: Statistiska centralbyrån, 2001), Table 45 and Table 237.
[23] Anna-Lena Lodenius and Stieg Larsson, *Extremhögern* (Stockholm: Tidens Förlag, 1994); Anna-Lena Lodenius and Mats Wingborg, *Slaget om svenskheten: Ta debatten med Sverigedemokraterna* (Stockholm: Premiss förlag, 2009).

example, the members of Finnish Sisu (*Suomen Sisu*) have been closely connected with the Sweden Democrats. The anonymous members of the Finnish right-wing website *Hommaforum* most likely have similar connections.[24] In the 2010s, the former members of Finnish Sisu became active in the populist Finns Party (*Perussuomalaiset*) and some of them are now members of parliament.

The Nordic neo-Nazis are also similarly networked. In 1997, Swedish militant neo-Nazis founded an organization called Swedish Resistance (*Svenska Motståndrörelsen*). It was founded by, among others, members of the White Aryan Resistance (*Vit Arisk Motstånd*), who engaged in violence. The movement also spread to Norway (2003), Finland (2008) and Denmark (2013), and together these four organizations have comprised the Nordic Resistance Movement (*Nordiska motståndsrörelsen*) since 2016. The movement deals with the white race and the Nordic community, which should aspire to fulfill the Nazi slogan *ein Reich, ein Volk, ein Führer.*[25] The Finnish Supreme Court banned the organization's activities in 2020 on the grounds that the organization is essentially acting against the law and good manners.[26] Apparently, its activities have continued under other names.[27]

*Suomen Uutiset* is an online news service maintained by the Finns Party that provides a voice for its supporters. The party established the online media site on Finland's Independence Day, in 2014.[28] The date symbolized the importance of nationalism to the party.

The publication emphasizes that it is not a member of the Finnish Council for Mass Media (*Julkisen sanan neuvosto*), which is a self-regulatory body set up by media publishers and journalists to interpret good journalistic practices and defend freedom of expression: practically all other Finnish newspapers and magazines belong to the Council. According to the editor-in-chief of *Suomen Uutiset*, a party's online media cannot be a representative of independent journalism, nor can *Suomen Uutiset* accept all of the Council's

[24] Dan Koivulaakso, Mikael Brunila and Li Andersson, *Äärioikeisto Suomessa* (Helsinki: Into, 2012), passim.
[25] Christer Mattsson, *Nordiska motståndsrörelsens ideologi, propaganda och livsåskådning* (Göteborg: Göteborgs universitet, Segerstedtinstitutet, 2018), 4–2; Magnus Ranstorp, Filip Ahlin and Magnus Normark, "Nordiska motståndsrörelsen – den samlande kraften inom den nationalsocialistiska miljön i Norden," in *Från Nordiska motståndsrörelsen till alternativhögern: En studie om den svenska radikalnationalistiska miljön,* eds. Magnus Ranstorp and Filip Ahlin (Stockholm: Försvarshögskolan, 2020), 146–47, 189, 191, 192; Henrik Holappa, *Minä perustin uusnatsijärjestön: Suomen Vastarintaliikkeen ex-johtajan muistelmat* (Helsinki: Into, 2016), 103–14, 128–46, 155–89.
[26] KKO: 2020:68. https://korkeinoikeus.fi/fi/index/ennakkopaatokset/kko202068.html.
[27] Tommi Kotonen and Daniel Sallamaa, "Pohjoismaisen Vastarintaliikkeen kieltäminen ja sen seuraukset," *Politiikassa,* November 10, 2020.
[28] *Suomen Uutiset,* no date. Hereafter *Suomen Uutiset* is shortened to SU in the footnotes.

views. He also believes that the *Guidelines for Journalists*, published and maintained by the Council, are overly binding for journalists and thus restrict their freedom of speech.[29]

The Finns Party is, by its own definition, "a patriotic [isänmaallinen] and Christian social party that promotes national interests."[30] It emphasizes Finnishness, nationalism and directness. Although the party's policy agenda does not directly criticize immigration, it for example states that "We want to support those in need primarily within their own country,"[31] which implies a criticism of immigration. In practice, however, the party's MPs have stated the matter directly, in some cases even succumbing to hate speech, which has led to legal action.[32]

### The concept of hate speech

Hate speech as a concept did not exist in the 1930s but, arguably, our current European understanding of hate speech, its nature and forms is based primarily on the European phenomenon of the 1930s, which culminated in the Holocaust.[33] Thus, speakers in the 1930s did not realize that they were using "hate speech" in the modern sense when denigrating other groups that they viewed as undesirable. Nowadays, hate speakers know that they are continuously testing the limits of current hate speech legislation and tolerance of society. However, since the phenomenon itself became noticeable in the 1930s, we have opted to also use the term *hate speech* for the speech of that time. We are not alone in adopting this strategy, as other researchers have also done so previously.[34]

Hate speech can be understood as an expression of one's ideology. It is always public and it also has listeners. The purpose of a hate speaker is to influence listeners and bend them to the speaker's own position. The aim is to get the audience to share the stigmatizing and contemptuous attitude of the hate speaker towards the object of the hate speech.[35] Due to such purposefulness,

---

[29] *SU*, November 13, 2016.

[30] Perussuomalaiset rp., *Periaateohjelma*.

[31] Perussuomalaiset rp., *Periaateohjelma*.

[32] E.g. Ari Haasio and Markku Mattila, *Suvaitsematon Suomi: Suvaitsemattomuuden historia* (Helsinki: Avain, 2021), 18.

[33] Mattila, Haasio and Ojaranta, "Vihapuhetta," 31.

[34] See, e.g. the research articles in Marja Vuorinen, ed., *Vihapuheen, viholliskuvien ja disinformaation historiaa: Vallan ja vastarinnan välineitä* (Turku: Turun Historiallinen Yhdistys, 2021).

[35] E.g. Markku Mattila and Ari Haasio, "Fake News, Fake Media and Hate Speech in Finnish MV-Magazine—How Can Libraries Fight Against the Lies?," in *New Trends and Challenges in Information Science and Information Seeking Behaviour*, ed. Octavia-Luciana Madge (Cham: Springer, 2021), 80.

hate speech can thus be considered a rhetorical activity since the basic function of rhetoric is to influence listeners and convince them to support the view of the speaker (author, presenter).[36]

Hate speech has been defined in many different ways. For a general definition of hate speech, we have chosen to use Bhikhu Parekh's formulation, according to which hate speech is defined via three characteristics: 1) hate speech is directed at a defined or easily identifiable individual or against a group, 2) hate speech stigmatizes an object either by implying or directly saying that the object has characteristics that are generally considered undesirable, and 3) as a result of these characteristics, the existence of the object is repugnant and the object can be viewed hostilely. The object deserves to be destroyed or deported, or at least oppressed and pushed to the margins of a decent society.[37]

While analyzing anti-Semitic hate speech in online discussions, we discovered that a significant portion of it was indirect. Anti-Semitism was not directly brought up verbally but instead referentially tied to the context of what was being said.[38] Other researchers have also noted a tendency for indirect hate speech.[39] Rather than taking a direct form, hate speech can also be described "as hate speech because of the intention and content."[40]

Indirect hate speech can therefore be understood as context-dependent content with the same purpose as direct hate speech: a stigmatizing and intolerant use of language targeting an individual or group. With indirect hate speech, the object of hate speech can be presented in as negative a light as possible, attaching to him/her or to the group that he or she represents irrelevant facts that may in themselves be true but that distort the context.

In this chapter, we start from the view that hate speech can be divided into direct and indirect hate speech. While their goal is the same, direct hate speech

---

[36] See also Aristotle, *Rhetorica*.

[37] Bhikhu Parekh, "Is There a Case for Banning Hate Speech?," in *The Content and Concept of Hate Speech: Rethinking Regulation and Responses,* eds. Michael Herz and Peter Molnar (New York: Cambridge University Press, 2012), 40–1; *Cf.* Katharine Gelber, *Speech Matters: Getting Free Speech Right* (St Lucia, Queensland, Australia: University of Queensland Press, 2011), 83–4.

[38] Michael Ridenhour, Arunkumar Bagavathi, Elaheh Raisi and Siddharth Krishnan, "Detecting Online Hate Speech: Approaches Using Weak Supervision and Network Embedding Models," in *Social, Cultural, and Behavioral Modeling,* eds. Robert Thomson, Halil Bisgin, Christopher Dancy, Ayaz Hyder and Muhammad Hussain (Cham: Springer, 2020), 209.

[39] E.g. Nedjma Ousidhoum, Zizheng Lin, Hongming Zhang, Yangqiu Song and Dit-Yan Yeung, "Multilingual and multi-aspect hate speech analysis," *arXiv preprint arXiv:1908.11049.*

[40] Naganna Chetty and Sreejith Alathur, "Hate speech review in the context of online social networks," *Aggression and Violent Behavior* 40 (May–June 2018): 108–18.

is more aggressive in its nature and even sub-style, relying on expressions that offend the object of the hate speech, for example. In contrast, indirect hate speech seeks the same result by hinting at and even subtly addressing issues out of context using correct language. The implicit hate speech mentioned by Parekh can be understood as indirect hate speech.[41] Current research deals with indirect hate speech primarily on the Internet and especially on social media,[42] but we are investigating it here also in printed media.

## Analysis

### Ajan Suunta

*Ajan Suunta* had a congruent view that the "arch villain" and "representative of all evil" is "the filthy rich Masonic, Soviet Jewish Communist that is puppeteering in the background."[43] The paper's propaganda against the Jews was directly lifted from contemporary German sources. *Ajan Suunta* directly referred to *The Protocols* in only seven newspaper articles in 1933, 1934, and 1937. In contrast, the claims based on them, i.e. the Jewish quest to destroy civilized nations, to start a world revolution and to achieve world domination, appeared in a total of 76 newspaper articles, which account for approximately 11 percent of the 1,015 anti-Semitic articles published in the journal.[44]

With respect to the topoi of hate speech (Table 2.1), we discovered a total of twelve used repeatedly by *Ajan Suunta*. Only the citizen always pays topos lacked direct use. It made use of such topoi in news reports, foreign letters, art reviews and letters from the public and political causeries. The paper did not include an actual editorial section. Instead, it included a political causerie column entitled "Tarkkailijan tähtäimestä" (From the Observer's Crosshairs), written over the years by authors using several pen names.[45] The column was published almost daily and usually located at the bottom of the front page. Due to its regular publication, uniform title and central location, the column can be considered representative of the paper's opinion, the equivalent of a formal editorial.

---

[41] Parekh, "Is There."

[42] E.g. Oğuz Kuş, "Documenting and Categorizing Hate Speech: Investigating Islamophobia in User Comments on Social Networks," in *International Symposium of New Media from the Past to the Future (May 10, 2017, Istanbul, TURKEY) Proceedings* (E-Book); Oana Ştefăniţă and Diana-Maria Buf, "Hate Speech in Social Media and Its Effects on the LGBT Community: A Review of the Current Research," *Romanian Journal of Communication and Public Relations* 23, no. 1 (2021): 47–55; Ridenhour et al., "Detecting."

[43] Salokangas, "Puoluepolitiikkaa," 306.

[44] Karhu, "Ajan Suunnan juutalaiskuva," 21, 34, 50, 57, 78, 80, 98.

[45] Karhu, "Ajan Suunnan juutalaiskuva," 21–2.

The paper stated in the spirit of the new world order topos that a historic battle was being waged over who ultimately would come to rule, Christ or Marx, the "5-angle blood-red Soviet star or white cross of Christ." The struggle was apocalyptic, for the seed of the Jewish "race gave birth to the prophet of the millennial Marxian kingdom, the new Saviour, the Messiah of Communism."[46] The conspiracy topos was supported by such claims as the freemasons and Jews are one and the same, the Jews are striving for world domination and to enslave all others, and furthermore that all "damage to the Western state order" or "waves [of leftist revolutions impacting] states" is because of the Jews.[47] "An international Jew laughs in his beard as the world of money has hidden its face. It plays everywhere and benefits from everything," states the paper,[48] in reference to the idea that Jewish people engage in usury and profiteering.

The nation in danger topos is represented by claims that the Jews own and control international (global) financial capital and that Jewish bankers determine the fate of nations. Finns should be aware of being pushed aside by all kinds of "yids." For the Jew does not hate anything so much as national thinking and its desire to make people healthy and powerful.[49]

The Jews carry out their plan by controlling international news agencies, the press and the film industry, which spread their lies (media topos).[50] Referring to foreign countries—Germany, Hungary and Czechoslovakia—the paper claimed that Jews controlled the legal profession (judiciary topos).[51] In Finland, on the other hand, a large number of lawyers ran on the Patriotic People's Movement platform in the elections.[52] Jews want to pit Christian nations against each other. Their goal is war, even a new world war. In addition to disorder (topos), war brings more wealth to Jews, who own the arms factories.[53] They also promote all kinds of criminality (topos), for example by controlling the European "white slavery" trade.[54] Jews promote such disintegrated ideas as "anti-Christian communism," (cultural) liberalism, "international Jewish-

---

[46] *AS*, March 24, 1933, 3; *AS*, August 29, 1938, 2.
[47] E.g. *AS*, June 29, 1933, 1; *AS*, September 6, 1933, 2; *AS*, October 7, 1935, 3; *AS*, September 15, 1936, 1, 4; *AS*, May 20, 1938, 2.
[48] *AS*, February 19, 1936, 3.
[49] E.g. *AS*, January 11, 1934, 3; *AS*, September 15, 1936, 1; *AS*, August 24, 1936, 4; *AS*, December 15, 1936, 9; *AS*, March 10, 1937, 1; *AS*, August 22, 1938, 3.
[50] E.g. *AS*, July 3, 1935, 3; *AS*, January 18, 1937, 1, 3, 4; *AS*, March 10, 1937, 1, 3; *AS*, May 27, 1937, 8; *AS*, March 23, 1938, 2.
[51] E.g. *AS*, April 28, 1938, 8; *AS*, August 29, 1938, 2; *AS*, December 13, 1938, 7.
[52] *AS*, June 3, 1936, 3.
[53] E.g. *AS*, January 11, 1934, 3; *AS*, October 7, 1935, 3; *AS*, September 15, 1936, 1; *AS*, December 15, 1936, 9.
[54] E.g. *AS*, January 22, 1934, 3; *AS*, July 1, 1943, 1.

Marxism," atheism, "'democracy'" and the "'peace movement'' [there were quotation marks in the original text to express scorn] (wrong ideals topos).[55] "Equality and brotherhood are [...] junk invented by the Jews," wrote the paper.[56]

The ideal of anti-Christian communism, or Marxism, fits the religion is in danger topos. Jews hate Christ and want to deprive people of their faith in God, thereby undermining the religious-moral foundation of society. However, the eastern brand of Marxist atheism is not the only danger: from the West comes a form of liberalism intent on debasing God's holiness.[57] The Jews are their own distinct race (ethnic "other" topos), a "chosen people of the world revolution" whose actions will have a devastating effect on the people among whom they live.[58] They are willing to advance their cause by all means necessary (topos).[59] They may even convert to Christianity and take Christian names, but still work "for the ideas adopted by Judaism, even to the point of often been more Jewish than the Jews themselves."[60] When Jews are promoting their cause, even their own people and allies are expendable (topos).[61]

The rhetoric employed in *Ajan Suunta* is very rudimentary. By its very nature, the rhetoric is declarative, not argumentative, as noted in previous research.[62] In general, it was sufficient to show the "Jewishness" of an idea or actor as a form of argument. Marxism is evil because Karl Marx had a Jewish background.[63] The businessman and swindler, who caused others to file for bankruptcy, is a Jew.[64] The Bolshevik leaders of the Soviet Union are Jews.[65] Here, *Ajan Suunta* also relied on the longstanding tradition of Finnish anti-Semitism and its strong connection with the Lutheran religion, which stems from Luther himself.[66] When Jews are already known to be untrustworthy in advance, it is enough to claim or show that someone is a Jew to prove they are not desirable neighbours or

---

[55] E.g. *AS*, January 2, 1933, 1, 3; *AS*, February 6, 1933, 2; *AS*, December 30, 1932, 1; *AS*, January 4, 1938, 3.

[56] *AS*, February 24, 1934, 5.

[57] E.g. *AS*, December 28, 1932, 1, 2; *AS*, January 2, 1933, 1, 3; *AS*, February 22, 1933, 5; *AS*, January 11, 1934, 3; *AS*, October 15, 1935, 2; *AS*, June 16, 1937, 3.

[58] E.g. *AS*, August 1, 1936, 3; *AS*, August 29, 1938, 2.

[59] E.g. *AS*, January 22, 1934, 3; *AS*, January 8, 1939, 8.

[60] *AS*, January 11, 1934, 3.

[61] E.g. *AS*, February 21, 1934, 1, 6.

[62] Salokangas, "Puoluepolitiikkaa," 305.

[63] E.g. *AS*, January 3, 1934, 1, 6.

[64] E.g. *AS*, March 27, 1937, 5.

[65] E.g. *AS*, August 23, 1935, 4.

[66] Hanski, *Juutalaisviha*; Haasio, Ojaranta and Mattila, *Valheen*, 41–2.

citizens. This essentialist thinking is inextricably linked to racism and ethnicity.[67]

The hate speech in *Ajan Suunta* was direct. For example, the paper blatantly used slurs like "jutku" (Jew), "ryssä" (Russian), and "rappari" (Freemason),[68] all commonly used sub-style words of the time. On the other hand, the paper's hate speech was kind of indirect. The slurs were repeated quite often and commonly in suspicious or reprehensible contexts and humiliating ways. This drumming repetition created a toxic, hate-speech-like atmosphere.[69]

### Suomen Uutiset

One of the journalistic methods used by *Suomen Uutiset* is the extensive use of interviews and raising a number of quotes and paraphrases to the main headline. A significant number of the interviewees are leading politicians in the party. On the pages of the online media, their views appear not only as personal statements but also as the Finns Party's policy on these themes.

Experts and "research-based knowledge" are used in many contexts. Academically trained people who agree with the party's agenda are consulted as experts, not, for example, as representatives of various research institutes or universities. When referring to research data, a large number of works from the Finns Party's own think tank are used. The think tank *Suomen Perusta* publishes trend-like studies, the scientific validity of which can be questioned. A closer analysis of the references shows that they are used in a one-sided manner and that only certain literature and studies supporting their agenda are used.

The Finns Party's own think tank publishes studies that support its ideology, with nationalism and non-immigration at the center. *Suomen Uutiset* also reproduces this ideological worldview. By doing so, the Finns Party tries to convince people of the "scientific" validity of their agenda. The studies are often questionable, like one study that says, "racist attitudes and behaviour can be seen more and more among immigrants, especially Muslims." This perspective is justified on the grounds that a large proportion of the racist beatings of immigrants are committed by people from the same area.[70] It is clear that assault statistics may show this to be true, but an act cannot be considered a racist crime if the motive is not racist. This erroneous circumstantial conclusion is a

---

[67] Maykel Verkuyten, "Discourses about ethnic group (de-)essentialism: Oppressive and progressive aspects," *British Journal of Social Psychology* 42, no. 3 (2003): 371–91.

[68] E.g. *AS*, April 2, 1938, 2.

[69] For more on the use of drumming repetition in hate speech, see Mattila, Haasio and Ojaranta, "Vihapuhetta," 39–40.

[70] Joona Räsänen, *Liberaalin dilemma: Monikulttuurisuus ja vapaa yhteiskunta* (Helsinki: Suomen Perusta, 2015), 57.

typical way in which party publications seek to stigmatize above all the Muslim population as well as other immigrants. It gives readers the impression that racism is just "left-green" propaganda.

Issues related to social security are also popular topics in *Suomen Uutiset*. Almost without exception, writings on this topic relate to the social security received by immigrants and the principles and alleged grievances associated with it. They either openly criticize social benefits for immigrants or use a critical tone to refer to immigrants receiving social benefits as part of a wider societal problem.

Some of the writings on social security for immigrants are quite sensationalistic, and above all references to Swedish sources and the ills of immigration in Sweden are cited in rather sensational fashion, such as in one story entitled "'The state paid for my gun'—Swedish Isis terrorists fought on social aid."[71] *Suomen Uutiset* sees Sweden as a warning sign of where things are headed in Finland, unless immigration is addressed. "We are on the road to [becoming] Sweden" is a much-repeated slogan.[72] The issues addressed in this regard—e.g. Islam, Islamization, immigration and especially crimes and violence in the suburbs committed by immigrants—are the same in both countries, and the hate speech is likewise quite similar.[73]

The Finns Party states in their party platform that they are on the side of the common people.[74] In its rhetoric, the party appeals to the disadvantaged by juxtaposing the benefits given to Finns in need and those paid to immigrants. For example, when the Ministry of Social Affairs and Health did not grant money to the traditional food aid organization Veikko Hursti, the news site prominently highlighted the fact that the funding was instead given, among others, to Sexpo, which promotes immigrants and sexual well-being.[75] Islam, immigrants and sexual minorities are the main targets of *Suomen Uutiset*. These themes are associated with most news in one way or another.

In terms of rhetoric, what is most striking are the quotes from interviews and speeches by political leaders of the party as well as examples of indirect hate speech. *Suomen Uutiset* publishes much interview-based material, in which

---

[71] *SU*, December 18, 2020.

[72] *SU*, September 24, 2021.

[73] For more on Swedish hate speech, see, e.g. Katrina Hirvonen, "Sweden: When hate becomes the norm," *Race & Class* 55, no. 1 (2013): 78–86; Sara Loredana Kiros, "Hate Speech: A Comparative Study of the Rhetoric in the Official Documents of the Sweden Democrats and the Rhetoric in Samtiden, a News Site Owned by the Sweden Democrats" (Bachelor's thesis, Malmö University, 2019).

[74] Perussuomalaiset rp, *Periaateohjelma*.

[75] *SU*, February 16, 2019; *SU*, February 14, 2020.

party MPs use offensive language that can be interpreted as hate speech. For example, the party chairman Jussi Halla-aho uses derogatory expressions about refugees, including the following:

> Gone are the days when the green leftists protested against the repatriation of *asylum tourists* and sabotaged police actions; they are now deeply offended when anyone questions the actions of the authorities.[76]

Resistance to immigration is a cornerstone of the party's ideology, and this theme is repeated both directly and indirectly in the paper. In some cases, the rhetoric takes the form of hate speech, as in an interview with MP Jukka Mäkynen published by the online media site:

> Finland is rapidly becoming especially a Somali colony, which will be settled by Somalis with Finnish taxpayers' money, which will also be sent to the colonial hosts in Somalia. The colonial hosts also go on holiday in their home country of Somalia [using the money].[77]

Mäkynen states that when the inhabitants of the colony grow tired of the role of net contributor, the colonial hosts will be in trouble, when money does not necessarily come from the "magic wall" anymore. In the quote, Finland is referred to as a Somali colony and colonial hosts refers to the family and kin left in the migrants' country of origin. The "magic wall" is also a typical expression of hate speech,[78] which includes the idea that an immigrant can withdraw any amount of money from an ATM.

When using the term "media," *Suomen Uutiset* is referring to media supported by the mainstream media, the truthfulness of which it regularly questions. The Finns Party and its members also believe that the leading Finnish media, above all the national broadcaster Yle and the country's largest media house Sanoma Corporation, are hostile to the party. According to a study commissioned by the party, that is due to the green-leftism of Finnish journalists.[79] The argument also implies that the Finnish media therefore do not present issues truthfully but emphasize instead their political nature based on the views of the so-called green-left alliance, even though the leading media are not officially engaged.

---

[76] *SU*, August 29, 2019.
[77] *SU*, August 12, 2019.
[78] See also Haasio, Ojaranta and Mattila, *Valheen.*
[79] Marko Hamilo, *Punavihreä kupla: Perussuomalaiset ja media* (Helsinki: Suomen Perusta, 2015).

When looking at the rhetoric of *Suomen Uutiset* from the perspective of topoi, several similarities can be observed with the topoi of *Protocols* and *Ajan Suunta*. All the topoi in *Protocols*, which also occur in *Ajan Suunta* in the 1930s, can also be found in the indirect hate speech of *Suomen Uutiset* in the early twenty-first century. In practice, this means that *Suomen Uutiset* uses the same themes as *Ajan Suunta* did in its day. In terms of content, the targets are different, but the rhetoric is the same.

For example, *Suomen Uutiset* references the topoi in a similar way as *Ajan Suunta* did in the past. In *Suomen Uutiset*'s case, the mainstream media, like Yle, gives leftist journalists silent permission to spread their propaganda.[80] The news site also suggests that the term "fake media" should be abolished.[81] According to MP Olli Immonen, "the elite censor you, your freedom of speech is threatened."[82] Criminality is also a good example of a similar topos employed in both *Ajan Suunta* and *Suomen Uutiset*. For instance, news especially about sexual crimes targeting children and women are a point of focus, even more so if the conviction is mild or the accused is acquitted of all wrongdoing.[83] These are just couple examples of some common topoi found in both publications: a full list is presented in Table 2.2.

The idea of just how the Finns Party defines hate speech is crystallized in a statement by MEP Teuvo Hakkarainen. According to him, hate speech is a new vocabulary used to attack nationalists. He sees racism as a fallback term used when one's own case lacks credibility.[84] The concept of racism as understood by the Finns Party differs from how it has traditionally been understood.[85] Instances of racism can certainly be found in the articles published in *Suomen Uutiset*. It more often takes the form of indirect hate speech, but also direct hate speech, targeting people of non-Finnish origin in a pejorative manner.

The examples presented above show that hate speech in *Suomen Uutiset* is characterized by the use of indirect hate speech. The use of sub-style words that are prohibited as outright hate speech (e.g., the n-word) is not noticeable. The online media site discusses various topics from an immigration policy perspective, consciously highlighting the adverse effects of immigration. In this way, indirect hate speech creates an image that can be interpreted as anti-immigration hate speech. The same phenomenon can be observed when religion is a topic of focus. Muslims and Islam are always presented in a

---

[80] *SU*, February 6, 2021.
[81] *SU*, November 28, 2017.
[82] *SU*, June 12, 2021.
[83] *SU*, November 19, 2020.
[84] *SU*, February 12, 2020.
[85] See also Jukka Hankamäki, *Totuus kiihottaa: Filosofinen tutkimus vasemmistopopulistisen valtamedian tieto- ja totuuskriisistä* (Helsinki: Suomen Perusta, 2020), passim.

negative light or a pejorative manner. On the other hand, the representatives of the party do use direct hate speech in public.

### Synthesis

Whereas the writing of the *Ajan Suunta* perceived Jews as the main threat, *Suomen Uutiset* considers Islamization to be a threat to the West and Finland. It is paradoxical that in a speech given in the EU Parliament and reported in *Suomen Uutiset*, MEP Teuvo Hakkarainen insisted on the rights of Jews, stating that "the persecution experienced by Jews must be tackled firmly."[86] Judaism is also a basic Finnish rhetorical tool for attacking Islam and the left.[87]

Since Islam and Islamization are a threat to Finland's independence and Finnishness, according to *Suomen Uutiset*, they must be addressed and the spread of Islam prevented. The key here is to prevent immigration, which the Finns Party is pushing. In the same vein, *Ajan Suunta* opposed Jewish refugees and demanded their expulsion from the country, to which "we have in the name of the nation's self-defence, not just a right but a duty."[88]

The key point here is that the forms of hate speech in the media have changed over the decades. Whereas the hate speech found in *Ajan Suunta* was usually very direct and stigmatizing, the hate speech of *Suomen Uutiset* is indirect. However, the goal is the same in both cases. Direct hate speech is not appropriate for columns published by a party's online media, but it is quite common in various social media forums. On the other hand, the themes of the hate speech have not changed. The same ideas and attitudes have been the motives of hate speech for decades.

**Figure 2.1.** Forms and motives of hate speech.

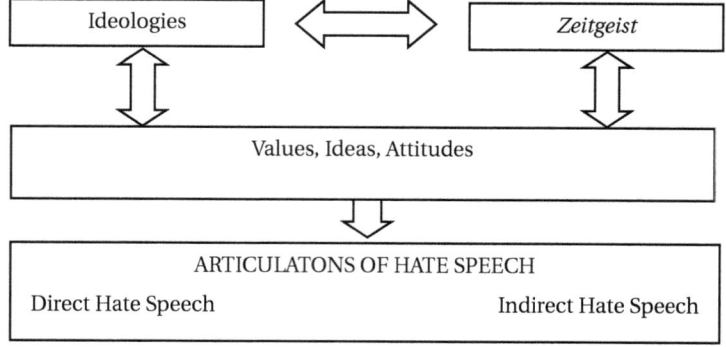

---

[86] *SU*, October 22, 2019; *SU*, February 12, 2020.
[87] E.g. *SU*, October 22, 2019.
[88] *AS*, February 11, 1939, 5.

As Figure 2.1 shows, the prevailing ideologies in society and the general *zeitgeist* influence an individual's values, attitudes and ideas. They materialize as hate speech, which can be both direct hate speech and indirect hate speech. It is assumed that the importance of indirect hate speech has grown and will continue to grow due to the increased sensitivity of society to, for example, the #MeToo campaign, anti-racism movements like Black Lives Matter and so forth.

Indirect hate speech appears to be correct and acceptable language precisely because its terminology is not offensive. For example, *Suomen Uutiset* tries to avoid direct hate speech due to the status of online media. As the supporter of a parliamentary party, it does not want to be stigmatized as a forum for outright hate speech. Direct hate speech, on the other hand, manifests itself in the statements of individuals, which online media sites quote more freely. Its stage is, above all, social media, in which individuals clearly comment on things using rhetoric that is seen as direct hate speech. This is evidenced by a number of cases, and even the leaders of the party perpetuate direct hate speech in social media.[89]

As noted above, *Ajan Suunta* used drumming repetition as an indirect hate speech technique. For example, whenever possible a person's Jewishness was mentioned—whether or not it was relevant to the matter at hand—creating an atmosphere in which the world seemed to revolve around Jews and their actions alone. At the same time, direct and indirect hate speech effectively complemented each other as direct hate speech was used to stigmatize them.

When comparing the topoi derived from the *Protocols* with the content of the data analyzed here (Table 2.2), many similarities emerge. Thus, the same topoi are repeated in societal hate speech regardless of time and target. The difference primarily has to do with the way in which the topos is expressed (linguistic expression) and its degree of directness/indirectness. In addition, the specifics of the hate speech topoi are still bound to a specific time. Whereas in the 1930s the religion in danger topos focused on (Jewish) communism and liberalism spread by Jews, in the 2010s the target was Islam.

**Table 2.2.** The topoi of hate speech in the analyzed data.

| TOPOS | *AJAN SUUNTA* | *SUOMEN UUTISET* |
|---|---|---|
| Conspiracy | Jews are behind all evils, striving for world domination | Islam is evil and its goal is to spread everywhere around the world |

[89] E.g. Vesa Sundqvist, "KKO kovensi Halla-ahon tuomiota," *YLE uutiset*, June 8, 2012; Pekka Loukkola, "Kansanedustaja Sebastian Tynkkysen tuomio kiihottamisesta kansanryhmää vastaan pysyi hovissa – aikoo valittaa Euroopan ihmisoikeustuomioistuimeen," *YLE uutiset*, July 2, 2020.

| Nation is at risk | International global Jewish capital determines the fate of nations | Islamisation, immigration, refugees |
|---|---|---|
| Media | Owned and controlled by Jews | *Helsingin Sanomat*, Finnish Broadcasting Company (Yle), Mainstream media |
| Disorder | Jews pit Christian nations against each other | Terrorism by Muslim people causes disorder |
| Wrong ideals | Communism, liberalism, atheism | Green, leftism, non-patriotism |
| Religion is in danger | Marxist atheism, Western liberalism | Islam |
| Ethnic "other" | Jewish race is harming the people they live with | All Muslim people, Africans |
| By any means necessary | For the Jews, the ends justify the means | Terrorist attacks and fear of them |
| Own people are expendable | When promoting the Jewish cause, the Jews are ready to make sacrifices | When promoting Islam, the terrorists are ready to make sacrifices |
| Criminality | Jews promote all kinds of criminality | Refugees promote criminality, especially rapes. Sweden as a cautionary example |
| New World Order | Jewish Marxism or Christianity? | Fear of Islam |
| Judiciary | In some countries, the legal profession is already controlled by Jews | Immigrants' sentences are shorter |
| Citizen always pays | — | Social security benefits paid to refugees |

## Discussion

The central theme addressed in this chapter is the permanence of the form, technique and content of hate speech, even if the target changes over time. According to our research, this hypothesis indeed seems to be true. The topoi of hate speech are quite constant, but the targets may vary. For example, in the 1930s the target was Jews, whereas today it is Muslims. However, this study does not reveal the extent to which the topoi of hate speech targeted, for example, sexual minorities, or whether they have always been the same as the topoi we identified. This needs to be studied further.

The research has focused above all on direct hate speech, but we think that a more detailed study of the rhetoric and structure of indirect hate speech would be necessary as well. Furthermore, the current research deals with indirect hate speech primarily on the Internet and especially on social media. It can also be observed in other media. For example, print newspapers can publish material that contains indirect hate speech. Also, the extent to which indirect hate speech has occurred over the decades is of research interest. Has society become more sensitive to hate speech, with such ideas thus being expressed more indirectly even though the goal is the same?

Nowadays, hate speech can be understood as a tool of propaganda in the Nordic countries. It is used to convince people about the correctness of an ideology, an ideology that is racist, Islamophobic and claims to be patriotic.

This chapter discusses the hate speech produced by the radical right. Comparing its rhetoric and topoi to the hate speech produced by another political extreme is also an area of research worth considering in the future. The results here are limited to Finnish hate speech, so an international comparison would also be necessary in the future. Our study of hate speech has emphasized the hate speech of the far right, namely the Finns Party, though analyzing the hate speech by another party (e.g. anarchists) and comparing it with the hate speech of the far right would be fruitful both at home and abroad, for there are also many specific cultural elements to hate speech.

Chapter 3

# Solidarity in a new guise:
# The concept of solidarity in the Swedish
# social democratic party press 1980–1990

Karin Jonsson

*Södertörn University, Sweden*

**Abstract:** Solidarity has a long history as one of the most central and elusive concepts in socialist language. This article aims to examine social democratic solidarity as a propagandistic and ideological concept in the 1980s, a time of political rupture when solidarity was being reassessed and redefined. The concept is examined in the monthly magazines of the Swedish social democratic youth and women's branch organizations, *Tvärdrag*, *Frihet* and *Morgonbris*. The study shows that the place and function of the concept of solidarity is ambiguous. On the one hand, the concept emerges as ideologically central in that its meaning is subject to struggle. The ambivalent relationship of social democracy to neoliberal influences exemplifies this. Solidarity could be presented as the antithesis of neoliberalism, while in other texts and contexts the concept was almost depoliticized by placing it in the sphere of the private or presented as the responsibility of the individual.

**Keywords:** Solidarity, social democracy, conceptual history, press, neo liberalism

\*\*\*

Solidarity has a long history as one of the most central and elusive concepts in socialist language. It has been used to put into words the specific form of imagined community existing between the working class within and across national borders.[1] The concept is descriptive at the same time as it is emotionally charged. It describes the basis of political organization and calls for the same. Solidarity has thus been seen both as a fact and as the goal of socialist politics. This chapter aims to examine social democratic solidarity as a propagandistic and ideological concept in a time of political rupture when it was being

---

[1] Benedict Anderson, *Imagined Communities: Reflections on the Origin and Spread of Nationalism* (London: Verso, 2016 [1983]).

reassessed and redefined. In the history of social democracy, solidarity did not occupy a central ideological place in the sense of being used in political manifestos or programs. Instead, it was in the political press, which at the time was very extensive, that the concept was found with the aim of convincing and enthusing potential supporters.[2]

The chapter examines the use of the concept of solidarity in the monthly magazines of the Swedish social democratic youth and women's branch organizations; *Tvärdrag—En tidning för debatt och kritik* (Cross Draft—A Magazine for Debate and Criticism), *Frihet* (Freedom) and *Morgonbris* (Morning Breeze). The magazines were the official organs of the branch organizations and were aimed primarily at their members. They can thus be regarded as an arena where social democratic ideology and concrete policies were debated. The magazines discussed democratic and party level ideology and also pondered how it corresponded to or contrasted with that of the branch organizations. Women's issues received more attention in *Morgonbris*, the magazine of the women's branch organization, whereas the youth organization's two magazines *Frihet,* and in particular the explicit debate magazine *Tvärdrag*, focused on young people but also on ideology in general to a greater extent. What the three magazines have in common is that they gave considerable space to interviews with various social democratic politicians and referred to other branch organizations in a way that shows that they perceived themselves as constituting a community in relation to the party. Both *Morgonbris* and *Frihet* also gave space to reports from the local associations of the branch organizations. In addition, trade union representatives were heard in the newspapers and authors often formulated their political position in relation to the ideology of the trade union movement and the party level respectively. It is worth noting that in all the studied magazines, the own branch organization, together with other branch organizations, is presented as the vanguard of the social democratic ideology.

Previous studies of solidarity as a social democratic concept have focused on the place and function of the concept in party programs and have thus mainly illuminated the official ideological level. By examining how the concept is used in the ideologically steeped materials of two different branch organizations, the study provides a more nuanced perspective on the social democratic concept of solidarity in an ideologically changing era.[3] The chapter therefore aims to study how the continuity and change of social democratic ideology are manifested and renegotiated through the use of the concept of solidarity in the magazines

---

[2] Sven-Eric Liedman, *Att se sig själv i andra: Om solidaritet* (Stockholm: Bonnier, 1999).
[3] Steinar Stjernø, *Solidarity in Europe: The History of an Idea* (Cambridge: Cambridge University Press, 2005).

of the branch organizations. The aim can be understood partly in relation to solidarity's long-established position as a key ideological concept for social democracy, and partly in relation to the socio-political conditions that characterized the 1980s. It was a period when Swedish social democracy renegotiated the content of social democratic ideology—most clearly expressed through the "politics of the third way."[4] During this period, the class and national welfare-based solidarity that had traditionally defined social democratic solidarity was questioned and renegotiated both within the party and in the external political debate.

It is particularly interesting to study the function, continuity and changeability of the concept of solidarity in the political press because the press, by its outward and mediated character, aimed to convey an ideological concept of solidarity through propaganda. The term "propaganda" is used here in a broad sense, encompassing party- or organization-bound democratic press aimed at convincing people of a certain ideological worldview. As a result, social democratic solidarity was expressed with rational as well as moral and emotional arguments in order to appeal to its readers. Thus, a study of the varying meanings and uses of the concept of solidarity in the monthly magazines of three social democratic branch organizations has the opportunity to examine the relationship between manifested ideology (press), political worldview and political arguments of a moral and emotional nature. Willibald Steinmetz and Michael Freeden have stressed the importance of studying the performativity of political concepts because, among other things, it allows the researcher to examine the emotive rhetoric that surrounds the use of political concepts.[5] Considering that emotive and moral rhetoric seem to be prominent features in the political concept of solidarity I want to stress the relevance of researching those connotations, as Sally J. Scholz has also done.[6]

---

[4] See e.g., Antony Giddens, *The Third Way: The Renewal of Social Democracy* (Cambridge: Polity Press, 1998); Tony Blair, *The Third Way: New Politics for the New Century* (Fabian Society, 1998); Jing Jing Huo, *The Third Way Reforms: Social Democracy after the Golden Age* (Cambridge: Cambridge University Press, 2009).

[5] Willibald Steinmetz and Michael Freeden, "Introduction," in *Conceptual History in the European Space*, eds. Willibald Steinmetz, Michael Freeden and Javier Fernández-Sebastián (New York: Berghahn Books, Incorporated, 2017) 2, ProQuest Ebrary.

[6] Sally J. Scholz, *Political Solidarity* (University Park. Pa.: Penn State University Press, 2008), 11.

## Conceptual history – temporality and politicization

In this study, the theoretical perspectives of temporality and politicization are central to understanding the importance of the past in the use of concepts, and how solidarity can be understood as a concept of propaganda and ideology.

Reinhart Koselleck has coined the now classic analytical concepts of *space of experience* and *horizon of expectations* to explain how different layers of time relate to each other and together form the basis from which political and social concepts are constructed. He argues that the relationship between the analytical concepts was changing during modernity. The space of experience became less important as the future began to be presented as disconnected, and in a sense independent, of the past. The widening gap between experience and expectations thus opened up political language, meaning that the function of language in legitimating a particular policy was now increasingly linked to the ability of politics to read the present and relate to the future.[7] Koselleck's conceptual-historical theory is formulated to understand the relationship between the political language that emerged during the Saddle time (*Sattelzeit*), i.e. the politically formative years around the Enlightenment, and the significance of politics in a Western society increasingly shaped by the idea of progress, less and less by the conservative worldview of Christianity.

The study focuses on the 1980s, a period temporally characterized by both modernity's and postmodernity's relationship to time. This means that Koselleck's assumptions about the relationship of temporal layers to each other cannot be assumed unconditionally. The idea of progress had not been completely dismissed but had been complicated and conditioned by the socio-political changes of the twentieth century. Francois Hartog argues that the postmodern 1980s were characterized by presentism, i.e., that the notion of the present was temporally stretched to include what had previously been placed in the future through the idea of progress. Hartmut Rosa, on the other hand, describes postmodern temporality as completely permeated by acceleration.[8]

In examining the use of the concept of solidarity in the magazines of the Swedish social democratic youth and women's branch organizations, particular focus will be placed on how different layers of time are activated. The 1980s were in many ways a turning point, illustrated by both the ideological and political challenges of social democracy and the political changes that

---

[7] Reinhart Koselleck, *Futures Past: On the Semantics of Historical Time* (New York: Columbia University Press, 2004).

[8] Rosa Hartmut, *Acceleration, modernitet och identitet: Tre essäer* (Göteborg: Daidalos, 2014); Francois Hartog, *Regimes of Historicity: Presentism and Experiences of Time* (New York: Columbia University Press, 2015).

characterized world politics. In the Soviet Union, East Germany and other Eastern states, the totalitarian system was softening. The scope of the social democratic welfare project began to be questioned and voices advocating private actors and the right and duty of the individual to provide for what had traditionally been the responsibility of the collective welfare project were also heard within the social democratic parties. The relationship with the history of the social democratic movements and the established notion of what constituted social democratic solidarity and its significance in the present and the future was thus at stake.

As a method, Koselleck's conceptual history focuses on the internal temporality of political concepts and how these concepts can be defined in a frozen now and over time, i.e. synchronically and diachronically. Following Koselleck, Helge Jordheim argues that concepts contain a pragmatic and polemical element that intervenes in the present and that they convey a prognosis or even a utopian meaning that anticipates the future.[9] For the purposes of this study, this means paying particular attention to how the concept of social democratic solidarity is explicitly or indirectly thematized in its past, present and future.

Furthermore, politicization is one of the functions that Koselleck argues characterizes modern political and social concepts. The expansion of political space that took place in the context of the Enlightenment, which included an explosion of politically oriented publications of various kinds, meant that more people had the opportunity to influence their own future and that more people could be recruited into political movements and convinced of the correctness of a certain social view.[10] This phenomenon is also applicable to the 1980s and implies for this study a sensitivity to the fact that the use of the political concept of solidarity in the Swedish social democratic press is not merely descriptive but is charged with political significance and explosive power precisely in order to convince of a certain social analysis.

### A few Words on Method and Sources

In order to study the changes and continuities during the 1980s, I have consulted *Frihet* and read all issues from 1980, 1982, 1984, 1987, 1989 and 1990. For *Morgonbris*, I have studied all issues from 1981, 1983, 1985, 1987, 1989 and 1990. Finally, I have also studied all the issues of *Tvärdrag* from 1983, 1984, 1986, 1987, 1989 and 1990. There is thus some variation in the issues of each magazine

---

[9] Helge Jordheim "Against Periodization: Koselleck's Theory of Multiple Temporalities," *History and Theory* 51, no. 2 (2012): 165.
[10] Melvin Richter and Michaela Richter, "Introduction: Translation of Reinhart Koselleck's Krise In Geschichtliche Grundbegriffe," *Journal of the History of Ideas* 67, no. 2 (2006): 349ff.

that I have chosen to study. It is a deliberate choice as I wanted to cover as many years in the 1980s as possible, rather than, for example, following a certain political debate in all the papers. 1990 is studied in all the magazines because it is not only a chronological breakpoint but also a clearly ideological one with the collapse of the Soviet Union. Special focus is placed on articles and interviews with people involved in the Social Democratic Party and the labor movement in the broad sense. It is in this material that the concept of solidarity is used most frequently and in a propagandistic and sometimes controversial way.

The study is structured according to the themes that emerge in the source material when the place and function of the concept of solidarity are studied on the one hand from the perspective of conceptual history, focusing on temporality and politicization, and on the other hand, the socio-political context and the ideological shift of social democracy is considered.

## A short history of the concept of solidarity

The socialists of the nineteenth and early twentieth centuries used solidarity and fraternity in parallel to put into words the specific form of community that they believed existed between workers, regardless of national borders. For Karl Marx, and for many socialists after him, the very concept of solidarity belonged primarily to political propaganda, where it has been used extensively ever since, even up to the present day. For social democracy, however, the very term solidarity became significant. In the first decades of the twentieth century, social democratic theorists developed a concept of solidarity that both reflected and transcended the economically based and class-based socialist concept of solidarity.[11] When the German social democratic theorists and politicians Karl Kautsky and Eduard Bernstein were formulating a concept of solidarity that reflected contemporary political realities, a similar conceptual discussion was taking place in Swedish social democracy. In the 1910s, Ernst Wigforss, theorist and later finance minister, published ideological texts in which he problematized an orthodox Marxist social analysis and presented a revision that, like Bernstein's, pointed towards a broader definition of solidarity. By emphasizing the importance of emotions and ethics for the emergence of solidarity, it became possible to include the entire nation's people in the same community of solidarity.[12]

In contrast to the mainly propagandistic concept of solidarity in early socialism, the social democratic concept was incorporated into ideological texts. In fact, over time, it developed into one of the key concepts of social democratic ideology. In the West-German post-war Bad Godesberg Programme

---

[11] Stjernø, *Solidarity in Europe*, 48–52.
[12] Stjernø, *Solidarity in Europe*, 50–2.

of 1959, the term was used in a variety of ways—to denote ethical perspectives, the common interest of the working class in relation to employers, as well as Germany's relationship with "underdeveloped" Third World countries. The 1990 Swedish Social Democratic Party program presents the general tenets under the three headings of freedom, equality and solidarity.

## Solidarity under neoliberal conditions

The place and function of the concept of solidarity in the 1980s need to be understood in relation to its immense popularity in the 1970s. In many ways, the 1970s was the decade of international solidarity. The organization of citizens by political parties was challenged by social movements, which put global issues before party politics. Environmental issues, the fight against nuclear power and, not least, international solidarity expressed through involvement in social movements against racist and other forms of undemocratic and repressive regimes attracted large groups of people, particularly younger people.[13] The new social movements were thus largely preoccupied with solidarity in a universalist sense, which can be linked to the emergence of human rights. According to Samuel Moyn, the seventies was the breakthrough of the more individualistic concept of human rights, that has become the fundamental legal and moral concept in international social movements.[14]

For the Social Democrats, it was thus a matter of demonstrating both concretely politically and rhetorically that they were still the subjects of international solidarity. In the first half of the 1970s, the congress material of the Swedish Social Democratic Party ( SAP) and its branch organizations used solidarity to denote both lost and actual as well as future communities between town and country, between different generations and social classes and not least between rich, privileged countries at peace and vulnerable, war-torn and poor countries in the so-called Third World.[15] Solidarity was also associated with security, as in the 1972 slogan "solidarity for security." In his analysis, Jens Ljunggren puts it as if security became the new eschatology of the SAP. During the 1960s and 1970s, the word security appeared "together with phrases about

---

[13] Kjell Östberg, "Sweden and the long '1968': Break or Continuity?," *Scandinavian Journal of History* 33, no. 4 (2008): 339–52.

[14] Samuel Moyn, *The Last Utopia: Human Rights in History* (Cambridge, MA: Belknap Press of Harvard University Press, 2010); Samuel Moyn, *Not Enough: Human Rights in an Unequal World* (Cambridge, MA: Belknap Press of Harvard University Press, 2018).

[15] Karin Jonsson, "Unifying Solidarity: The Concept of International Solidarity in Swedish Social Democracy 1972–1985," *Redescriptions: Political Thought, Conceptual History and Feminist Theory* 25, no. 1 (2022): 27–48, http://doi.org/10.33134/rds.371.

rising production, economic democracy, equality, social policy in solidarity, planned housing, peace, disarmament and solidarity."[16]

The last years of the 1970s saw the beginning of a shift in Swedish social democracy's concept of solidarity, which meant that it was both formulated as the ideological opposite of neoliberalism and incorporated the logic of neoliberalism. The conceptual shift and ambivalence were most clearly expressed in the rhetoric of Social Democratic Party leader Olof Palme. Against neoliberalism's suppression of people's natural instinct for solidarity, Palme, on the one hand, asserted the superiority of social democratic ideology by stressing that it was rooted in the "morality of justice."

> The labor movement wants to replace the morality of power with the morality of justice. It is a morality that has grown out of the labor movement itself and the conditions under which it has been forced to work. It was founded in the early labor movement and a number of other popular movements, where people came together in struggle for fairer conditions.[17]

On the other hand, the influence of neoliberalism was felt in his expressions such as "social solidarity as a personal drive" and an increasing focus on the individual's personal responsibility for the establishment of solidarity.[18]

### Solidarity in the 1980s – For the Salvation of Our Time

The above ambivalence can also be read in the magazines of the Swedish social democratic branch organizations from the 1980s. In *Morgonbris*, President of the women's league Lisa Mattson stated on the eve of May Day 1981 that "[w]e need more than usual this May Day to realize that cooperation and solidarity, the abandonment of private egoism is the only way to get the country out of the crisis."[19] Under the heading "Letters to Morgonbris," Disa Svanström's column "Neoliberalism" was published the same year. Like Palme, Svanström contrasted solidarity with neoliberalism. While solidarity was associated with democracy, and one may assume, real social democratic politics, neoliberalism was equated with misanthropy.

---

[16] Jens Ljunggren, *Den uppskjutna vreden: Socialdemokratisk känslopolitik från 1880- till 1980-talet* (Lund: Nordic Academic Press, 2015), 163.

[17] Olof Palme, SAP Congress 1981, book 2/CD, 188.

[18] Olof Palme SAP Congress 1981, book 2/CD: 192; Jonsson, "Unifying Solidarity," 44–5.

[19] Lisa Mattson, *Morgonbris*, no. 3, 1981, 4.

In a society where the strong are given the right to rule over the weak, where elitism is pitted against humanity, is there room for the disabled, the congenitally disabled, the long-term sick and the elderly? ...]

In the society that neoliberalism dreams of and works to make a reality, there is no place for democracy and solidarity. Its main characteristic will be contempt for human beings.[20]

For Svanström, solidarity appears to be the contemporary salvation from the elitism and destructive individualism of neoliberalism. But solidarity was not only invoked as the opposite of neoliberalism, it was also presented as a salvation in relation to environmental and women's issues.

Throughout the 1980s, *Morgonbris* published texts of various kinds highlighting the women's movement's special responsibility and ability to work for a present and future characterized by solidarity. In the first issue of 1981, Margareta Persson noted that class consciousness had declined sharply. People's interest in social issues was not channeled through party politics as it had been in the past but was expressed through an interest in the environment, women's issues and children's issues. In this development, Persson attributed particular responsibility to the women's branch organization, arguing that the previous class consciousness that had permeated the party's policies, and thus underpinned its concept of solidarity, was beginning to be replaced by "a dawning women's consciousness."

But the great hope I place in the women's movement. [...] The women's branch organization has an enormous responsibility right now We have to be able to respond to the dawning of women's consciousness. If we had class consciousness before, we're starting to have women's consciousness now.[21]

We see how Persson attributes to women's consciousness an emancipatory and almost revolutionary potential, better suited to meet contemporary demands than the earlier class consciousness. In this way, she rhetorically ties in with a politically radical rhetoric that has permeated the political language of social democracy even when the policies pursued have been reformist and based on compromise.

In several texts in the magazines of both the women's and the youth's branch organizations,' solidarity was presented as salvation in relation to an approaching

---

[20] Disa Svanström, "Nyliberalismen," *Morgonbris*, no. 4, 1981, 31.
[21] Margareta Persson, "Varför gör vi inte revolt?," *Morgonbris*, no. 1, 1981, 24.

environmental disaster. As a concept, solidarity was extended in time and space and described as absolutely necessary in relation to both global injustice and the well-being of future generations in a way that shows points of contact with the 1970s concept of solidarity. In the opinion piece "For an ecosocialist holistic view" by Roger Rådström and Lennart Weiss published in *Tvärdrag* in 1987, the relationship between social democratic values, the solution to the environmental crisis and international solidarity was expressed in the following way:

> Our environmental policy must be international and based on solidarity. Solidarity not only with future generations but also with the people of the Third World. Just as humanity today cannot take the liberty of depleting the earth's finite natural resources, neither can the rich part of the world take the majority of these resources for themselves.
>
> [...]
>
> The environmental threats are a clear confirmation that socialist values are needed for a good social development.[22]

In the text "Environment is about solidarity," an excerpt from the joint environmental manifesto of the SAP branch organizations published in *Morgonbris* in 1985, solidarity was similarly presented as a community across national and generational boundaries. Through solidarity, contemporary people took responsibility for inequalities between rich and poor countries and ensured that future generations could survive.

> For us social democrats, environmental policy is about building a society based on sustainable management of natural resources. For us, this issue is one of the most urgent and pressing.
>
> [...]
>
> For environmental issues are a matter of solidarity with people in our immediate environment, in foreign countries and with future generations.[23]

---

[22] Roger Rådström and Lennart Weiss, "För en ekosocialistisk helhetssyn," *Tvärdrag*, no. 3, 1987, 14–5.
[23] "Environment is about solidarity," *Morgonbris*, no. 5, 1985, 4.

In the examples above, solidarity appears both particular and all-er compassing. Solidarity emerges as an absolutely necessary relationship for solving socio-political problems. The rhetoric has an air of radicalism and the concept is emotionally charged, but beyond that, it has few points of contac with a more traditional social democratic concept of solidarity based on class analysis.

### Everyday solidarity and the increasing responsibility of the individual

Steinar Stjernø has shown that a deradicalization took place wher. the concept of solidarity was both democratized and extended to particular communities of various kinds.[24] The concept found its way into the program of practically every political party, but at the same time lost its radical character in favor of more everyday use. In the Swedish social democratic press from the 1980s, there are several examples that show how a neoliberal understanding of the relationship between the individual and the collective changed the way the concept of solidarity was used, and how, even in cases where a more traditional understanding of the concept was put forward, solidarity was rooted in people's everyday lives and feelings.

In a 1983 interview in *Tvärdrag*, the future social democratic leader and prime minister Ingvar Carlsson associated traditional social democratic politics with "everyday solidarity morality." Additionally, Carlsson presented it as the solution to the erosion of welfare over the past decade, which he argued had occurred as a result of economic recession, a dysfunctional and rigid public sector and the demoralizing influences of individualism.

> The last decade has seen an order of speculative cliques, bureaucrats, drug dealers and a self-legitimizing with often impotent public sector. That sort of thing passes during expansions but now it's worse. The waste and tragedies sting the eyes of people who want to see a different order.

> A traditional social democratic policy, with its pursuit of an everyday *morality of solidarity* [author's italics] and an unfair but at best acceptable distribution of social burdens, is not the worst option.[25]

Carlsson's argument illustrates how solidarity in the 1980s became less and less associated with the security discourse discussed by Ljunggren and more and more associated with the individual's own responsibility and sacrifices.

---

[24] Stjernø, *Solidarity in Europe*, 178–85.
[25] Martin Viredius, "Framtidsgruppen: samma uppdrag nu som 1932," *Tvärdrag*, no. 1, 1983, 32.

In the third issue of the magazine from the same year, a rhetoric similar in concept but different in content was repeated when Minister of Civil Affairs Bo Holmberg was asked to speak about alternatives to the unwieldiness of the public sector:

> For me, it is important that the safety net society should offer is complemented by an *everyday solidarity* [author's italics], preferably called compassion, which leads to people working together to solve many of the problems that arise—not waiting for society to step in and deal with the situation. The use of experts must not go too far.[26]

While Carlsson's "solidarity morality" was associated with traditional social democratic welfare policies, Holmberg used the expression "everyday solidarity" to point out an alternative social democratic policy, formulated according to the specific needs of the time. Holmberg's reasoning was thus influenced by a neoliberal critique of traditional social democratic welfare policy. Solidarity is therefore partly lifted out of its bureaucratic and political context by defining it as a relationship that should belong to the everyday and thus to the private human relationship.

When the new district president of the women's branch organization in Västerbotten was interviewed in *Morgonbris* in 1983, she used solidarity as a synonym for community in an everyday and almost depoliticized sense: "The best thing is the community and solidarity that exists between the girls in Västerbotten."[27] In this context, solidarity appears as an emotional relationship between women, a "women's community" which may constitute the basis from which political struggle can develop.

In the examples above, solidarity emerges as a pre-political as well as a political and everyday concept. The meaning and specific significance of the concept for social democracy thus seems to be determined in relation to how the different spheres' relationship to each other is articulated and changes over time. While proponents of the classical social democratic concept of solidarity placed its core in economic or socio-political relations, it is possible to understand "everyday solidarity" as arising primarily from the sphere of private relations.

### Particular solidarity

The above reasoning leads us on to an examination of how social democratic solidarity was both challenged and expressed through particular solidarities, as

---

[26] Bo Holmberg, "Vad anser jättarna om självförvaltning?," *Tvärdrag*, no. 3, 1983, 18.
[27] "Tre nya distriktsordförande," *Morgonbris* 1983, no. 4, 1983, 23.

discussed earlier in "women's community." In the third issue of *Morgonbris* in 1989, Annica Frisk argued that "tougher action was needed against male supremacy within the party."

> It is high time to abandon the strategy of patience and take tougher action against male domination in the party. We also need more open and fearless debate about solidarity, democracy and ideology in general. [...]
>
> Solidarity with men and the party is all well and good, but the price is high: the important 6-hour day has been replaced by a sixth week of holidays, childcare is still not sufficiently developed and women have the lowest wages and unsustainable working conditions.[28]

In the quote above, Frisk used the concept of solidarity in two different but related senses. On the one hand, she referred to it as a key ideological concept for social democracy under threat from conservative and neoliberal forces, and on the other hand, she described how "solidarity with men" within the party was devastating because acceptance of their political line excluded politically central issues for women and thus for society as a whole. To put it a little more bluntly, solidarity with men within the party undermined political, social democratic solidarity. Patriarchal structures within the social democratic organization thus risked standing in the way of the realization of social democratic policy.

That the way to real, universal solidarity was through particular solidarity was a recurring theme in the publications of the branch organizations during the years under study. The perspective was discussed in different ways, based on the common denominator that the political issues in which the women's branch organization was particularly interested—equality, care and international solidarity—made real, universal solidarity a reality. In the 1989 text "Third World Poverty—a Women's Issue," Minister for Development Lena Hjelm-Wallén argued for "women's solidarity in practice" through international solidarity in the form of "aid in solidarity."

> Poverty in the world has been "feminized." Therefore, women's issues can never be seen in isolation from the fight against poverty and social justice.
>
> If we are ever to see a world in which people are not stratified by gender and class, we must work for a just world order and ensure that aid to poor

---

[28] Annica Frisk, "Tuffare tag mot mansväldet inom partiet," *Morgonbris*, no. 3, 1989, 16.

people is increased and based on solidarity. But it is important, within the framework of a just world order, to emphasize more clearly the role of women in development.[29]

Hjelm-Wallén thus identified international solidarity as a central social democratic concern. It was through international and particular solidarity directed towards women in the Third World that universal, social democratic solidarity based on class analysis could be realized. Hjelm-Wallén's reasoning bears several similarities to the rhetoric of international solidarity in the 1970s.

The increasing portrayal of women as subjects and objects of solidarity in the 1970s and 1980s, and whether this implied any real shifts in power and focus, was commented on laconically by Inger Krantz in the first issue of *Tvärdrag* in 1989 under the heading "The Church's Decade:"

> 1975 was proclaimed the UN Year of Women! That year, the situation of women all over the world was highlighted. Does anyone remember that?
>
> Already at the end of that year, it was decided that a women's decade was needed if women's issues were to have an impact and solutions in politics in the member states [...]
>
> In 1988 at Easter, the World Council of Churches decided to declare a Decade for Women 1988–1998. "The Ecumenical Decade of Churches in Solidarity with Women"—and that means a new twist. Now it is the churches who are to be in solidarity with women – not just the men with the women within the churches![30]

Krantz's reasoning illustrates how the relationship between the one who solidarizes and the one who is solidarized with could shift depending on whose gaze was guiding the narrative. Unlike the examples above, it was not women's agency that was the focus of the World Council of Churches' Declaration on the Decade of Women. Instead of being the subjects of solidarity, they were portrayed as its objects and the Church thus as a supposedly male or gender-neutral actor.

---

[29] Lena Hjelm-Wallen, "Tredje världens fattigdom: en kvinnofråga," *Morgonbris*, no. 7, 1989, 9.
[30] Ingen Krantz, "Kyrkans årtionde," *Morgonbris*, no. 1, 1989, 23.

## Solidarity as an emotional and moral foundation

As the social democratic concept of solidarity was associated with the sphere of the everyday and the individual from different lines of argument, its emotional as well as moral connotations were reinforced. When the controversial issue of solidaristic wage policy[31] was discussed in *Tvärdrag* in 1987, Åke Wiklund expressed himself in a way that illustrates how the political concept of solidarity was based on an emotional commitment.

> We must face this [the business community's attack on the solidarity wage policy, *author's comment*] by starting to think with our hearts. Try to bring back solidarity. We must learn to share, to feel solidarity with the weak. Otherwise, we are heading for a dark society. If we succeed in this, we will not only save the solidarity-based wage policy, but we will also achieve a lot of other positive things.[32]

According to Wiklund's reasoning, it seems that social democracy has lost the political power of solidarity that it once possessed. The phrase "start thinking with the heart" blurs the boundaries between solidarity as politics and emotion on the one hand, and history and the present on the other. According to the argument, real social democratic politics is as much ideological social analysis as emotional engagement with the weak in society.

Similar reasoning can be found in Anders Jonsson's contribution in the same magazine in 1989 on the abolition of the collective membership of the members of the Trade Union Organization (Landsorganisationen – LO) in the SAP.[33] The precarious political situation of Swedish social democracy, with an ever smaller part of the population that could or would be described as working class in the traditional sense, meant, Jonsson argued, that "[s]ocial democracy's great challenge [...] is to try to make this middle class feel solidarity with the underclass that does exist; with the unemployed, immigrants, low-paid single mothers and so on."[34] The reasoning brings to mind a more traditional social democratic rhetoric, from which solidarity emerges as the unifying concept that expresses the social democratic welfare policy or the rhetoric of the

---

[31] The solidaristic wage policy was an economic policy pursued by the Swedish Trade Organization in the 1960s and 1970s. It entailed striving for equal pay for equal work and thus a leveling out of wage differences.

[32] Håkan Bengtsson, "Smedens återkomst," *Tvärdrag* no. 3, 1987, 11.

[33] In 1987, SAP Party Congress, it was decided to end the collective affiliation of the members of the Trade union organization LO to the Social Democratic Party. The decision came into force in 1990/91 and resulted in a significant reduction in party membership.

[34] Christer Mattson, "Rikets finanser och socialismens idé," *Tvärdrag*, no. 4 1989, 11.

people's home, the vision of community between the classes of the nation. Jonsson seems to place his hope in the fact that the concept of solidarity itself carries an emotional power capable of enthusing and convincing primarily middle-class voters of the superiority of social democratic ideology.

In some texts—such as "Love and Socialism" by Tomas Wennström, also published in *Tvärdrag* in 1989—the writer even expresses it as the strength of social democratic ideology that, unlike the bourgeois ideology, it binds the private and public spheres together through "the morality and ethics of love." Socialism, Wennström argues, "seeks to unite and develop the private and public ethics in a spirit of altruism and solidarity."[35]

The statement is not unique, but similar arguments are found in various forms in the studied magazines. When Helle Klein argues about the Bible as a classic and basis for the idea of solidarity in both a broader and narrower social democratic sense in *Tvärdrag*'s thematic issue on the political right in 1990, she invokes the necessary foundation of the concept of political solidarity in ethical and emotional convictions:

> But throughout the Bible there is a common thread of righteousness and love for our neighbor. For both Amos and Jesus, the ethos is based on a bottom-up perspective, where solidarity with those who have the least power is the starting point.
>
> Perhaps a good benchmark for us in the labor movement in our efforts to raise the moral and ethical issues in politics?
>
> Whether you believe in God or not, the biblical stories urge us to think.
>
> What is our driving force? What is our solidarity really for? How do we get the "heart's commitment" back into the Strong Society?[36]

### Solidarity as nostalgia or future – the ideological choices of social democracy

The intra-organizational struggle for the ideological future of social democracy was thus partly reflected and conducted through the concept of solidarity. In the third issue of *Tvärdrag* in 1990, Vidar Andersson argued that the SAP could be "a new party for peace, solidarity and justice." Although Andersson's concept of solidarity was placed in an established semantic field for the social democratic

---

[35] Tomas Wennström, "Kärlek och socialism," *Tvärdrag*, no. 5, 1989, 8.
[36] Helle Klein, "Ur kärleken till nästan föddes solidariteten," *Tvärdrag*, no. 5–6, 1990, 49.

concept of solidarity, where it was associated with peace and justice, he questioned the significance of history for contemporary and future social democratic politics.

> As young people, we cannot base our political lives on what previous generations in the party have achieved, created and shaped. Our task is to create a social democratic policy that is fit for today's and tomorrow's society. [...]
>
> Forget history, tradition and politics. Ask yourself: why are we forming the party and what will be the main features of our 1990s policy of solidarity, justice and peace?[37]

From a temporal perspective, the historical experience and continuity of social democracy appear irrelevant to the pragmatic and future-oriented politics he claims the party should pursue. Ideologically, the argument is permeated by the presentism discussed by Hartog. An ambivalence arises in how the concept of solidarity should be understood ideologically. On the one hand, historical experience is presented as meaningless when formulating future policy; on the other hand, the continuity of the concept emerges as central when it is placed in a long-established semantic field for social democracy.

A similar argument is made by Göran Bolin in the same issue of *Tvärdrag*. In the text "After Feldt's dead end. Forget the dogmas and create a modern labor movement," Bolin takes aim both at the total capitulation to neoliberalism represented by the social democratic finance minister's statement that "the task of socialism is to give capitalism a human face" and at the nostalgic rhetoric of the trade union movement: "Many in the unions and the party are now talking about a return to traditional values, justice and solidarity."[38] For Bolin himself, solidarity appears to be an instrumental concept where it is written in the context of making the public sector more efficient. "In order to maintain equality, while efficient production requires competition, the fight for solidarity-financed consumption of health, education and care will become increasingly important."[39]

In the programmatic paper "Socialism in our time" written by Håkan Bengtsson and Lennart Weiss and published in the fourth issue of *Tvärdrag* in 1990, the formulation of a third way between nostalgic social democratic dogmatism and neoliberal pragmatism was further deepened and complicated.

---

[37] Vidar Andersson, "Ett nytt parti för fred, solidaritet och rättvisa," *Tvärdrag*, no. 3, 1990, 30.
[38] Göran Bolin, "Efter Feldts återvändsgränd. Glöm dogmerna och skapa en modern arbetarrörelse," *Tvärdrag*, no. 3, 1990, 32.
[39] Bolin, "Efter Feldts återvändsgränd," 32.

The experience of history is dismissed with—to quote Hartog—presentist statements such as "[i]t is no longer enough to look back and refer to tradition or some hero of times past. Tomorrow's politics must be shaped by the present—not by yesterday's bygone reality and increasingly allusive political victories."[40] The ideological function of the concept of solidarity as a key concept was relativized by replacing it with the concept of fraternity and placing it in the everyday sphere discussed earlier and in a depoliticized semantic field together with concepts such as spirituality, personal creation and cooperation:

> Does social democracy have the basic ideas for this new society? Is there a new modernism in the movement capable of revitalizing the eternal ideas of equality, fraternity and democracy?
>
> That is definitely the case.
>
> [...]
>
> What politics needs is a new pattern, a new basic melody, which shows the way to a new and warm welfare society based on participation, practical everyday solidarity, social justice and gentle social structures.
>
> [...]
>
> A new welfare policy must necessarily be based on what today is popularly called "spirituality," which puts the personal and human aspects of politics at the center. [...]
>
> Put simply, it is a policy that respects the human condition and allows for personal creation and interaction.[41]

At the same time, the rhetoric also tied in with the history of social democracy and the Enlightenment by stating that contemporary social democratic politics needed to be anchored in "the eternal ideas of equality, fraternity and democracy." Whereas the Enlightenment and the French Revolution had been about "liberty, equality and fraternity," Bengtsson and Weiss replaced equality with democracy. The authors' rhetoric thus expresses both the presentism discussed by Hartog and a more retrospective, almost cyclical notion of solidarity, associated with modernity's ambivalent relationship with history and the future.

---

[40] Håkan Bengtsson and Lennart Weiss, "Socialism i vår tid," *Tvärdrag*, no. 4, 1990, 26.
[41] Bengtsson and Weiss, "Socialism i vår tid," 32.

## Final discussion

Solidarity has had both an elusive and central place in the history of social democratic concepts. During the formative years of socialism and early social democracy the concept itself was not accorded any ideologically central significance. However, its meaning of community and responsibility within a transnational working class formed an important basis of social democratic ideology and self-understanding. In this article, I have studied the place and function of the concept of solidarity in three magazines associated with the SAP youth and women's branch organizations—*Frihet, Tvärdrag* and *Morgonbris* during the 1980s. The 1980s were in many ways a turning point, illustrated by both the ideological and political challenges of social democracy and the political changes that characterized world politics. The scope of the social democratic welfare project began to be questioned and the established notion of what constituted social democratic solidarity and its significance in the present and the future was thus at stake. In the post-war period, and particularly in the 1970s, solidarity was established as a key social democratic concept, prominent both in ideological texts such as party programs and in propaganda materials such as the political press. By studying the concept of solidarity it is therefore possible to examine how contemporary ideological schisms took shape, and by doing so on the basis of Koselleck's theory of conceptual history, with particular attention to the temporality and politicising function of the concept, it has been possible to examine more closely the ideological function of the concept of solidarity during a period of political rupture.

The study shows that the place and function of the concept of solidarity in the press studied is ambiguous. On the one hand, the concept emerges as ideologically central in that its meaning is subject to struggle. The ambivalent relationship of social democracy to neoliberal influences exemplifies this. Solidarity could be presented as the antithesis of neoliberalism, while in other texts and contexts, the concept was almost depoliticized by placing it in the sphere of the private or presented as the responsibility of the individual. To put it a little more bluntly, the ideological battle over the influence of Third Way politics was fought, among other things, as a less heated battle over the meaning of the concept of solidarity.

The study has also shown that real social democratic solidarity was presented as necessary to be realized through particular solidarities such as women's solidarity in particular. The results confirm Stjernø's observation that during the 1980s the concept of solidarity was democratized and considered to be a matter of concern for almost every community. Just as Stjernø stated, the democratization meant that the concept was also depoliticized, which my study partly confirms.

The ambivalent position of the concept of solidarity is most evident in the very texts that dealt with whether or not the social democracy's ideological turnaround was necessary. In these texts, the temporalization of the concept of solidarity also emerges as ideologically central. While some writers highlighted the concept of solidarity as a core concept for contemporary political challenges, others attributed a more nostalgic meaning to the concept.

# Promoting and discussing feminism

Chapter 4

# *Hertha*: A women's rights magazine that did not see the light of day

Tiina Kinnunen

*University of Oulu, Finland*

**Abstract:** In 1901, Aleksandra Gripenberg, the figurehead of the Finnish Women's Association, announced that a new women's rights magazine, *Hertha*, would be started. The plan was not realized, but it is interesting from several viewpoints. The initiative is indicative of the central role of the press in the women's rights movement's communication and the activists' strong commitment to journalism, and, in addition, of the restrictions with regard to the freedom of press in the early twentieth century Finland. Behind the initiative were ideological conflicts within the women's movement, and Gripenberg's goal was to create not only a transnational (Finnish-Swedish) magazine, but also an ideologically correct mouthpiece that was directly in opposition of the views of Swedish writer Ellen Key. The article asks why Key was so dangerous that a separate magazine was planned, and what kind of network Gripenberg planned in order to implement her initiative.

**Keywords:** Aleksandra Gripenberg, Ellen Key, transnational feminism, Scandinavian feminism, early twentieth-century feminist journalism, women's rights magazine Hertha.

\*\*\*

At the beginning of December 1901, Aleksandra[1] Gripenberg, the figurehead of the Finnish Women's Association (Finsk kvinnoförening—Suomen Naisyhdistys), told her Swedish activist friend Maria Cederschiöld in a letter that the Finnish press had just reported about her plan for a new women's rights magazine.[2] The *Uusi Suometar* newspaper reported that a Swedish-language magazine called *Hertha* would be published from the beginning of 1902 if it got the "relevant" authorizations. Authorizations were needed because the press was regulated at

---

[1] I use the form "Aleksandra" in my article unless a reference uses the alternative "Alexandra."
[2] Gripenberg to Cederschiöld, December 2, 1901. The letters from Gripenberg to Cederschiöld are preserved in the Archives of Suomen Naisyhdistys, City Archives of Helsinki, Hd:3.

the time. The magazine was supposed to discuss "women's aspirations in the home and in society."[3] Aleksandra Gripenberg would be the editor-in-chief of the journal, and contributors would include Selma Lagerlöf, for example, in addition to Maria Cederschiöld.

The Finnish newspaper press was highly politicized at the beginning of the century, and *Uusi Suometar* represented the Fennoman movement and the Finnish Party that the movement had initiated. Gripenberg, alongside the Finnish Women's Association, represented this movement. Even its offshoot, the Young Finnish Party, reported the initiative in its *Päivälehti* newspaper,[4] but it was ignored in the Swedish-language press, even in the women's rights magazine *Nutid*. In *Nutid*, the name *Hertha* was mentioned in connection with Swedish writer Fredrika Bremer's identically named novel. The novel, published in 1856, was a pioneer for Nordic discourse about the status of especially unmarried women. For both Finnish- and Swedish-speaking contemporary audiences, the message of the initiative's commitment to Fredrika Bremer's legacy contained in the name of Gripenberg's magazine likely did not remain unclear.

Gripenberg's magazine initiative (henceforward initiative or *Hertha* initiative) was not realized, but it is interesting from several different points of view, which is why it is the subject of this chapter. The initiative is indicative of the central role of the press in the women's rights movement's (henceforward women's movement) communication and in the related building of collective identities, of the activists' strong commitment to journalism, and, in addition, of Finland's exceptional situation with regard to the freedom of press. As part of the Russification efforts that began in the late nineteenth century, Finnish press was subjected to censorship, and journalists who were critical of the efforts even had to flee the country.[5] One of the reasons why Gripenberg's initiative was not realized was precisely the situation Finland was in. Its authorization was postponed; the executor of the Russification efforts, Governor-General Bobrikov, who oversaw press matters, was "at times away, other times unwilling."[6]

The initiative is also interesting because the goal was a transnational women's publication. In addition to having a readership in Finland and Sweden, readers would also have been found in Norway, Denmark, and Iceland, where

[3] *Uusi Suometar*, December 1, 1901.
[4] *Päivälehti*, December 1, 1901.
[5] Pirkko Leino-Kaukiainen, "Kasvava sanomalehdistö sensuurin kahleissa," in *Suomen lehdistön historia I*, ed. Päiviö Tommila (Kuopio: Kustannuskiila, 1988), 554–60. See also Reetta Hänninen, *Tulisydän: Maissi Erkon kiihkeä elämä* (Helsinki: Otava, 2022).
[6] Tyyni Tuulio, *Aleksandra Gripenberg: Kirjailija, taistelija, ihminen* (Porvoo, Helsinki: Werner Söderström Osakeyhtiö, 1959), 245.

Scandinavian languages are spoken (Swedish, Norwegian, Danish, and Icelandic). Even before Gripenberg's initiative, women's rights magazines in Scandinavian languages spread from one Nordic country to another, and also to Finland because educated persons in Finland spoke Swedish well even if they were native in Finnish. However, these magazines were usually connected to and published by a national women's rights organization. *Hertha*, meanwhile, was designed to be transnational and not connected to any specific organization.[7]

Behind the *Hertha* initiative were ideological conflicts within the women's movement, where Gripenberg stood out as a strong leader. In my chapter, I argue that Gripenberg's goal was to create not only a transnational, but also an ideologically correct mouthpiece for the women's movement that was directly in opposition to the views of Swedish writer Ellen Key. At the turn of the century, the field of women's movements and female activists contained different, even conflicting, interpretations of women's rights and the nature of equality. Different players had different emphases as to whether there was a difference or a similarity between the genders. Among the most controversial topical issues were, for example, gender-specific labor legislation and sexual morality. These differences reflected divides over general political and ideological stances, such as liberalism and socialism. Similarly, stances on Christianity were divisive: For some, Christianity's message of equality was an integral part of the feminist message, while others distanced themselves from Christianity or, at least, the Church as an institution.[8]

In my chapter, I will answer the following questions: What conflicts did Gripenberg's initiative arise from and why did Gripenberg consider Key so dangerous as to want to combat her using a separate magazine? What kind of women's identity did she want to build and what kind of transnational network was she planning in order to implement her initiative? Were there any other non-ideological goals behind it? Before I address these questions, I will provide context for my discussion with an overview of Gripenberg's feminist activism and Finland's and Sweden's women's rights press around 1900. Central to my chapter are the concepts of women's rights and feminism. The concept of feminism, of improving women's rights and status in society and gender equality— approached using different emphases—began to spread from French to other

---

[7] In her correspondence, Gripenberg did not discuss the economics of the journal, but apparently, it would have been funded using subscription fees.

[8] E.g. Ulla Wikander, Alice Kessler-Harris and Jane Lewis, eds., *Protecting Women: Labor Legislation in Europe, the United States, and Australia, 1880–1920* (Urbana and Chicago: University of Illinois Press, 1995); Sue Morgan, ed., *Women, Religion and Feminism in Britain, 1750–1900* (Basingstoke: Palgrave Macmillan, 2002).

languages at the end of the 1800s but was commonly used alongside the concept of women's rights. It was also common to talk about women's emancipation.[9]

I will answer these questions by examining correspondence. Gripenberg discussed her initiative in her correspondence with a few Swedish activist friends.[10] I also draw on Gripenberg's writings published in various forums to examine the ideological conflicts underlying the initiative. One of the main forums was the women's rights magazine *Koti ja Yhteiskunta* (Home and Society), which Gripenberg edited between 1889 and 1911, and in the columns of which she took a firm stance in favor of the women's rights she saw as correct. Another key publication channel was Gripenberg's book on the history of feminism, *Reformarbetet för förbättrandet af kvinnans ställning* (Finnish: *Naisasian kehitys eri maissa*; The development of women's rights in different countries).[11]

The *Hertha* initiative has not received much attention in earlier studies. Tyyni Tuulio's biography of Gripenberg briefly mentions it.[12] Indeed, the initiative does seem a rather insignificant part of her personal history, but I suggest that it can be viewed as a prism that enables us to view the press as a supplier and producer of feminist ideology, as well as feminists' journalistic activism and feminist transnationalism. These themes are central to telling feminist history, whether it be from a media, a political, or a transnational point of view.

### Aleksandra Gripenberg—a national and international women's rights activist and pioneer in the Finnish women's rights press

Researchers who have studied early Finnish women journalists have noticed that this group shared a common feature, i.e., often, they were also (fiction) writers, literary translators, and organizational activists. Many had a background

---

[9] E. g. Karen Offen, *European Feminisms, 1700–1950: A Political History* (Stanford: Stanford University Press, 2000), 19.

[10] These are unpublished letters, some of which are in Gripenberg's Collection, located in the Archives on Literature and Cultural History of the Finnish Literature Society (in this article: GC), and some in the Archives of Suomen Naisyhdistys (Finnish Women's Association) within the Helsinki City Archives (in this article: FWAA). Letters to the following recipients are cited: Maria Cederschiöld (FWAA, Hd:3), Ellen Fries (GC, 306:3), Anna Hierta-Retzius (FWAA, Hd:4), and Toini Topelius (GC, 305:7).

[11] The work was originally published in Swedish in three volumes in 1893–1903. The Finnish version was expanded into four volumes that were published in 1905–1909. In the original work, Finland was included in the third volume. When the work was translated, the text concerning Finland was revised and given a volume of its own. In this article, I refer to the Finnish version, but note that in the early twentieth century, when the *Hertha* initiative was relevant, only the Swedish version had been published.

[12] Tuulio, *Aleksandra Gripenberg*, 244–46.

as teachers, and the journalists were also alike in their extens ve language skills.[13] The personal history and activism of Aleksandra Gripenberg, born in 1857, reflected many aspects of this characterization. Thanks to he: aristocratic family background, she was taught at home and achieved a considerable level of education despite lacking formal degrees. The inheritance she received enabled her to live a relatively modest but stable lifestyle. Partly inspired by her siblings, Aleksandra became involved in current ideological trends. She was a native Swedish speaker, but at the beginning of the 1880s, she became a Fennoman and adopted a pro-Finnish mindset aiming for the imp rovement of the status of the Finnish language and the Finnish-speaking population, and the women's rights in connection to this. She joined the Finn sh Women's Association, founded in 1884, and soon rose to its leadership. Gripenberg did not marry and life without family responsibilities liberated her tc take part in diverse social action both in Finland and internationally.[14]

In 1887, Gripenberg traveled to England and from there to the United States, sent by the Finnish Women's Association. During her trip, she became convinced of the leading role played by England and the United States in women's emancipation.[15] In England, she was impressed by *The Englishwoman's Review* and its editor, Caroline Ashurst Biggs. In her letters to Finland, Gripenberg writes admiringly about how energetic and intellectually vigilant Biggs was.[16] Biggs died soon after Gripenberg's return home, and in a memorial in *Koti ja Yhteiskunta*, Gripenberg stresses that Biggs had sacrificed herself for what she considered to be a costly woman's rights cause by abandoning her dreams of being a fiction writer. Gripenberg writes that she herself had been 'awoken and supported" by Biggs.[17]

Gripenberg also thought personally about the idea of sacrificing personal dreams and aspirations for the sake of a cause. Before her travel to England and the United States, she had published fictional texts, and a career as a fiction writer was particularly attractive.[18] However, when she returned home, she fully devoted herself to organizational work for women's rights, both in Finland and internationally. Gripenberg's main medium at a national level was the *Koti ja*

---

[13] Henrika Zilliacus-Tikkanen, *När Könet började skriva: Kvinnor i finländsk press 1771–1900* (Helsingfors: Finska Vetenskaps-Societeten, 2005), 164–65.

[14] Tuulio, *Aleksandra Gripenberg*, 49–67.

[15] Tiina Kinnunen, "The National and International in Making a Feminist: The Case of Alexandra Gripenberg," *Women's History Review* 25, no. 4 (2016): 661–63.

[16] Gripenberg to Topelius, January 4, 1888 (GC, 305:7).

[17] Aleksandra Gripenberg, "Caroline Ashurst Biggs," *Koti ja Yhteiskunta*, October 15, 1889.

[18] Pia Forssell, "Från skrivande damer till yrkesförfattrinnor," in *Finlands svenska litteraturhistoria*, ed. Johan Wrede (Helsingfors: Svenska Litteratursällskapet i Finland, 1999), 454–55.

*Yhteiskunta* magazine. The magazine was founded in 1889 for the Finnish Women's Association, but "at the same time, particularly to serve as the Finnish Women's Association's chairperson Gripenberg's magazine,"[19] to borrow Maija Töyry's characterization. Gripenberg did not begin editing *Koti ja Yhteiskunta* unexperienced in the press industry. For example, she had edited children's magazines together with her friend writer Toini Topelius.[20] In 1894, *Koti ja Yhteiskunta* literally became Gripenberg's magazine, as at that time she took full financial responsibility for it. This was made possible by her financial independence as an unmarried and reasonably wealthy woman.

In the early 1900s, Aleksandra Gripenberg was one of the most internationally well-known Nordic women's rights activists. The International Council of Women (ICW), established in 1888, represented an appropriate internationality for her, and she attended its conferences, networked with its key players, and served on its board. At the same time as Gripenberg promoted her *Hertha* initiative in Finland and Sweden, she was considering moving abroad to spread ICW's message. However, she felt obligated to stay due to the situation in her home country. She felt that the Russification efforts eroding Finland's autonomy were particularly grave and that women also had to be mobilized against them.[21]

As a multilingual and frequent traveler in Europe, Gripenberg was able to study women's rights journals published in different languages. She shared the information she had gathered from them and reviewed the journals in both *Koti ja Yhteiskunta* and in her book, *Naisasian kehitys eri maissa.* She described the German journal, *Neue Bahnen,* as distinguished,[22] and stated that France's "most influential women's rights friends" gathered around the journal *Le droit des femmes.*[23] She used *The Englishwoman's Review* as a key source to describe the history of women's rights in different countries.[24] Gripenberg was not an impartial observer in her reviews, but a participant who made very specific use of the women's rights press. She was a fierce opponent of gender-specific labor legislation, and accordingly, she very carefully quoted, for example, Danish magazine *Kvinden og Samfundet*'s stance against a government bill in 1899.

---

[19] Maija Töyry, *Varhaiset naistenlehdet ja naisten elämän ristiriidat: Neuvotteluja lukijasopimuksesta* (Helsinki: Helsingin yliopisto, 2005), 206.

[20] Janina Orlov, "'Var glad som sparven kvittrar' – barnlitteraturen," in *Finlands svenska litteraturhistoria,* ed. Johan Wrede (Helsingfors: Svenska Litteratursällskapet i Finland, 1999), 349.

[21] Kinnunen, "The National and International," 659–61, 664.

[22] Aleksandra Gripenberg, *Naisasian kehitys eri maissa I* (Porvoo: Werner Söderström Osakeyhtiö, 1905), 111.

[23] Aleksandra Gripenberg, *Naisasian kehitys eri maissa II* (Porvoo: Werner Söderström Osakeyhtiö, 1906), 27.

[24] E.g. Gripenberg, *Naisasian kehitys I,* 74, 115, 140; Naisasian kehitys *II,* 82.

The magazine was particularly praised for being "the first to raise the alarm for this bill, which, under the guise of protection, interferes in the gainful employment of women."[25]

## Finnish and Swedish women's rights press at the turn of the century

In the early twentieth century, the press in the Western world played a key role in political communication and related activism. Women's movements were no exception in this respect. In her study on nineteenth-century suffrage journals, Linda Steiner states that "no national movement — can survive, much less succeed, without publicly shared discourse, without 'media.'"[26] Research on the history of feminism has increasingly focused on the role of media in both national and transnational communication regarding women's rights and in building imagined communities of sisterhood. In their study on the media history of Anglo-American feminism, Lucy Delap and Maria DiCenzo point out that participation in the women's movement was primarily through reading.[27]

In Sweden, the history of the country's feminist press from the nineteenth century to the present day has been duly charted, in addition to the history of some individual journalist women.[28] *Tidskrift för hemmet*, launched in 1859 and suppressed in 1886, was the first women's rights journal published in the Nordics. The *Hertha* initiative originated in Alexandra Gripenberg's dissatisfaction with the majority of Swedish and Finnish women's rights press at the turn of the nineteenth and twentieth centuries. In contrast, she gave a high rating to *Tidskrift för hemmet*: "This great journal, the first mouthpiece of women's rights, had an almost unlimited impact on the women of Scandinavia and Finland."[29] In 1886, a magazine called *Dagny* replaced *Tidskrift för hemmet*. *Dagny* was the voice of Fredrika Bremer Association (Fredrika Bremer-förbundet),

---

[25] Aleksandra Gripenberg, *Naisasian kehitys eri maissa III* (Porvoo: Werner Söderström Osakeyhtiö, 1908), 388.
[26] Linda Steiner, "Nineteenth-Century Suffrage Journals: Inventing and Defending New Women," in *Front Pages, Front Lines: Media and the Fight for Women's Suffrage*, eds. Linda Steiner, Carolyn Kitch and Brooke Kroeger (Urbana and Chicago: Illinois University Press, 2020), 55.
[27] Lucy Delap and Maria DiCenzo, "Transatlantic Print Culture: The Anglo-American Feminist Press and Emerging 'Modernities,'" in *Transatlantic Print Culture, 1880–1940: Emerging Media, Emerging Modernisms*, eds. A. Ardis and P. Collier (London: Palgrave Macmillan, 2008), 55.
[28] E.g. Ulrika Holgersson, "Från tågresor till social medier: Rösträttens mediehistoria," in *Rösträttens århundrade: Kampen, utvecklingen och framtiden för demokratin i Sverige*, eds. Ulrika Holgersson and Lena Wängnerud (Stockholm: Makadam, 2018), 103–28; Anna Nordenstam, ed., *Nya Röster: Svenska kvinnotidskrifter under 150 år* (Möklinta: Gidlunds förlag, 2021).
[29] Gripenberg, *Naisasian kehitys III*, 54

founded in 1884. The magazine and the Association had a moderate policy, simultaneously emphasizing women's rights and duties,[30] in line with the Finnish Women's Association. Meanwhile, *Framåt* magazine was writing in favor of a more liberal sexual morality. *Framåt* was a short-lived project, lasting a few years in the mid-1880s, but its existence reflects the differences within the women's movement.[31]

Feminist media history has also been researched in Finland, both the woman's rights press and early journalist women.[32] In her study of the earliest women's rights journals, Maija Töyry examines Gripenberg's *Koti ja Yhteiskunta* magazine. According to her, the magazine's stance reflected the status of women in the tension between the home and society. The role of women in the private sphere was not problematized and referred to as if "in passing."[33] The magazine shared a great deal of recipes, crafting patterns, and gardening advice, but interpreting them as non-emancipatory—as Töyry does[34]—because they did not challenge the gender division of labor in the private sphere does not, in my opinion, adequately recognize the historical contexts that affected the publication policy of the magazine. The women's movements—both in Finland and internationally—did not consider the complementary roles of the genders to be the main problem. A counter-discourse was created in which the home was defined as the heart of society and women's participation in society as a social motherhood. The Fennoman commitment of Gripenberg and the Finnish Women's Association added an additional component to this whole: In addition to theoretical reflections upon women's emancipation ordinary Finnish-speaking women—peasant women and from urban lower classes—was to be directed to participate in the building of the Finnish nation. A key part of this participation was proficiently raising children and meticulous housekeeping.[35]

In 1889, another women's rights magazine was founded in Finland, the Swedish-speaking *Hem och Samhället*, which, despite its name, was not a translation of the magazine edited by Gripenberg. *Hem och Samhället* ceased operation in 1894, and *Nutid* was founded the next year to be the Swedish-language mouthpiece of women's rights and a challenger to *Koti ja Yhteiskunta*. Arja Turunen has examined women's magazines as a whole in Finland, and she

[30] Lina Samuelsson, "Dagny: En tidskrift för den nya dagens kvinna," in *Nya Röster: Svenska kvinnotidskrifter under 150 år*, ed. Anna Nordenstam (Möklinta: Gidlunds förlag, 2021), 19–27.

[31] Lisbeth Stenberg, "Tidskriften Framåt: Två åsiktsriktningar möts i unika debatter," in *Nya Röster: Svenska kvinnotidskrifter under 150 år*, ed. Anna Nordenstam (Möklinta: Gidlunds förlag, 2021), 49–67.

[32] On journalist women, e.g. Zilliacus-Tikkanen, *När Könet började*.

[33] Töyry, *Varhaiset naistenlehdet*, 227–28.

[34] Töyry, *Varhaiset naistenlehdet*, 231.

[35] Gripenberg to Cederschiöld, September 20, 1900 (FWAA, Hd:3).

highlights that the breakthrough of so-called consumer magazines took place slowly due to the slow formation of a consumer society. As a result, early women's rights journals were primarily association journals. *Nutid* was affiliated with The Finnish Women's Association Unioni (Naisasialiitto Unioni, henceforward Unioni), which broke away from the Finnish Women's Association in 1892.[36] Unioni did not have a radically different emancipation policy from the Finnish Women's Association; there were other reasons behind the conflict, such as a more tolerant attitude towards Finnish bilingualism and criticism of Gripenberg as a person. A few other women's rights magazines were also established in Finland, but only after Gripenberg's *Hertha* initiative was buried.

Lucy Delap and Maria DiCenzo show in their research how women's rights journals published in both the United States and England, when traveling across the Atlantic, created a single reading community.[37] Also in other contexts, comparable transnational communities emerged, based on both reading journals and producing their contents. This was evident in Finland and Sweden by the fact that when reporting about women's emancipation in different countries or international encounters, individual women's rights journals utilized the corresponding press in other countries by translating texts from one language to another, for example. Translating foreign articles was also typical for the rest of the press in the early 1900s. According to Margareta Stål, who has written about the history of Swedish journalist women, they often launched their professional careers by translating articles from foreign press.[38] Associations also obtained periodicals from outside their own country, especially from other Nordic countries, for their readers. For example, the women's discussion club in the Norwegian town of Horten subscribed to the Finnish magazine *Nutid*.[39] Meanwhile, in 1889 in *Koti ja Yhteiskunta*, women were encouraged to form reading and discussion clubs to familiarize themselves with women's rights. In addition to literature, they were also urged to read the Swedish *Dagny*, the Norwegian *Nylaende*, and the Danish *Kvinden og Samfundet* magazines. The latter was particularly recommended.[40] Mobilization had

36 Arja Turunen, "Naistenlehdet Suomessa 1880-luvulta 1930-luvulle," *Media ja viestintä* 37, no. 2 (2014): 44–5.
37 Delap and DiCenzo, "Transatlantic Print Culture," 56. See also Lucy Delap, *The Feminist Avant-Garde: Transatlantic Encounters of the Early Twentieth Century* (Cambridge: Cambridge University Press, 2007), 44–56.
38 Margareta Stål, "Kvinnorna i det offentliga samtalet: Om hur pennskaften blev reportrar," *Kvinnovetenskaplig tidskrift* 24, no. 2 (2003): 71.
39 Rita Paqvalén, *Queera minnen: Essäer om tystnad, längtan och motstånd* (Helsingfors: Schildts & Söderströms, 2021), 131.
40 Aleksandra Gripenberg, "Niille naisille," (Editorial), *Koti ja Yhteiskunta*, December 15, 1889.

already taken place in different parts of Finland before this suggestion. For example, in Sortavala, a town of about 1,300 inhabitants in eastern Finland, the local women's rights association had already commissioned foreign literature and periodicals about women's rights for its members as early as from the mid-1880s. The magazines were sourced from Sweden and Norway: *Tidskrift för hemmet, Framåt, Dagny* and *Nylaende.*[41]

### Journalism for the correct women's rights cause and in opposition to Ellen Key

According to Aleksandra Gripenberg, women's rights—that is, the question of economic, legal, social, and political equality between the genders—was "a matter of humanity, a question of the emancipation and harmonious advancement of the whole of humanity."[42] She considered Christianity to be the basis for women's emancipation of women and the general advancement of humanity.[43]

*Koti ja Yhteiskunta* was a vital tool for Gripenberg to promote her vision of "true emancipation." The magazine sought to reach women across class boundaries, which is why the material ranged from educational texts, including home and childcare advice, to articles discussing women's rights issues in a more theoretical sense and raising awareness of their international nature. Suffrage was not a key issue around 1900, it became topical in the years 1904–1905. In a letter sent to Maria Cederschiöld in 1900, Gripenberg describes the magazine—"my magazine"—as representing "an old-fashioned strict woman's rights" without concessions to any kind of "stupidity."[44] By stupidity, Gripenberg meant the radicalism that had spread from one country to another—support for a liberal sexual morality and socialism—and she identified as a firm opponent of these. The majority of feminists extended the demand for an absolute sexual morality tied to marriage to encompass men as well, but to the shock of Gripenberg, dissidents, from her point of view, "opponents of the correct women's rights cause," were also present in the women's movement. One of the most influential was the Swedish writer and educator Ellen Key (1849–1926). According to Gripenberg, Key must be opposed as well because she was in favor of labor legislation that restricted women's work in order to protect their

---

[41] "Oman maan kuulumisia," *Koti ja Yhteiskunta*, March 15, 1891.
[42] Gripenberg, *Naisasian kehitys* I, 9.
[43] E.g., Tiina Kinnunen, "Alexandra Gripenberg's Feminist Christianity," in *Finnish Women Making Religion: Between Ancestors and Angels*, eds. Terhi Utriainen and Päivi Salmesvuori (Basingstoke: Palgrave Macmillan, 2014), 61–79.
[44] Gripenberg to Cederschiöld, September 20, 1900 (FWAA, Hd:3).

function as mothers. According to Gripenberg, the right to work was a prerequisite for women's emancipation and this right was not to be restricted.[45]

In the 1880s, Key was still considered a credible friend to women's rights in Sweden and Finland, but the relationship between Key and the organized women's movement suffered a crisis in the 1890s when Key began to publicly distance herself from some of the common principles. In particular, the *Missbrukad kvinnokraft* booklet, published in 1896, agitated women's rights proponents. In the booklet and in subsequent works, Key criticized the women's movement for ignoring the "natural" difference between the sexes in its goal for a formal equality. Key did not oppose women's right to education, employment, or political engagement, but she stressed the unique importance of motherhood as a cultural force. Key, who was critical of Christianity, did not consider Christian marriage to be a necessary institution, but instead emphasized the omnipotence of love as the basis of family life.[46]

Gripenberg reacted to Key's ideas not only ideologically, but also deeply emotionally, even losing sleep.[47] She thought that buried in Key's speeches and writings was a radicalism against the interests of society and women—"a gospel of the flesh," as she wrote to Maria Cederschiöld[48]—that left her no alternative but to fight back. To another Swedish women's rights activist, Ellen Fries, she writes that Key's ideas were so dangerous that she had to be perceived as "the enemy."[49]

The anger Key incited was reflected in Gripenberg's private correspondence. She was not silent about Key in public either. She condemned Key's ideas in *Koti ja Yhteiskunta*, but also in international contexts. For example, she spoke at an anti-Key rally in Stockholm in 1896, and she challenged Key on the issue of the special labor legislation at the International Congress of Women in London in 1899.[50] Gripenberg hoped to find the time to write critically of Key

45 Gripenberg, *Naisasian kehitys III*, 166–70. See also Tiina Kinnunen, "'Fighting Sisters': A comparative biography of Ellen Key (1849–1926) and Alexandra Gripenberg (1857–1913) in the contested field of European feminisms," in *Biography, Gender and History: Nordic Perspectives*, eds. Erla Hulda Halldórsdóttir, Tiina Kinnunen, Maarit Leskelä-Kärki and Birgitta Possing (Turku: k&h, 2016), 143–64.
46 On Key's life work and thinking, see e.g. Ronny Ambjörnsson, *Ellen Key. En europeisk intellektuell* (Stockholm: Albert Bonniers förlag, 2012). In particular, chapter three "Samhällsmodern" deals with Key's stance on women's rights issues but it is notable that her thinking was an entity in which the various aspects are closely intertwined.
47 Gripenberg to Hierta-Retzius, March 7, 1899 (FWAA, Hd:4).
48 Gripenberg to Cederschiöld, July 19, 1901 (FWAA, Hd:3).
49 Gripenberg to Fries, August 23, 1897 (GC, 306:3).
50 Tuulio, *Aleksandra Gripenberg*, 192–200.

in women's rights magazines internationally to avoid the impression that she was generally accepted as a representative of Nordic women's movement.[51]

Gripenberg did not consider her own actions to be sufficient to stop Key's harmful influence and desired a fiercer resistance. In September 1901, Gripenberg wrote to Maria Cederschiöld that she considered it important to start a Swedish-language women's rights magazine that took a clear stance against Key. She did not feel that people in the Nordics were sufficiently committed to resisting Key.[52] The Swedish Fredrika Bremer Association (Fredrika Bremer-förbundet) had basically the same take as Gripenberg and the Finnish Women's Association: A key element of "true women's emancipation" (*sann frigörelse*) was a call for a strict sexual morality, both for women and men.[53] However, Gripenberg considered the "Fredrikas"—members of the Association—and their magazine *Dagny* powerless in relation to Key, and was also critical of Danish women's rights activists—they were so enthusiastic about Key.[54] Gripenberg thought that it was easier for Finns than Swedes to launch a campaign against Key because, for Swedes, it was a question of a countrywoman. Swedish critics of Key could then subscribe to the magazine to support the campaign.[55]

Key's growing popularity in both Sweden and Finland increased the pressure to act, and she became more well-known elsewhere in Europe in the early 1900s as well. In Finland, Gripenberg noted with concern, Key was garnering positive attention among Unioni activists, as well as in their Swedish-language magazine *Nutid*. The undeniable proof that the Unionists, whom Gripenberg already found objectionable, thought favorably of Key was that she was one of *Nutid*'s contributors.[56]

Feeling an extreme sense of duty, Gripenberg could not stand by and watch the spread of Key's ideas and reputation, but she was aware of the difficulties involved in her initiative. She had been assured by those in the know that under the Russification measures, she would not be allowed to start a new magazine. She also feared that she did not have sufficient time to dedicate to the new initiative.[57] Time was a legitimate concern as Gripenberg had many irons in the

---

[51] Gripenberg to Cederschiöld, July 19, 1901 (FWAA, Hd:3).

[52] Gripenberg to Cederschiöld, September 26, 1901 (FWAA, Hd:3).

[53] Ulla Manns, *Den sanna frigörelsen: Fredrika-Bremer-förbundet 1884–1921* (Stockholm: Brutus Östlings Bokförlag Symposion, 1997), 80–102.

[54] E.g. Gripenberg to Fries, March 17, 1897 (GC, 306:3); Gripenberg to Hierta-Retzius, September 22, 1901 (FWAA, Hd:4); Gripenberg to Cederschiöld, March 8, 1903 (FWAA, Hd:3).

[55] Gripenberg to Cederschiöld, September 26, 1901 (FWAA, Hd:3).

[56] Tuulio, *Aleksandra Gripenberg*, 202.

[57] Gripenberg to Cederschiöld, December 5, 1901 (FWAA, Hd:3).

fire. Editing *Koti ja Yhteiskunta* took resources, time, and strength, as did her other written work. Even when Gripenberg was abroad, she had to take care of *Koti ja Yhteiskunta*. There was a third volume of *Reformarbetet för förbättrandet av kvinnans ställning* underway concerning the Nordics. Writing took time, but Gripenberg was also able to include criticism against Key in this third volume.[58] In addition to her written work, association work throughout Finland was time-consuming, and her international commitments required travel abroad

The core of the "true emancipation" defended by Gripenberg can be found in Fredrika Bremer's novel *Hertha* published in 1856: women's rights and responsibilities to build society, whether it be employment, raising children, or political participation. The name Gripenberg gave to her magazine demonstrated that she identified with Bremer's legacy. Elisabeth Löfgren, a close activist friend of Gripenberg, came up with the name[59] but Gripenberg could just as well have penned it. Gripenberg characterized Bremer's novel as a book that had "foresight, depth, and compassion," and was to be "spotlighted in the overall history of women."[60] Overall, Bremer was a key inspiration and role model for Gripenberg in the fight to promote women's rights in a Christian sense. In her speech at Bremer's centennial memorial service in August 1901—about a month before publishing the magazine initiative—Gripenberg emphasized Bremer's exemplarity.[61]

If realized, *Hertha* would have enabled Gripenberg to engage in journalistic activities in her native language, Swedish. When editing *Koti ja Yhteiskunta*, she was reliant on assistants, even though she was good at Finnish. I am not suggesting that Gripenberg intended to create a new magazine in order to write in Swedish, but the question of language was not insignificant in her activism either. She was a Fennoman, which meant that at a political level, she had to fight against the domination of her native language in Finland. As a representative of Fennoman women's movement, she had to work in Finnish to appeal to the Finnish-speaking women population. However, as a writer, her native language was important for her, and she reflected on this issue even in her correspondence.

---

[58] Gripenberg, *Naisasian kehitys III*, 166–79.
[59] Tuulio, *Aleksandra Gripenberg*, 245.
[60] Gripenberg, Naisasian kehitys III, 41.
[61] "Eräs satavuotismuisto," *Koti ja Yhteiskunta*, September 15, 1901. The name of the writer is not given but it is obvious that it was Gripenberg. See also Tiina Kinnunen, "History as Argument – Alexandra Gripenberg, Ellen Key and the Notion of True Feminism," in *Gendering Historiography. Beyond National Canons*, eds. Angelika Epple and Angelika Schaser (Frankfurt and New York: Campus Verlag, 2009), 181–207.

To Maria Cederschiöld she wrote that she was very tempted to write in Swedish. It was the language to which she had a strong emotional bond.[62]

The Russification measures were also directed at the press and getting authorization to publish *Hertha* was buried in 1902. In October 1904, Gripenberg, in a letter to Maria Cederschiöld, guesses that it could be possible to obtain the authorization, but says she doubts whether the initiative will be realized.[63] Reasons for the doubts can at least be found in Gripenberg's heavy workload. She also had some health concerns at times. The danger of "deterioration" caused by Ellen Key had not disappeared, but new objectives had also emerged. Since 1904, for example, the issue of women's suffrage began to require more attention. *Hertha* was never realized as a journal edited by Gripenberg. Instead, a Swedish *Hertha* saw the light of day in 1913 when *Dagny* journal was suppressed and was succeeded by a new journal. The first volume of Hertha was published in 1914. Aleksandra Gripenberg did not live long enough to read it. She died in 1913.

### Constructing a network of like-minded contributor

With the launch of *Hertha* in mind, Aleksandra Gripenberg assembled a network of contributors composed of Finnish and Swedish women who had expressed critical views on Ellen Key.[64] Some of them were also personally close to Gripenberg. Criticality of Key could even be said to have been a prerequisite for Gripenberg to consider someone close to herself. Maria Furuhjelm from Finland and Selma Lagerlöf, Mathilda Roos, and Annie Quiding from Sweden were named as contributors in an announcement in the newspaper *Uusi Suometar*. The Swedish Elisabeth Elkan had also promised to support it but did not allow her name to be published.[65] The women were connected to each other: Cederschiöld and Roos were childhood friends, and Lagerlöf and Elkan lived together.[66]

---

[62] Gripenberg to Cederschiöld, October 19, 1901 (FWAA, Hd:3). See also Tiina Kinnunen, "Alexandra Gripenberg and Lost Faith in National Belonging," in *Nineteenth-Century Nationalisms and Emotions in the Baltic Sea Region: The Production of Loss*, eds. Anna Bohlin, Tiina Kinnunen and Heidi Grönstrand (Leiden and Boston: Brill, 2021), 361–65.

[63] Gripenberg to Cederschiöld, October 23, 1904 (FWAA, Hd:3).

[64] On criticism towards Key in the Swedish feminist movement, see Manns, *Den sanna frigörelsen*, 134–53.

[65] *Uusi Suometar*, December 1, 1901; Gripenberg to Cederschiöld, December 18, 1901 (FWAA, Hd:3).

[66] Eva Helen Ulvros, "Sophie Elkan och Selma Lagerlöf – kärlek och kvinnorörelse," in *Den kvinnliga tvåsamhetens frirum: Kvinnopar i kvinnorörelsen 1890–1960*, eds. Eva Borgström and Hanna Markusson Winkvist (Stockholm: Appell förlag, 2018), 33–75.

In a letter to Cederschiöld, Gripenberg mentions receiving promises of pieces for *Hertha* "from abroad."[67] The wording is interesting because it reflects Swedish-speaking Gripenberg's attitude towards Sweden. It was not abroad for her in the same sense as England, for example, which she so admired in terms of women's emancipation, was. There are no references in her correspondence to any collaboration in the Nordics beyond Sweden. As previously noted, Gripenberg was suspicious of the Danes because of their favorable attitudes towards Key. Of the Norwegians, she especially admired Gina Krog. Krog was an editor for *Nylaende* magazine and thus a colleague of Gripenberg in the field of feminist media. Krog visited Finland at the end of 1900 to give a lecture, and *Koti ja Yhteiskunta* describes her as "one of the most esteemed representatives of women's rights" in Norway.[68] During the visit, the Finnish Women's Association organized a reception in honor of Krog. In her speech Gripenberg praised Krog for being a representative of the fight against the deterioration in the women's movement. By deterioration, Gripenberg meant praising sexual radicalism.[69] The *Koti ja Yhteiskunta* quote of Gripenberg's speech is descriptive of her strategy against Key: Gripenberg did not necessarily refer to Key by name in her speeches or writings, but instead referred to her using the concept of decline. Her contemporaries knew who and what dispute she was referring to.

Gripenberg highlighted Lagerlöf, Roos, Quiding, and Elkan in the third volume of her book *Reformarbetet för förbättrandet av kvinnans ställning* and emphasized their literary talent.[70] The most notable of them was Lagerlöf. She achieved an international breakthrough with her *Jerusalem* novel at the beginning of the 1900s, at the same time as Gripenberg's magazine initiative was launched. Lagerlöf's promise to be a contributor was a particular victory for Gripenberg—of course, in the planning stages, it was not essential whether Lagerlöf actually wrote in the magazine. What was important was that she gave her promise. *Nutid*, a competitor of *Koti ja Yhteiskunta*, which was more favorable to, though not uncritical of, Key in comparison to Gripenberg and her circles, would have been delighted to count Lagerlöf among its contributors. Thus, Gripenberg's "capture" was notable among the Finnish competition.[71]

According to Eva Helen Ulvros, annoyance at Ellen Key was a common theme in the correspondence between Elkan and Lagerlöf. They opposed how Key

---

[67] Gripenberg to Cederschiöld, January 12, 1902 (FWAA, Hd:3).

[68] "Oman maan kuulumisia," *Koti ja Yhteiskunta*, November 15, 1900, 100.

[69] "Neiti Gina Krog'in esitelmä," *Koti ja Yhteiskunta*, December 15, 1900. The name of the writer is not given but it is obvious that it was Gripenberg.

[70] Gripenberg, *Naisasian kehitys III*, 138–39.

[71] Annie Furuhjelm, *Den stigande oron* (Helsingfors: Söderströms Förlagsaktiebolag, 1935), 283.

emphasized motherhood as the fulfillment of women's lives.[72] According to Louise Lindblom, who studied the correspondence between Ellen Key and Selma Lagerlöf, the relationship between Key and Lagerlöf went through various stages. Lindblom emphasizes that the relationship contained positive elements—mutual encouragement and respect—contrary to what previous studies have often suggested. For example, the Nobel Prize for Literature Lagerlöf received in 1909 was a great source of joy for Key. However, Lindblom also notes that it was precisely at the turn of the century when the *Hertha* initiative began to take shape that Lagerlöf took on critical tones towards Key.[73]

The media coverage overseen by Gripenberg highlighted the promised contributors' open opposition to Key. Mathilda Roos reacted very critically to Key's ideas in the 1890s, and in a eulogy written by Maria Cederschiöld in *Koti ja Yhteiskunta* (1908), Roos is described as follows: "She (Roos), who had always been a friend of the true emancipation of women, rose against Ellen Key and the false women's emancipation that she had started to defend."[74] Roos emerged in the 1880s with her work on women's emancipation,[75] whereas Annie Quiding was a new talent at the beginning of the century and at that stage very respected. She received, among other things, a medal from the Swedish Academy.[76] Her novel *En droppe ur havet* was described in *Koti ja Yhteiskunta* in 1901 as a wholesome counterforce to the world view Key represented, which "prioritizes pleasure in life." Furthermore, the novel uses "great skill" to describe the battle between "the representatives of the gospel of pleasure and the representatives of Christian morality."[77]

Of those who promised to be contributors, Maria Furuhjelm and Maria Cederschiöld were the closest to Gripenberg personally. The former was Gripenberg's sister and wrote children's literature and material aimed at public enlightenment. In addition to newspapers, it was also published in *Koti ja*

---

[72] Ulvros, "Sophie Elkan och Selma Lagerlöf," 61–5.

[73] Louise Lindblom, *Ellen Key & Selma Lagerlöf – Breven* (Stockholm: Blue Publishing, 2022), 100–1.

[74] Maria Cederschiöld, "Mathilda Roos," *Koti ja Yhteiskunta*, October 15, 1908, 107. See also Margareta Stål, "'För quinnans framåtskridande': Idun – de första 25 åren," in *Nya Röster: Svenska kvinnotidskrifter under 150 år*, ed. Anna Nordenstam (Möklinta: Gidlunds förlag, 2021), 94–5.

[75] Eva Heggestad, "Anna Mathilda Roos," in *Svenskt kvinnobiografiskt lexikon* (https://skbl.se/en/article/MathildaRoos).

[76] Sif Bokholm, "Annie Åkerhielm," in *Svenskt kvinnobiografiskt lexikon* (https://skbl.se/en/article/AnnieAkerhielm). Quiding (Åkerhielm since 1906) was a conservative nationalist and, for example, an opponent of women's right to vote. In 1901, however, she was not yet active on this issue.

[77] "Kirja vanhoista ja nuorista," *Koti ja Yhteiskunta*, February 15, 1901, 18.

*Yhteiskunta.*[78] Cederschiöld, meanwhile, was a close friend of Gripenberg. She worked as the head of the international news section of the *Aftonbladet* newspaper and was thus a pioneer in the history of Swedish journalist women. She also wrote in *Dagny* and contributed to *Koti ja Yhteiskunta* and promoted the spread of Gripenberg's writings in Sweden.[79]

## Conclusion

This chapter takes part in the topical discussion on the role of the press in feminism in the early twentieth century. The initiative launched in 1901 by Aleksandra Gripenberg of a new women's rights magazine, *Hertha*, demonstrates the key role the press played in the communication within the women's movement and in the building of collective identities and transnational communities. The initiative also demonstrates that feminism was a contested field with competing views, and characterized by solidarity and sisterhood, on the one hand, and disunity and rivalry, on the other hand. It was through the press—the main communication channel of social and political movements—that Gripenberg believed she could create a counterforce to Ellen Key's ideas that she saw as dangerous for "true emancipation."

The initiative with its Finnish-Swedish starting point reflects the transnational nature of feminism in Northern Europe. It was based on a shared Scandinavian language community and the circle of promised contributors consisted of pre-existing connections that Gripenberg had established across borders over decades. At the same time, if realized, *Hertha* would have strengthened and created a new layer in the transnational community of Nordic women's rights activists.

This chapter is about an unfulfilled history. Because *Hertha* never saw the light of day, the feminist periodical community that Gripenberg envisioned never took shape. We cannot know exactly how the content of the magazine would have been formed and how opposing Key—the main objective of the magazine—would have been reflected in its content. What we can conclude is that the journal would have enabled Gripenberg to focus on women's rights from an ideological point of view—what she could not do when editing *Koti ja Yhteiskunta* with its nationalistic aim to reach women from all social classes. We also do not know to what extent and how the promised contributors would have been involved in the magazine. It also remains unanswered how the magazine would have addressed its Nordic readership and how enthusiastically it would have been read. However,

---

[78] Forssell, "Från skrivande damer," 454.
[79] Lisbeth Stenberg, "En 'lifsmakt för kvinnan' – Toini Topelius, Alexandra Gripenberg och Maria Cedeschiöld," in *Den kvinnliga tvåsamhetens frirum: Kvinnopar i kvinnorörelsen 1890–1960*, eds. Eva Borgström and Hanna Markusson Winkvist (Stockholm: Appell förlag, 2018), 95–102.

it can be concluded from Gripenberg's public and private reflections that she would not have pulled her punches as the editor of *Hertha* either. Women's rights had to be defended against "enemies" and the triumph of "decline" had to be stopped.

Chapter 5

# Parisian fashion or functional style? Ideal dress of the modern woman in Finnish women's magazines in the 1920s and 1930s

Arja Turunen

*University of Jyväskylä, Finland*

**Abstract:** The 'New Woman' of the 1920s with her modern dress was a controversial figure. In this article I analyze, how the new dress style was discussed in Finnish women's magazines in the 1920s and 1930s. The article reconstructs the genre of women's magazine by showing that in addition to commercial women's magazines there were also several bulletins published by different kind of women's organizations. The analysis shows that many of the political magazines discussed also fashion, and political content was typical also for the commercial women's magazines, which makes them mixtures of political and fashion (consumer) magazines. Each magazine formulated its own version of an ideal dress style that represented its political goals. Additionally, each magazine reconstructed its own version of a 'women's magazine'. The concept of women's magazine also changed during the time period under study, which underlines the need to carefully contextualize each magazine when they are used as research material.

**Keywords:** women's magazines, feminism, dress history, fashion, Finland

\*\*\*

*Isn't it humiliating that magazines that aim to boost women and raise them [their political awareness] are dying from lack of support, but those magazines that turn women into slaves of fashion and vanity overgrow like weeds? Those magazines are the source of all those disgusting, half-naked women with sleeveless dresses with bare backs and low-cut necklines.[1]*

---

[1] *Naisten Ääni* 17/1924, 256.

Women's fashion underwent dramatic changes during the first decades of the twentieth century. The long and cumbersome dress and the mature feminine figure of the turn of the century were replaced by a short and loose-fitting dress and a boyish figure by the mid-1920s. In fashion magazines, the new style was celebrated as representing the emancipated "modern women" who—with increased employment opportunities—lived an active and independent life. In other forums of public discussion, the new style was mostly criticized. Short hemlines and low necklines were seen as indecent and unhealthy, and social observers such as the Finnish feminist magazine *Naisten Ääni* cited above were also worried that young women were more interested in the hedonistic lifestyle of a dancing "jazz girl" than the role of a mother or questions of women's political rights. Women's associations and other educators sought to control the social change by defining new standards for women's behavior, duties, and responsibilities.[2]

In this chapter, I analyze how Finnish women's magazines discussed contemporary women's fashion in the 1920s and 1930s.[3] I ask what role fashion journalism played in each magazine, and what kind of dress style was seen as ideal for modern women. I understand the concept of "women's magazine" as an umbrella category referring to periodicals that were addressed to women and discussed "women's concerns."[4] This broad understanding of women's magazines means that the study is not limited to the genre of commercial women's magazines (women's consumer magazines) that typically discuss fashion, beauty care and domestic matters but also includes other magazines that address "women" as their readers. It also allows the analysis of the similarities and differences between different sub-genres of women's magazines.

---

[2] See e.g. Mary Louise Roberts, *Civilization without Sexes: Reconstructing Gender in Postwar France, 1917–1927* (Chicago: The University of Chicago Press, 1994); Kaisa Vehkalahti, "Jazz-tyttö ja naistenlehtien siveä katse," in *Modernin lumo ja pelko: Kymmenen kirjoitusta 1800–1900-lukujen vaihteen sukupuolisuudesta,* eds. Kari Immonen, Ritva Hapuli, Maarit Leskelä and Kaisa Vehkalahti (Helsinki: SKS, 2000); Birgitte Soland, *Becoming modern: Young Women and the Reconstruction of Womanhood in the 1920s* (Princeton: Princeton University Press, 2000); Emma Severinsson, *Moderna kvinnor: Modernitet, femininitet och svenskhet i svensk veckopress 1920–1933* (Lund: Historiska institutionen, Lunds universitet, 2018).

[3] This chapter is based on my PhD thesis: Arja Turunen, *Hame, housut, hamehousut! Vai mikä on tulevaisuutemme? Naisten päällyshousujen käyttöä koskevat pukeutumisohjeet ja niissä rakentuvat naiseuden ihanteet suomalaisissa naistenlehdissä 1889–1945* (Helsinki: Suomen muinaismuistoyhdistys, 2011).

[4] Kathryn Shevelow, *Women and Print Culture: The Construction of Femininity in the Early Periodical* (London: Routledge, 1989).

Feminist and commercial magazines are usually seen to invo.ve two very different and even opposite ideologies: women's consumer magazir.es represent the fashion industry and consumerism and reinforce "unrealistic standards of beauty," whereas feminist magazines are critical towards the afo:ementioned "traditional" women's magazines and offer their readers an alternative, feminist perspective on society and women's lives.[5] A closer reading of *Naisten Ääni*, however, reveals that its readers were recommended to dress according to the latest Parisian style.[6] This kind of combination of feminist or political and fashion content was also typical of other Finnish women's magazines in the early twentieth century.[7] In my analysis, the critical views expressed in political women's magazines such as the *Naisten Ääni* also represent "fashior. journalism" because they participated in interpreting fashion.

Internationally and historically, the boundaries between different types of women's magazines have not been clear. Since the establishment of the genre in the late seventeenth century, women's magazines have represented a wide variety of forms and ideologies. Besides fashion and feminism, the market of women's magazines has also consisted of periodicals associated with leisure, career, domestic matters, religion, literature, philosophy, various political aims, and moral conduct, for example.[8] The history of women's magazines is, therefore, a history of a changing society, changing meanings of femininity, and changing meanings and forms of journalism and publishing. As a genre, women's magazines are not a simple and homogeneous concept; rather, they

---

[5] See Kathleen R. Endres, "Women's Magazines: Fashion," in *Encyclopedia of Gender in Media*, ed. Mary Kosut (Thousand Oaks, California: Sage, 2012); Andrea Bergstrom, "Women in Magazines: Feminist magazines," in *Encyclopedia of Gender in Media*, ed. Mary Kosut (Thousand Oaks, California: Sage, 2012).

[6] See e.g. *Naisten Ääni* 19/1925, 301.

[7] Raili Malmberg, "Naisten ja kotien lehdet aikansa kuvastimina," in *Suo nen lehdistön historia 8: Aikakauslehdistön historia*, ed. Päiviö Tommila (Kuopio: Kustannuskiila oy, 1991), 193–291; Maija Töyry, *Varhaiset naistenlehdet ja naisten elämän ristiriidat: Neuvotteluja lukijasopimuksesta* (Helsinki: Helsingin yliopisto, 2005); Maija Töyry, "Gender Contract and Localization in Early Women's Magazines in Finland Since 1782," *Media History* 22, no. 1 (2016): 13–26; Turunen, *Hame, housut, hamehousut!*; Erkka Railo "Women's Magazines, the Female Body, and Political Participation," *NORA: Nordic Journal of Women's Studies* 22, no. 1 (2014): 52–3.

[8] Shevelow, *Women and Print Culture*; Ros Ballaster, Margaret Beetham, Elzabeth Fraser and Sandra Hebron, eds., *Women's Worlds: Ideology, Femininity and the Woman's Magazine* (Basingstoke: Macmillan, 1991); Margaret Beetham, *A Magazine of her own? Domesticity and Desire in the Woman's Magazine 1800–1914* (London: Routledge, 1996); Margaret Beetham and Kay Boardman, *Victorian Women's Magazines: An anthology* (Manchester and New York: Manchester University Press, 2001); Töyry, *Varhaiset naistenlehdet*; Töyry, "Gender Contract," 13–26; Rachel Ritchie, Sue Hawkins, Nicola Phillips and Jay S. Kleinberg, "Introduction," in *Women in Magazines: Research, Representation, Production and Consumption*, eds. Rachel Ritchie et al. (London: Routledge, 2016), 1–22.

are an active, ideologically and historically changing modifier of texts, meanings, and social actions.[9]

The genre of women's consumer magazines was established in the United States and the United Kingdom and also in Sweden during the late nineteenth century but in Finland, only during the 1920s and 1930s. In each country, the development of the genre took place in the context of the wider growth of the publishing industry and the development of consumer culture. It also coincided with the emergence of the bourgeois family model, which emphasized women's domestic role as the opposite to men's public role. At the same time, consumption patterns were redefined based on gender. Women were recognized as the target market of household items, fashion, and other women's products, including women's magazines. As a genre, commercial women's magazines represented this new ideology and femininity and were also instrumental in articulating and redefining them.[10]

Throughout their history, commercial women's magazines have been criticized for representing consumerism and promoting the interests of the fashion industry only.[11] The starting point for this chapter is, however, the notion that women's magazines are an institution that participates in defining the characteristics of femininity and producing gender relations in a given society at a given point of time. By paying attention to women and "women's concerns" such as dress and fashion, women's magazines also make claims about women's identities, capabilities, and social importance for both women themselves and society. [12]

As this chapter will show, women's magazines do not simply mediate fashion; they have a crucial role in representing and interpreting it to consumers through text and image.[13] Women's magazines of the 1920s and 1930s adopted an active role in making the new style meaningful in a way that suited their ideology. The aim of this chapter is to discuss how women's magazines reconstructed the meaning of fashion and the ideas and norms of dress of class society in the inter-war period.

---

[9] Töyry, "Gender Contract," 13–5.

[10] Beetham, *A Magazine of her own?*; Shevelow, *Women and Print Culture*; Ballaster et al., *Women's Worlds*.

[11] See e.g. Ellen McCracken, *Decoding Women's Magazines: From Mademoiselle to Miss* (Basingstoke: Macmillan, 1993); Töyry, *Varhaiset naistenlehdet*, 39–44.

[12] Shevelow, *Women in Print Culture*; Ballaster et al., *Women's Worlds*; Beetham, *A Magazine of her own?*

[13] Joanne Entwistle, *The Fashioned Body: Fashion, Dress and Modern Social Theory* (Cambridge: Polity, 2000), 235; Yunuya Kawamura, *Fashion-ology* (Oxford: Berg, 2005), 4, 20, 80; Endres, "Women's Magazines: Fashion," 437.

## Methodology: Femininity in women's magazines

The ideologies of women's consumer magazines have been studied since the 1960s, particularly by feminist scholars, who have drawn different conclusions about their role in society. Especially in early studies, women's magazines were seen as repressive institutions maintaining patriarchal values and women's domestic role, but more recent studies have demonstrated their role as spaces for negotiation or even resistance for women.[14] These contradictory conclusions can be partly explained by the fact that study results have depended on the material analyzed. Women's magazines have developed as a mixed form containing various text types, genres, and voices that construct different and multiple meanings. The discussion and representation of femininity within a single issue therefore involves many ambivalent, fragmentary, competing, and even contradictory notions.[15]

This means that the chosen magazines and individual text samples need to be contextualized in terms of text types and genres as well as the historical context because each magazine and its content are also part of culture-specific political, economic, and other local discussions.[16] As Maija Töyry has argued, women's magazines build their content around the contradictions in women's lives. She suggests that the success of women's magazines seems to lie in their ability to address readers in a way that resonates with the ongoing public discussions and negotiations, as well as with the private lives of readers.[17]

The material for this article consists of 14 Finnish women's magazines, which are presented in Tables 5.1, 5.2, and 5.3. I have analyzed all articles and fashion columns published in these magazines in the period under study. In analyzing the ideologies that they represent, I used the method of discourse analysis[18] to scrutinize how the magazines represent and give meaning to femininity as they discuss dress. I also determined the "implied reader" of each magazine, meaning the reader produced and subjected by the text.[19] By defining their readers "as women," women's magazines construct their implied reader based on her

---

[14] Ballaster et al., *Women's Worlds*, 4–25; Beetham, *A Magazine of her Own?*, 1–3; Richie et al., "Introduction," 5.

[15] Ballaster et al. 1991, *Women's Worlds*, 4–25; Beetham, *A Magazine of her Own?*, 1; Beetham and Boardman, *Victorian Women's Magazines*, 4; Richie et al., "Introduction," 5.

[16] Töyry, "Gender Contract," 13–5.

[17] Töyry, "Gender Contract," 22–3.

[18] Donald Matheson, *Media Discourses: Analysing Media Texts* (Maidenhead: Open University Press, 2005).

[19] Ballaster et al., *Women's Worlds*, 2; Töyry, *Varhaiset naistenlehdet*, 61, 36; Porter. H. Abbot, *The Cambridge Introduction to Narrative*. Second edition (Cambridge: Cambridge University Press, 2008), 84–6, 235.

gender; she is "not a man." Although women's magazines are often addressed to "all women," they seek to differentiate themselves from other magazines by defining their readers as certain kinds of women such as middle-class women or working-class women. The positioning of readers "as women" in women's magazines is ideological because it offers individuals social identities and, through them, ways of making sense of the world. They also give a particular meaning to gender difference and femininity. Additionally, different texts may construct different implied readers within one magazine.[20]

In magazines, femininity is usually represented simultaneously as a given and as something still to be achieved. Femininity is also often portrayed as a difficult process of "becoming a woman" that includes learning the skills of beauty care and dressing oneself stylishly and fashionable. For the process, they characteristically provide recipes, patterns, narratives, and models both in the journalistic content and advertisement. Therefore, I read and analyze the women's magazines under study as agents of socialization that tell women what to think and do about themselves, and keep them up to date on the arts and skills of femininity such as fashion.[21]

### Finnish women's magazines of the 1920s and 1930s

The very first Finnish women's magazine was published in 1782, but only the establishment of the Finnish-language *Koti ja Yhteiskunta* (Home and Society) and the Swedish-language *Hemmet och samhället* in 1889 started the boom of women's magazine publishing in Finland. They were bulletins of the bilingual (Finnish- and Swedish-language) women's rights organ Finnish Women's Association (Finsk kvinnoförening—Suomen Naisyhdistys), and they institutionalized the genre of women's magazines in Finland in the form of feminist magazines. The women's association had been established in 1884 by upper-class (bourgeois) women.[22] The labor movement emerged in Finland

---

[20] Ballaster et al., *Women's Worlds*, 25, 43–4, 82–3; Beetham, *A Magazine of Her Own?*, 2, 5, 12–3; Beetham and Boardman, *Victorian Women's Magazines*, 4–5; Töyry, *Varhaiset naistenlehdet*, 82, 253–54, 263.

[21] Beetham, *A Magazine of her Own?*, 1.

[22] Turunen, *Hame, housut, hamehousut!*, 139–41; Arja Turunen, "Naistenlehdet Suomessa 1880-luvulta 1930-luvulle," *Media & Viestintä* 37, no. 2 (2014): 47–8; Töyry, "Gender Contract," 17–9. For the history of the Finnish women's rights movement, see Irma Sulkunen, "Suffrage, Nation and Citizenship – The Finnish Case in an International Context," in *Suffrage, Gender and Citizenship – International Perspectives on Parliamentary Reforms*, eds. Irma Sulkunen et al. (Newcastle upon Tyne: Cambridge Scholars Publishing, 2009), 83–105; Riitta Jallinoja, *Suomalaisen naisasialiikkeen taistelukaudet: Naisasialiike naisten elämäntilanteen muutoksen ja yhteiskunnallis-aatteellisen murroksen heijastajana* (Helsinki: WSOY, 1983); Irma Sulkunen, *Naisen kutsumus: Miina Sillanpää ja sukupuolten*

at the turn of the twentieth century, and the first bulletin of labor women, the newspaper *Palvelijatar* (Domestic worker), was established in 1905. The following year, it was renamed *Työläisnainen* (Labor woman, 1906–1925).[23]

**Table 5.1.** Women's political magazines published in Finland in the 1920s and 1930s.

| Publisher | Title | Publishing period |
|---|---|---|
| Finnish Women's Union (Suomalainen Naisliitto) | *Naisten Ääni* (Women's Voice) | 1907–1949 |
| National Coalition Party | *Suomen Nainen* (Finland's woman) | 1913–1990 |
| Swedish People's Party | *Astra* | 1919–1992 |
| Women's Association of the Social Democratic Party | *Toveritar* (Female comrade) | 1922–1943 |
| Women's Association of the Communist Party | *Työläisnainen* (Labour woman) | 1906–1923 |
| Women's Association of the Communist Party's | *Naistyöläinen* (Female worker) / *Työläis- ja talonpoikaisnaisten lehti* (Worker and peasant women's magazine) | 1925 / 1925–1930 |
| Lotta Svärd Organization | *Lotta Svärd* | 1928–1944 |

In 1906, Finnish women got the vote and the right to stand as candidates in parliamentary elections. The following year, several leading figures of both the bourgeois and labor women's movements were elected as members of parliament. Thereafter, the bourgeois feminist associations were united with

*maailmojen erkaantuminen* (Helsinki: Hanki ja jää, 1989); Minna Hagner and Teija Försti, *Suffragettien sisaret* (Helsinki: Unioni Naisasialiitto, 2006); Anne Ollila, *Suomen kotien päivä valkenee... Marttajärjestö suomalaisessa yhteiskunnassa vuoteen 1939* (Helsinki: SHS, 1993); Anne Ollila, "Women's voluntary associations in Finland during the 1920s and 1930s," *Scandinavian Journal of History* 20, no. 2 (1995): 97–107; Pasi Saarimäki, "Bourgeois Women and The Question of Divorce in Finland in The Late 19th and Early 20th Centuries," *Scandinavian Journal of History* 43, no. 1 (2018): 64–90.

[23] Turunen, *Hame, housut, hamehousut!*, 154; Turunen "Naistenlehdet Suomessa," 48. For the history of the women's associations of the labor movement, see Sulkunen, *Naisen kutsumus*; Maria Lähteenmäki, *Vuosisadan naisliike: Naiset ja sosialidemokratia 1900-luvun Suomessa* (Helsinki: Sosialidemokraattiset naiset, 2002).

the women's associations of the conservative political parties, and the feminist women's magazines became their bulletins.[24] In the 1920s and 1930s, altogether eight women's political magazines were published in Finland. Three of them represented the bourgeois political agenda: *Suomen Nainen* (Finland's Woman, 1913–1990) and *Astra* (1919–1992) were bulletins of the women's associations of the Finnish-language and Swedish-language conservative parties (National Coalition Party and Swedish People's Party). *Naisten Ääni* (Women's Woice, 1907–1949) represented the politically unaffiliated Finnish Women's Union (Suomalainen Naisliitto), which had, however, close connections to party politics as it was established by women members of the Young Finnish Party (Constitutional-Fennoman Party) to support and promote the political participation of Finnish-speaking women.[25]

Labor women had altogether four bulletins in the 1920s and 1930s. After the Finnish Civil War in 1918, the Finnish Labour Party was divided into the Social Democratic Party and the Communist Party. *Työläisnainen* (Labour woman) was published by communist women, and social democratic women established their own bulletin *Toveritar* (Female comrade) in 1922. In the 1920s, the publishing of the Communist Party's bulletins and newspapers faced difficulties due to the political situation.[26] *Työläisnainen* was first replaced by *Naistyöläinen* (Female worker) in 1925 and then by *Työläis- ja talonpoikaisnaisten lehti* (Worker and peasant women's magazine) in 1925–1930.

The eighth women's political journal *Lotta Svärd* was established in 1929 and represented the women's voluntary auxiliary paramilitary organization Lotta Svärd. The Lotta Svärd organization was founded to support the White Guard, a voluntary militia, by providing food supplies and medicine, for example, and to promote patriotic values among women.[27]

---

[24] These women's associations were closely connected to party-political activism even before this. The Finnish Women's Association was established by bourgeois Fennoman (Finnish nationalist) women, and the Finnish Women's Association Unioni was established by Svecomans (Swedish nationalists in Finland) and liberal Fennomans. See Jallinoja, *Naisasialiikkeen taistelukaudet*; Hagner and Försti, *Suffragettien sisaret*; Tanja Ohtonen, *Oikeuden, laillisuuden ja ihmisyyden hengessä: Suomalainen naisliitto vuosina 1907–1939* (Helsinki: Suomalainen naisliitto, 2007), 14–20.

[25] Ohtonen, *Oikeuden, laillisuuden*, 14–20. The political participation and activism of Swedish-speaking women was supported and promoted by the women's association of the Swedish People's Party. See Ohtonen, *Oikeuden, laillisuuden*, 15.

[26] Sulkunen, *Naisen kutsumus*, 68–70; Lähteenmäki, *Vuosisadan naisliike*, 110–11; Tauno Saarela, *Suomalainen kommunismi ja vallankumous 1923–1930* (Helsinki: SKS, 2008), 306.

[27] Pia Olsson, *Eteen vapahan valkean Suomen* (Helsinki: Suomen muinaismuistoyhdistys, 1999); Seija-Leena Nevala-Nurmi, *Perhe maanpuolustajana: Sukupuoli ja sukupolvi Lotta Svärd- ja suojeluskuntajärjestöissä 1918–1944* (Tampere: Tampere University Press, 2012).

**Table 5.2.** Domestic women's magazines published in Finland in the 1920s and 1930s.

| Publisher | Title | Publishing period |
|-----------|-------|-------------------|
| Martha Organization | *Emäntälehti / Husmodern* (Farm women's magazine) | 1902– |

The genre of domestic women's magazines, which focused on discussing cooking, cleaning, gardening, needlework, child-rearing, and other duties of housewives, was established in 1902 when the magazines *Emäntälehti* (Farm women's magazine, est. 1902) and *Husmodern* (Farmer's wife, est. 1902) were founded. They were bulletins of the popular educational Martha Organization, which had been established in 1899 to provide domestic economic advice to farmer and worker women.[28]

### Fashion as a harmful phenomenon in political women's magazines

Corresponding to the international feminist movement,[29] nineteenth-century feminist women's magazines were very critical towards fashion. They criticized corsets and suggested that women should wear so-called "reform dresses" as an alternative to fashionable dresses.[30] The women's rights movement was part of a larger bourgeois women's movement in Finland, which consisted of several prominent and powerful associations. The bourgeois women's movement demanded more political rights for women, but it also aimed at to emancipate women through the idealization of the domestic women. It emphasized the social importance of the housewife's role by arguing that by raising children, taking care of the household, and ensuring the emotional stability of the home, women advanced society as a whole.[31] The fashionable "new woman" of the 1920s posed a threat to both of these objectives. In the 1920s and 1930s, the feminist bulletin *Naisten Ääni* continually criticized contemporary fashion as impractical and argued that the wearing of fashionable clothes made women look silly and illogical, which defeated the feminist argument that women were as intelligent as men. *Naisten Ääni* was especially worried about young women

---

[28] See Ollila, *Suomen kotien*; Ollila, "Women's voluntary."

[29] See e.g. Gayle V. Fischer, *Pantaloons and Power: A Nineteenth-Century Dress Reform in the United States* (Kent: The Kent State University Press, 2001); Patrick Steorn, "Konstnärligt antimode: Svensk Reformdräkt kring sekelsskiftet 1900," in *Mode – en introduktion: En tvärvetenskaplig betraktelse*, eds. Dirk Gindt and Louise Wallenberg (Stockholm: Raster Förlag, 2009), 225–49.

[30] Töyry, *Varhaiset naistenlehdet*, 225–27; Turunen, *Hame, housut, hamehousut!*, 143–48.

[31] Ollila, *Suomen kotien*, 338–39, 342; Ollila, "Women's voluntary;" Saarimäki, "Bourgeois Women," 73–4.

who were easily lured by the whims of fashion and were more interested in reading fashion magazines than educating themselves and joining the women's rights movement.[32] To encourage young women to read *Naisten Ääni* instead of fashion magazines, the magazine established a new column addressed to them in the late 1920s.[33]

On the other hand, members of the feminist movement were expected to follow fashion in their dress style. The bulletin advertised fashion houses and published reports of fashion shows. The Stockmann department store in Helsinki was praised for paying attention "to us who need to dress well and follow both fashion and good taste."[34] By reading *Naisten Ääni*, young women too would hopefully learn to dress in good taste.

In the early 1920s, other political women's magazines representing either the labor movement or the conservative political parties equally criticized contemporary fashion with arguments similar to those voiced in *Naisten Ääni*: fashionable dresses were impractical, unhealthy, and ridiculous. Especially in the winter, light dresses caused serious colds and other problems.[35] In *Toveritar*, fashion was also discussed as a political question: the fashion industry exemplified the capitalist system that lured young girls astray.[36]

### *Kotiliesi* and the modern rational dress style

In Sweden, the first women's consumer magazines *Svensk Damtidning* and *Idun* were established in the late 1880s and the genre became more diversified as *Husmodern* and *Charme* were established in 1917 and 1921.[37] In Finland, the establishment of the first women's consumer magazines *Naisten Lehti* and *Kotiliesi* took place only in the early 1920s. They did not, however, dramatically change the market of women's magazines. Their mission was similar to the one pursued by the bulletins of the bourgeois women's movement. They both called

---

[32] See e.g. *Naisten Ääni* 19/1923, 268; *Naisten Ääni* 17/1924, 256; *Naisten Ääni* 1/1926, 12; *Naisten Ääni* 18–19/1929, 367–68.

[33] Turunen, *Hame, housut, hamehousut!*, 153.

[34] *Naisten Ääni* 22/1936, 318.

[35] *Suomen Nainen* 8–9/1920, 128; *Suomen Nainen* 22–23/1920, 340; *Toveritar* 11/1924, 130; *Työläis- ja talonpoikaisnaisten lehti* 5/1928, 4.

[36] *Toveritar* 11/1924, 130; *Työläis- ja talonpoikaisnaisten lehti* 5/1928, 4.

[37] Emma Severinsson, *Moderna kvinnor: Modernitet, femininitet och svenskhet i svensk veckopress 1920–1933* (Lund: Historiska institutionen, Lunds universitet, 2018), 44–52; Lisbeth Larsson, *En annan historia: Om kvinnors läsning och svensk veckopress* (Stockholm: Symposion, 1989), 105; Lisbeth Larsson, "Trender i svensk veckopress," in *Veckopressbranschens struktur och ekonomi*, ed. Karl Erik Gustafsson (Göteborg: Handelshögskolan vid Göteborgs universitet, 1991), 25–7.

themselves "organs of Finnish women and homes" and aimed to bring women's voice to the political discussion. In addition to political questions, the magazines covered art and literature and gave advice on housekeeping, health care, and dress. Their content was therefore a mixture of feminist, domestic, and fashion magazines.[38]

**Table 5.3.** Women's consumer magazines published in Finland in the 1920s and 1930s.

| Publisher | Title | Publishing period |
|---|---|---|
| Edistysseurojen Kustannus (Progressive societies' publishing) | *Naisten Lehti* (Women's Magazine) | 1921 |
| WSOY / Yhtyneet Kuvalehdet (United Magazines) | *Kotiliesi* (Hearth and home) | 1922– |
| Otava | *Oma Koti* (Home of one's own) | 1932–1934 |
| (Publisher unknown) | *Kauneudenhoitolehti* (Beauty care magazine) | 1931–1933 |
| Kustannus oy Eeva (Publishing Ltd Eeva) | *Eeva* | 1933– |
| United Magazines | *Hopeapeili* (Silver mirror) | 1936–1971 |

*Naisten Lehti* was published by the publishing company Edistysseurojen Kustannus, which represented Finnish educational civic organizations. It was suppressed within a year but *Kotiliesi* which was established at the end of 1922 by the publishing company Werner Söderström Osakeyhtiö (WSOY) became the most long-lived commercial women's magazine in Finland. *Kotiliesi* was a Finnish version of the American *Good Housekeeping* and the Swedish *Husmodern* that represented domestic women's magazines, a consumer magazine genre, but the editorial team had close connections to the women's rights movement and represented its goals in educating Finnish women, emancipating them as experts of household matters, and professionalizing the status of housewives.[39] The

---

[38] Turunen, *Hame, housut, hamehousut!*, 160.

[39] The editor-in-chief of *Kotiliesi* was Alli Wiherheimo, who had previously worked as a copy editor at WSOY. The editorial team included four members: Laura Harmaja was a teacher (and later a professor) of home economics, Hedwig Gebhard was a founder of the

motto of the magazine was "for better housekeeping, rational domestic economics, and cultivated homes."[40]

*Kotiliesi* was targeted at middle-class women who made most of their clothing themselves. The magazine's educational role through which it aimed to modernize the Finnish way of life also dominated the way dress was discussed: the magazine did not merely present new fashion trends, but it strove to "translate" the ideals of Parisian fashion into a dress style suitable for the daily life of "ordinary" (middle-class) Finnish women. While fashion magazines used fashion photography to convey fashion ideals to their readers, *Kotiliesi* relied on written columns in which readers were taught how to dress: columnists provided detailed instructions on how to choose patterns and fabrics for dresses, how to sew clothes, and, most importantly, how to wear them.[41] Dressing well did not only mean wearing fashionable and expensive clothing; rather, each person was supposed to know her personality, style and social class and dress accordingly. When choosing what kind of clothing to purchase or make and wear, women were advised to pay attention to the occasion on which the clothing would be worn and their own body type and personality.

> A dress that suits Maija does not suit Kaija. A dress that looks very good on one occasion, is tasteless in another. A wonderful-looking dress can make a woman look terrible. A dress that is beautiful in a fashion magazine might look very different when worn by somebody with a different body type.[42]

---

cooperative movement Pellervo, which was established to modernize Finnish agriculture, Mandi Hannula was one of the leading figures of the Finnish Martha Organization, and Eva Somersalo and her successor Mary Ollonqvist were specialists of dress and handicrafts. They were both teachers at the Helsinki Handicraft School. Gebhard, Hannula, and Somersalo were also members of the parliament representing conservative parties. See Leena Löyttyniemi, "Harmaja, Laura (1881–1954)," in *Kansallisbiografia: Studia Biographica 4* (Helsinki: SKS, 2000); Anna-Liisa Sysiharju, "Gebhard, Hedvig (1867–1961)," in *Kansallisbiografia: Studia Biographica 4* (Helsinki: SKS, 2007); Ulpu Marjomaa, "Hannula, Mandi (1880–1952)," in *Kansallisbiografia: Studia Biographica 4* (Helsinki: SKS, 2004); Päivi Aikasalo, *Alli Wiherheimo: Uranaisen sydän* (Helsinki: Otava, 2004).

[40] Malmberg, "Naisten ja kotien lehdet," 197–200; Töyry, *Varhaiset naistenlehdet*, 251–53; Turunen, *Hame, housut, hamehousut!*, 161–63.

[41] See e.g. *Kotiliesi* 23/1923, 699–702; *Kotiliesi* 5/1924, 120; *Kotiliesi* 6/1928, 175–76.

[42] *Kotiliesi* 3/1923, 82.

Before buying new clothing, the implied reader was supposed to critically evaluate her existing clothing. For example, when the season changed, it was time to check the condition of one's existing clothes and remodel them if necessary:

Clean and iron them if they are still usable. In most cases, you can undo the seams and wash, iron, and sew the pieces together again to make a dress with a new style. If the colors have faded, dye the fabric with a dark color, which will make it look almost like new.[43]

The educational role adopted by *Kotiliesi* also meant that it taught its readers how to be economical consumers and dress in a civilized manner. Dressing oneself was represented as a skill involving various detailed aspects that all needed to be mastered to be a well-dressed modern citizen. Especially in the 1920s, *Kotiliesi* actively discussed why appearance mattered:

There are countless people who think that it's a sin to enhance one's appearance, that beautiful clothes mean superficiality and vanity, and that good manners are a sign of dishonesty and falseness But why should a noble soul hide under a scary exterior? Aren't ugly clothes rather a sign of recklessness and a lack of a sense of beauty than of a prestigious character? Isn't it more pleasant to socialize with loveable and civilized people than with inconsiderate and clumsy people?[44]

In *Kotiliesi*, the implied reader followed fashion although the magazine also warned against the whims of fashion. The most important aspects of dress were rationality, functionality, and hygiene. Firstly, readers were advised to buy clothing that had a classic style that would not soon go out of fashion. Secondly, clothing had to be functional: winter clothes, for example, had to be warm and protect the body from wind and cold weather. Thirdly, clothing had to be easy to wash because a clean and tidy appearance was an important characteristic of a modern woman. With these instructions, *Kotiliesi* taught its readers the idea of a modern woman as a rational woman who was an economical consumer, understood the principles of hygiene in preventing disease, and valued the ideas of modern functional design.

## Establishment of fashion magazines in the 1930s

The publishing of *Kotiliesi* proved successful for WSOY. The circulation grew from 9,500 in 1923 to nearly 80,000 in the late 1920s.[45] The publishing of

---

[43] *Kotiliesi* 17/1928, 581–82.
[44] *Kotiliesi* 20/1923, 592.
[45] Malmberg, "Naisten ja kotien lehdet," 200.

magazines was modernized during the 1920s: publishing houses started to publish new kinds of periodicals that targeted new audiences and the genre of a periodical developed from a literary journal into a magazine consisting of various text types, a casual journalistic style and photojournalism.[46] These changes paved the way also for new Finnish women's magazines. Otava, WSOY's main rival, established its first women's magazine *Oma Koti* (Home of One's Own) in 1932. *Oma Koti* was also a domestic magazine that aimed to elevate the status of housewives and make homes more pleasant, but its assumed reader was an urban middle-class housewife, and therefore gardening and farming of domestic animals were not discussed in it as in *Kotiliesi*.[47]

A year later, the publisher Amos Anderson decided to modernize the market of women's magazines by establishing *Eeva*. It revolutionized the genre of women's magazines in Finland: instead of a domestic magazine, *Eeva* was a true fashion magazine. As the Swedish *Charme* that was established already in 1921, *Eeva* was targeted at modern, independent women. It was also a Finnish version of foreign women's magazines targeted at upper-class ladies. *Eeva* addressed modern educated women, including career women, who were interested in art, literature, movies, sports, fashion, and beauty care. Domestic issues and handicrafts were not covered in *Eeva*. The editor Lempi Torppa was the former editor of *Kauneudenhoitolehti* (Beauty care magazine, 1931–1933), which focused on fashion, beauty care, and cosmetics. The readers of both these magazines represented urban upper- and upper-middle-class women.[48] While *Kotiliesi* was very critical towards the wearing of make-up, *Eeva* and *Kauneudenhoitolehti* advised women to look after their appearance:

> The claim that beauty means power, applies especially to working women. Actresses, fashion models, saleswomen, women working in offices, house servants—they all must look as young and fresh as possible in order to keep their jobs and their position in life. No matter how talented and skilled they are at their profession, they might be replaced by younger and more beautiful women if they age too soon.[49]

In 1934, WSOY and Otava united their magazine publishing into one publishing company called Yhtyneet Kuvalehdet (United Magazines), and *Oma Koti* was

---

[46] Uino 1991, 42–3, 81–93; Leino-Kaukiainen 1992, 220–21.

[47] Turunen, *Hame, housut, hamehousut!*, 165–66; Malmberg, "Naisten ja kotien lehdet," 201–2.

[48] Turunen, *Hame, housut, hamehousut!*, 191–96: Malmberg, "Naisten ja kotien lehdet," 203–4. For Charme, see Severinsson, *Moderna kvinnor*, and for ladies' magazines, see e.g. Ballaster et al., *Women's Worlds*, 93ff.

[49] *Kauneudenhoitolehti* 1 / 1931, 6.

integrated into *Kotiliesi*. The editor of *Oma Koti*, Ida Pekari became a member of the editorial board of *Kotiliesi*. Her ideas of *Kotiliesi's* profile dissented from the views of the editor-in-chief and the editorial board and disagreements hampered the editorial work. The difficult situation was solved by Jorma Reenpää, the managing director of the Yhtyneet Kuvalehti. He decided to establish a new women's magazine *Hopeapeili* (Silver mirror, 1936–1971) and asked Pekari to be its editor-in-chief. *Hopeapeili* was similar to the *Oma Koti* and it addressed the same audience as *Eeva*: the urban upper-middle-class women and career women who were interested in fashion, beauty care, and literary issues. *Hopeapeili* covered however also handicrafts, cooking, and interior design.[50]

*Kauneudenhoitolehti, Eeva*, and *Hopeapeili* can be labeled as fashion and beauty magazines. Their readers were not given a list of domestic tasks, they were taught the routines of daily beauty care instead. For example, in the article "A career women's week," *Hopeapeili* instructed women to have a manicure every Monday, a pedicure every Tuesday, facial care on Wednesdays, shaping of eyebrows on Thursdays and to wash their hair on Friday.[51] *Kauneudenhoitolehti, Eeva*, and *Hopeapeili* reported on the latest trends of Parisian fashion and featured fashion from Berlin, Stockholm, and America as well. Readers were informed about the materials, styles, and colors that were currently in fashion, and they were also acquainted with famous fashion houses and designers. For example, in the spring 1935, *Eeva* informed that the next summer, dresses will be much shorter than last year, "but not as narrow as we expected." The language of fashion was international:

Dresses of the summer 1935 were made of "crépe de chine" fabric and they represented the style of a "georgette dress."

> The fabrics of Chanel are the most beautiful, they include dark colors with butterfly and star patterns. The most common color combination consists of black and rose-red and it is typically used in the fabric called "mousse-line de soie" (in Finnish it is often called chiffon). Dresses made of linen, lustex or piqué usually include a small coat or a cape.[52]

The fashion industry and fashion as a phenomenon were never questioned. The magazines' implied readers kept themselves up to date with the latest fashion trends. Although the Stockmann department store was highly praised for providing high-quality fashion, the implied readers purchased their dresses

---

[50] *Kauneudenhoitolehti* 1/1931, 166, 196–97; Malmberg, "Naisten ja kotien lehdet," 204–6.

[51] *Hopeapeili* 2/1938, 36.

[52] *Eeva* 4/1935, 25.

first and foremost at fashion houses: "In the summer, we need a beautiful evening dress for the casino, and we will only find one at a fashion designer's salon."[53]

## Fashion journalism in political women's magazines in the 1930s

In parallel with the establishment of *Kotiliesi* in the early 1920s, *Astra*, the bulletin of the women's association of the conservative Swedish People's Party, started to publish fashion columns representing Swedish and Parisian fashion.[54] By doing so, it abandoned the critical tone against fashion characteristic of political women's magazines and started to develop into a fashion magazine. *Suomen Nainen* underwent a similar transformation during the 1930s. At first, readers of *Suomen Nainen* were given advice in a similar fashion to *Kotiliesi*— with an emphasis on choosing practical clothing[55]—but since 1934, the fashion columnist focused on reporting on the latest trends of high fashion and the collections of Finnish fashion salons. Parisian fashion was represented as the norm of dress for readers of *Suomen Nainen*.[56] Next to the fashion column appeared the ads of Finnish fashion houses. *Astra* also published a column entitled "Sew by yourself" (Sy själv), which provided advice on home sewing and advertised dress patterns published by the *Revue des Modes* store.[57] The relatively small amount of political journalism and the decision to develop the bulletin into a fashion magazine reflected women's political role in conservative parties: their role was to focus on traditional women's concerns and leave the ideological work to men.[58]

The readers and editors of *Toveritar*—the labor women's bulletin—also noticed how the establishment of *Kotiliesi* changed the market of women's magazines. *Toveritar* had been very critical towards fashion, but in 1925, its readers expressed a wish that it would include sections on fashion and domestic matters as well. Readers explained that this might make the magazine interesting enough to subscribe also for those labor women who were not members of the women's association of the Social Democratic Party. Additionally, labor women needed an alternative to *Kotiliesi*, "whose recipes and fashion pages are unfeasible for us working women."[59]

---

[53] *Eeva* 4/1934, 13.

[54] *Astra* 14/1922, 8–9; see also *Astra* 1930, 17–8; *Astra* 1/1939, 36–7.

[55] E.g. *Suomen Nainen* 1/1932, 13; *Suomen Nainen* 10/1933, 143.

[56] E.g. *Suomen Nainen* 4/1935, 63.

[57] E.g. *Astra* 17/1927, 288.

[58] Vesa Vares and Ari Uino, *Suomalaiskansallinen Kokoomus: Kansallisen Kokoomuspuolueen historia 1929–1944* (Helsinki: Edita, 2007), 298–306.

[59] *Toveritar* 5/1925, 62–4.

To respond to its readers' wishes, the magazine started to publish a fashion column and sewing patterns in 1928. The fashion columnist gave advice on what kind of clothing suited different body types—that a short dress did not suit a bandy-legged woman, for example.[60] The publishing of sewing patterns was explained by noting that the modern style was so simple that every woman could now make her own dresses.[61] The contemporary style was also praised for being healthy and practical:

> Our [modern] dresses are loose-fitting and short. Young women might go too far with these. In our everyday dress, the pattern is not capricious but straight and as simple as possible, so that it would be very easy and economical to sew your dresses yourself![62]

The *Toveritar* fashion column ended with a hidden advertisement: "When you buy a *Revue des Modes* pattern, you can easily sew yourself a nice everyday dress and even an evening dress."[63] During the 1930s, *Toveritar* transformed from a political bulletin into a domestic magazine similar to *Kotiliesi*. *Toveritar* started purposefully to compete for readers with *Kotiliesi*, but the change also resulted from an ideological change in the Social Democratic Party. In the early twentieth century, the labor movement had criticized the bourgeois ideal of domestic women, but in the 1930s, it started to support it.[64]

A similar transformation also took place in *Emäntälehti*. While *Naisten Ääni* was worried that farm women would replace their traditional dress style and domestic materials with international fashion and imported fabrics,[65] *Emäntälehti* did not discuss dress and fashion until the late 1920s. At first, the magazine only gave advice on cleaning and repairing clothes. In 1924, it started to offer advice on how to darn underwear, aprons, and children's clothes.[66] In the late 1920s, *Emäntälehti* began to recommend that farm women should wear the national costumes that had been recently designed based on traditional Finnish peasant dresses.[67] Farm women were also educated about the importance of hygiene in everyday life. From the perspective of the upper-class educators, working-class and agrarian people's dress and homes were untidy. By emphasizing the importance of cleanliness and hygiene in

---

60 *Toveritar* 3/1928, 47.
61 *Toveritar* 7/1928, 104–5.
62 *Toveritar* 7/1928, 104.
63 *Toveritar* 7/1928, 104.
64 Sulkunen, *Naisen kutsumus*, 83–4.
65 See e.g. *Naisten Ääni* 6/1930, 136.
66 Turunen, *Hame, housut, hamehousut!*, 177.
67 E.g. *Emäntälehti* 1/1927, 10–1; *Emäntälehti* 2/1928, 38–41.

appearance and at home, the Martha Organization and its periodicals taught their audience the modern middle-class standards of civilized manners.[68]

A column advising on how to dress was established in *Emäntälehti* in 1931. Readers were taught that their most important dresses were their work and everyday dresses. The ideals of dress were similar to the ones expressed in *Kotiliesi*: the material and style for these dresses had been carefully selected to guarantee their functionality, easy care, and long-lasting use. The main difference between the two magazines was their attitude towards consumption. *Kotiliesi* represented consumer culture. The dresses of the implied *Kotiliesi* reader were made by herself or a seamstress, but the fabric was purchased in a fabric store. *Emäntälehti*, in turn, promoted the idea of self-sufficiency: farm women were supposed to make their family's clothing themselves by using wool and other materials that could be produced and processed at home. An evening dress was an unnecessary item of clothing for farm women; a simple black wool dress fulfilled the need for a Sunday dress, *Emäntälehti* reminded its readers.[69]

In the late 1930s, a fashion column was established in *Emäntälehti*. It discussed the latest fashion trends, but it continued to emphasize the virtues of rationality and economical consumption: instead of making new dresses, women were supposed to mend their old dresses by patching them up with pieces of new fabric.[70] *Lotta Svärd* included a fashion column that gave its readers advice similarly to *Kotiliesi*. When performing official duties, members of the Lotta Svärd organization wore a Lotta dress, which was a simple grey uniform-like dress that symbolized patriotism, discipline, and moral purity.[71]

### Conclusion: Fashion journalism reconstructed the identities and consumption patterns of class society

In the United Kingdom, United States and also in Sweden, the genre of women's magazines was established in the late nineteenth century as the genre of women's consumer magazines that discuss fashion, beauty care, and domestic matters. The establishment and development of this magazine genre have been closely linked to the development of consumer society and the bourgeois family

---

[68] Ollila, *Suomen kotien päivä*; Arja Turunen, "Nykyaikaista naista luomassa: Kotilieden, Emäntälehden ja Toverittaren pukeutumisohjeet kansalaiskasvatuksena 1920–1930-luvuilla," *Kasvatus ja Aika* 13, no. 4 (2019): 14–5; Kati Mikkola, *Tulevaisuutta vastaan: Uutuuksien vastustus, kansatiedon keruu ja kansakunnan rakentaminen* (Helsinki: SKS, 2009), 239–52.

[69] *Emäntälehti* 6/1931, 303; *Emäntälehti* 7–8/1931, 346.

[70] *Emäntälehti* 4/1937, 118.

[71] Turunen, *Hame, housut, hamehousut!*, 187.

model. The ideologies of women's magazines are therefore often interpreted as representing consumerism, capitalism, and conservative values, but in this chapter, I have demonstrated that in the Finnish context of the 1920s and 1930s, various sub-genres of women's magazines were published that represented differing and even conflicting ideologies.

In Finland, the genre of women's magazines was established in the form of political magazines. The first Finnish women's magazines were published by bourgeois women's rights associations. As their main goal, the vote for women, was reached, women's political activism was channeled through political parties, and the feminist bulletins were replaced by the bulletins of the women's associations of the conservative political parties. Their political agenda was twofold: upper-class women demanded more political rights, whereas lower- and middle-class women were supposed to focus on their duties as mothers and housewives. The latter agenda was disseminated to farm and working-class women through the domestic women's magazines *Emäntälehti* and *Husmodern*. The conservative political ideology and bourgeois family model were criticized and challenged by the women's associations of the labor party and the communist party. It was common for all these magazines to criticize fashion and warn readers about the dangers of becoming a fashion victim. In their journalism, they reproduced and reconstructed fashion as a frivolous phenomenon that was also harmful to women. In *Työläisnainen*, fashion was also closely associated with the problems of capitalist society.

Due to the late establishment of consumer society in Finland, the publishing of consumer magazines for women became a profitable business only in the 1920s and 1930s. The first one of them, *Naisten Lehti*, was published only for a year, but *Kotiliesi*, established in 1922 proved to the successful and it is published even today. They renewed the journalism and publishing of women's magazines, but they did not revolutionize the market of women's magazines. Firstly, the previous and existing political women's magazines had also included fashion pages and advertisements. Secondly, the new consumer magazines, especially *Kotiliesi*, continued the tradition of political bulletins by discussing women's position in society and other political questions.

Most of Finnish women's magazines published in the 1920s and 1930s can be described as a mixture of political and fashion (consumer) magazines as they represented the ideology of consumer culture as well as the political ideology of bourgeois or labor feminism. The women's magazines *Kauneudenhoitolehti* and *Eeva*, which were established in the early 1930s, were the only ones representing a women's consumer (fashion) magazine without political content or connections to the bourgeois women's rights movement. However, they were not the only representatives of the genre of women's fashion magazines: the political magazines *Astra* and *Suomen Nainen*, which were published by Swedish- and Finnish-language conservative political parties, kept the political content to a minimum and offered their readers a substantial amount of fashion journalism.

In all the women's magazines, fashion journalism reflected and reconstructed the ideas and norms of dress of class society. The feminist magazine *Naisten Ääni*, the political bulletins *Astra* and *Suomen Nainen*, and the consumer magazine *Eeva* were targeted at upper-class women who were supposed to dress according to their social standing: to follow fashion, purchase their clothing at fashion salons, and be familiar with the principles of good taste. In these magazines, modern dress meant the latest style designed by fashion designers.

In the magazines of the Martha Organization, which were targeted at farm women, the ideal dress was a simple self-made dress. On the one hand, it was an economical option for poor agrarian women who could not afford imported fabrics or ready-made clothes. On the other hand, this kind of advice served to keep farm women out of modern consumerism and maintain traditional needlework skills. In dress, modernity meant functionality and hygiene.

*Kotiliesi, Oma Koti, Hopeapeili,* and *Lotta Svärd* were targeted at middle-class women, and the ideal dress in these magazines represented the ideals of a middle-class lifestyle. Fashion was portrayed as something that women must follow in their dress, but the implied readers were also expected to be rational consumers. Instead of buying clothing at fashion salons, the readers of these magazines made their clothing by themselves or had it made by a seamstress. Consuming fashion meant first and foremost consuming fabrics and women's magazines, which reported on the new styles of dress. In these magazines, a modern dress was a dress that was functional in style and chosen carefully to suit the wearer and the occasion on which it was to be worn. The modern dress was also a clean, tidy, and hygienic dress.

In the labor women's magazine *Toveritar*, the fashion journalism of the 1920s reconstructed a clear difference between working-class and middle-class women. The simplicity of the modern dress meant that it was easy to sew at home, which also made it a cheaper option for working-class women. In the 1930s, the magazine began to promote middle-class style as an ideal that also applied to working-class women.

My analysis shows that each magazine formulated its own version of a "women's magazine" and "modern dress." Both these concepts also changed during the time period under study, which underlines the need to carefully contextualize each magazine when they are used as research material.

Chapter 6

# Producing and distributing feminist counterpublics: Magazines of the Nordic new women's movements

Hannah Yoken

*University of Jyväskylä, Finland*

**Abstract:** This chapter examines the production and distribution of Nordic feminist magazines from the early 1970s into the mid-1990s. It adds to the history of new women's movements in the region by focusing on the media practices of two magazines: the Swedish *Kvinnobulletinen* and the Finnish *Akkaväki*. I argue that these magazines are best interpreted as subaltern counterpublics, focused on elevating women's voices. Furthermore, I contend that despite their anti-authoritarian characteristics, *Akkaväki* and *Kvinnobulletinen* were in constant dialogue with the public sphere and conventional institutions, including the state. This chapter makes an intervention in the existing historiography, which has largely focused on Nordic feminist magazine's social and political contents, by positing that the ideological and practical choices that went into producing and distributing Nordic feminist magazines—or activist media practices—are worthy of historical analysis in their own right.

**Keywords:** feminism, new women's movement, magazine, counterpublics, activist media practices

\*\*\*

In the summer of 1982, feminist activists from the Nordic countries gathered at the Hanaholmen Finnish-Swedish Cultural Center in Espoo, Finland. The aim of the gathering, arranged by the Finnish Women's Association Unioni (Naisasialiitto Unioni, hereafter referred to as Unioni) in conjunction with the editorial team of the Finnish feminist magazine *Akkaväki: Naisten ääni* (Hag Crew: Women's Voice), was to place Nordic women who produced feminist periodicals into transnational dialogue. In addition to its organizers, the meeting was attended by representatives from the bilingual Finnish-Swedish feminist magazine *Aikanainen–Kvinnotid* (Woman Time) as well as the Norwegian feminist magazines *KjerringRåd* (Old Woman's Remedy) and *Sirene* (Siren).

Swedish attendees were also present, representing feminist periodicals such as *Kvinnobulletinen* (Women's Bulletin) and *Vi Mänskor* (We Humans), as well as the women's studies journal *Kvinnovetenskaplig Tidskrift* (Women's Studies Journal), and *Anna: Ny kvinnotidning* (Anna: New Women's Magazine) produced by a Stockholm-based women's shelter. No attendees from Denmark or Iceland were present.

The women in attendance found much common ground. All editorial teams had faced economic hardship and encountered problems regarding the distribution and collection of information relevant to new women's movement publications.[1] After the meeting, attendee Lillemor Kälfors Örneland fittingly described the weekend-long gathering as "a small conference with large ambitions." Though the Finnish organizers' initial aim had been to host a conference on a European rather than Nordic scale, these intentions did not materialize, with most European feminist magazines turning down the invitation citing financial difficulties. Ultimately though, the strictly Nordic configuration of the meeting was seen by attendees as a strength rather than a weakness, enhancing the formation of close interpersonal bonds. The gathering resulted in plans to hold another similar seminar in Oslo the following summer and hopes for a European-wide meet-up during the 1985 United Nations World Conference on Women held in Nairobi, Kenya.[2] While these plans do not appear to have materialized, the significance of the Hanaholmen meeting for Nordic activists was in its ability to foster transnational camaraderie among the activists present. In the words of Swedish activist Cecilia Örnfelt: "What is most important about these seminars is that one meets other feminists."[3]

This chapter examines the production and distribution practices of Nordic feminist magazines during feminism's so-called second wave. It adds new perspectives to the history of feminism in the Nordic region by focusing on the media praxes of two feminist periodicals: *Kvinnobulletinen*, the magazine of the Swedish feminist organization Group 8 (Grupp 8), and the Union-affiliated magazine *Akkaväki*. During their contemporaneous lifespans, from the mid-1970s into the mid-1990s, both magazines circulated a myriad of ideas, presenting feminism as a tenet, practice, and overall force for sociopolitical good. However, the focus of this chapter is not on the magazines' content. Instead, I specify the principles and practicalities according to which *Akkaväki*

---

[1] Erja Lempinen, "Meitä on monta: Feministilehdet kokoontuivat ensimmäistä kertaa," *Akkaväki: Naisten ääni*, 3/1982, 30; Lillemor Kälfors Örneland, "Helsingfors: Liten konferens med stora ambitioner," *Kvinnobulletinen*, 4–5/1982, 54.

[2] Kälfors Örneland, "Helsingfors," 54.

[3] Lempinen, "Meitä on monta," 30.

and *Kvinnobulletinen* were produced and distributed, and analyze what led feminist activists in the Nordic region to choose these specific media practices.

The Hanaholmen gathering encapsulates the three main topics discussed in this chapter. Firstly, in addition to circulars internal to new women's movement groups, such as local newsletters and pamphlets, Nordic grassroots feminist activists produced numerous outward-facing magazines meant for the public at large at the national level. Secondly, an examination of Nordic feminist magazines demonstrates that despite the new women's movements' anti-establishment characteristics, their media practices were not devoid of connections to conventional institutions, including the state. Thirdly, the European-wide ambitions of the meeting showcase that Nordic feminist magazines' media practices were transnationally motivated and aimed at fostering dialogue across national borders, especially within the Nordic region. As an illustrative example of how grassroots activism, transnationalism, and the state collided, the site chosen for the 1982 gathering, the Hanaholmen Cultural Center, was itself the outcome of transnational cooperation at the state rather than grassroots level: the center was opened in 1975 by the Finnish government in honor of Sweden canceling Finland's wartime debt of 100 million Swedish crowns eight years prior.[4]

Within Nordic scholarship, second wave grassroots feminist activism is referred to as 'the new women's movement' paralleling concepts such as 'new feminism' in Italy and France and 'the women's liberation movement' in Anglophone contexts.[5] The groups and organizations that made up the new women's movements in the Nordic region were characterized by their initial proximity to New Left and Marxist socialist thought, their radical, extra-parliamentary, and party-politically unaffiliated protest tactics, and their anti-hierarchical organizational structures.[6] During the 1970s–1980s, the sociopolitical position of women in the Nordic region was also significantly shaped by state feminism, or the institutionalization of woman-friendly gender equality policies via governmental means. Nordic grassroots feminist approaches to state feminism varied, with some activists working alongside

---

[4] Johanna Luhtala, Markus Manninen and Sari Schulman, "Hanasaari: Raken-nushistoriaselvitys," accessed August 1, 2022, https://www.senaatti.fi/app/uploads/2017/05/31702013_Schulman_Espoo_Hanasaari_RHS.pdf.

[5] See e.g., Maud Anne Bracke, *Women and the Reinvention of the Political: Feminism in Italy, 1968–1983* (New York and London: Routledge, 2014), 1–5; Claire Duchen, *Feminism in France From May '68 to Mitterrand* (London: Routledge, 1986), 1–4.

[6] For more see Hannah Yoken, "Nordic Transnational Feminist Activism: The New Women's Movements in Finland, Sweden and Denmark, 1960s–1990s" (PhD diss., University of Glasgow, 2020).

professional politicians, party-political affiliates, and civil servants, while others lacked confidence in these top-down interventions.[7] Feminism's second wave in the Nordic region was formed by manifold clusters of activists characterized by plurality and change over time. Yet, certain groups and their respective media outputs were undeniably the largest in visibility and following, both in their time and from a historiographical perspective. In addition to the Swedish and Finnish feminist enclaves examined in this chapter, significant groups include the Danish Redstockings (Rødstrømperne), the Norwegian Women's Front (Kvinnefronten) and the Icelandic Redstocking Movement (Rauðsokkahreyfingin).[8]

The production and distribution of second wave feminist media has been studied from multiple angles, with a notable strand of scholarship focusing on unpacking the popularization and commercialization of grassroots activism.[9] For example, Anthea Taylor has discussed how feminist authors who chose to publish with for-profit publishers rather than niche feminist publishing houses were labelled by some activists as "selling out."[10] In recent years, historians charting the history of feminist publishers have begun to break down these dichotomies: Lucy Delap has termed bookstore owners who balanced relentless feminist politics with the financial needs of their business ventures

---

[7] See e.g., Joyce Outshoorn and Johanna Kantola, *Changing State Feminism* (Basingstoke and New York: Palgrave Macmillan, 2007); Helene Ahl, Karin Berglund, Katarina Pettersson and Malin Tillmar, "From feminism to FemInc.ism: On the uneasy relationship between feminism, entrepreneurship and the Nordic welfare state," *International Entrepreneurship and Management Journal* 12 (2016): 369–92; Anette Borchorst and Birte Siim, "Woman-friendly policies and state feminism: Theorizing Scandinavian gender equality," *Feminist Theory* 9, no. 2 (2008): 207–24.

[8] See e.g., Drude Dahlerup, *Rødstrømperne: Den danske Rødstrømpebevægelses udvikling, nytænkning og gennemslag 1970-1985, bind I & II* (Copenhagen: Gyldendal, 1998); Auður Styrkársdóttir, "From Social Movement to Political Party: The New Women's Movement in Iceland," in *The New Women's Movement: Feminism and Political Power in Europe and the USA*, ed. Drude Dahlerup (London: Sage, 1986), 141–57; Hilde Danielsen, *Da det personlige ble politisk: Den nye kvinne- og mannsbevegelsen på 1970-tallet* (Oslo: Scandinavian Academic Press, 2013).

[9] For more see Hannah Yoken, "Transnational Transfers and Mainstream Mappings: Women's Liberation Calendars of the 1970s and 1980s," in *Translating Feminism: Interdisciplinary Approaches to Text, Place and Agency (1945–2000)*, eds. Maud Bracke, Julia C. Bullock, Penelope Morris and Kristina Schulz (Cham: Palgrave Macmillan, 2021), 117–46.

[10] Anthea Taylor, *Celebrity and the Feminist Blockbuster* (London: Palgrave Macmillan, 2016).

as "movement entrepreneurs."[11] Beyond feminist historiography but staying within the Nordic region, Thomas Hvid Kromann has argued that the short-lived Danish cultural initiative Arena Sub-Pub, a subdivision of the publishing house Arena, which from 1969 to 1970 made printing equipment readily available and alternative publishing affordable and swift, existed both inside and outside traditional media institutions. Arena Sub-Pub functioned as a fully independent printing house, yet its publications entered mainstream literary circulation. Hvid Kromann posits that within the Scandinavian context, unlike in the United States, major publishing houses never represented conformity, nor were alternative publication strategies synonymous with challenging the establishment.[12] As this chapter will establish, Hvid Kronmann's assertion holds true for Nordic feminist publishing: both *Kvinnobulletinen* and *Akkaväki* applied for and received state funding and sought to standardize their media practices, as well as broaden their societal reach, while simultaneously holding on to their anti-establishment roots and countercultural ethos.

To best make sense of these dynamics, I have turned to the concepts of the public sphere and counterpublics.[13] Jürgen Habermas famously defined the bourgeois public sphere as a critical discursive space within which socio-political discourse is openly circulated. The individuals belonging to this public sphere form a civil society, where opinions regarding common affairs can be formulated.[14] In the late 1980s, exactly which individuals are allowed to exercise influence within the bourgeois public sphere became a topic of discussion among feminist thinkers. The existence of a feminist counterpublic sphere was first proposed by Rita Felski, who interpreted it as "an oppositional

---

[11] Lucy Delap, "Feminist Bookshops, Reading Cultures and the Women's Liberation Movement in Great Britain, c. 1974–2000," *History Workshop Journal* 81, no. 1 (2016): 171–96. See also e.g., D. M. Withers, "Enterprising Women: Independence, Finance and Virago Press, c.1976–93," *Twentieth Century British History* 31, no. 4 (2019): 1–24; Simone Murray, *Mixed Media: Feminist Presses and Publishing Politics* (London: Pluto Press, 2004).

[12] Thomas Hvid Kromann, "Subpublications from a Basement in Snaregade 6, Copenhagen – Arena Sub-Pub (1969–1970)," in *A Cultural History of the Avant-Garde in the Nordic Countries 1950–1975*, eds. Tania Ørum and Jesper Olsson (Leiden: Brill, 2016), 175–80.

[13] For scholarship that combines feminist history, 'the public sphere' and 'counterpublics' see e.g. Jocelyn Olcott, "Empires of Information: Media Strategies for the 1975 International Women's Year," *Journal of Women's History* 24, no. 4 (Winter 2012): 24–48, Bec Wonders, "Mapping second wave feminist periodicals: Networks of conflict and counterpublics, 1970–1990," *Arts Libraries Journal* 45, no. 3 (2020): 106–13; Heidi Kurvinen and Arja Turunen, "Radical sex role ideology and the Finnish gender role movement in the late 1960s," *Women's History Review* 32, no. 1 (2023): 62–81.

[14] Jürgen Habermas, *The Structural Transformation of the Public Sphere: An Inquiry into a Category of Bourgeois Society* (Cambridge: MIT Press, 1991); See also Michael Warner, *Publics and Counterpublics* (New York: Zone Books, 2002), 46–51.

public arena for the articulation of women's needs in critical opposition to the valued male-defined society."[15] Nancy Fraser furthered this definition, stating that counterpublics are best understood as subaltern, or "discursive arenas where members of subordinated social groups invent and circulate counterdiscourses, which in turn permit them to formulate oppositional interpretations of their identities, interests, and needs."[16] In this chapter, I am particularly interested in the relational tension between the public sphere and feminist counterpublics. *Kvinnobulletinen* and *Akkaväki* were significant forces within their countries' feminist media landscape and became the public faces of the new women's movements in Sweden and Finland respectively. The magazines' editorial teams acted in opposition to the public sphere and were constantly working to better the subordinate sociopolitical status of women. Simultaneously, the counterpublics created by feminist magazines were in direct dialogue with the public sphere, persistently attempting to widen their readerships from small enclaves of activists to the public at large. By emphasizing women's voices, feminist magazines challenged the public sphere's exclusionary practices via the introduction of alternative woman-led perspectives into civil society's patriarchal and male-dominated discursive arena.[17]

As a final conceptualizing note, the analysis in this chapter is grounded in social scientist Alice Mattoni's concept of activist media practices. Defined as the "routinized and creative social practices in which activists engage [...] through which activists can generate and/or appropriate media messages," a focus on these practices emphasizes the agency activists have in producing and distributing media, rather than activism and activists simply acting as media subjects or audiences.[18] This offers an avenue into studying feminist magazines in a manner where discourse does not become disjoined from its creators, nor is the agency of media-producing activists erased from the historical narrative. By considering media as social movement practice and activists as media practitioners, we are alerted to the complex web of scenarios and settings within which Nordic feminists produced media content.

---

[15] Rita Felski, *Beyond Feminist Aesthetics: Feminist Literature and Social Change* (Cambridge: Harvard University Press, 1989), 166.
[16] Nancy Fraser, "Rethinking the Public Sphere: A Contribution to the Critique of Actually Existing Democracy," *Social Text* 25/26 (1990): 67.
[17] Fraser, "Rethinking the Public Sphere," 61, 67; Felski, *Beyond Feminist Aesthetics*, 167–68; Warner, *Publics*, 56.
[18] Alice Mattoni and Emiliano Treré, "Media Practices, Mediation Processes, and Mediatization in the Study of Social Movements," *Communication Theory* 24, no. 3 (2014): 260; Alice Mattoni, *Media Practices and Protest Politics: How Precarious Workers Mobilise* (Farnham: Ashgate, 2012), 19–20.

## The face of a movement

In 1990, *Kvinnobulletinen* celebrated its twentieth anniversary. Long-standing contributor Inga-Lisa Sangregorio described the magazine as offering a counterpublic within which women could converse, unfiltered by the patriarchal norms of the public sphere:

> *Kvinnobulletinen* wants to be "a room of one's own" for the women's movement. Where we can do what we want, without having to ask permission from dad (or mom!), where the ceilings are high and where we can have the conversations that are otherwise overruled by the male choir of public discourse.[19]

Established in 1968, Group 8 defined itself as a party-politically unaligned socialist women's organization working towards ending the oppression of women, which they understood as stemming from both bourgeois society and patriarchal culture. Initially Stockholm-based, during the early-to-mid 1970s local offshoots of the organization were founded across Sweden, in larger cities and small towns.[20] *Kvinnobulletinen* was first envisioned in 1970 by activists in Stockholm and launched nationally the following year. The magazine became Sweden's most popular and longstanding new women's movement periodical, running until 1996. During its lifecycle, *Kvinnobulletinen* transformed from a manually duplicated black and white circular into a semi-professional glossy magazine, which nevertheless held on to its anti-establishment content.

The Finnish feminist magazine *Akkaväki* ran from 1975 to 1995 and was produced in close proximity to Unioni, a women's rights organization established in 1892. *Akkaväki* began as an amateurish circular edited by a group of Helsinki-based activists. In its first issue, the editorial team published an article sarcastically titled "Give me back my money right away! This wasn't a real women's magazine after all," in which readers' negative responses were pre-emptively resolved. The article made clear that *Akkaväki* was not a commercial venture, it did not strive for consistency in tone or layout, nor had it been produced by experts with specialist knowledge. The article closed with the optimistic statement:

> By publishing our thoughts already now, when we ourselves are still in the midst of searching, we hope that you—our fellow sisters—join us on

---

[19] Inga-Lisa Sangregorio, "Kvinnobulletinen 20 år," *Kvinnobulletinen*, 1/1990, 5.
[20] See e.g., Emma Isaksson, *Kvinnokamp: Synen på underordning och motstånd i den nya kvinnorörelsen* (Stockholm: Atlas, 2007); Elisabeth Elgán, *Att ge sig själv makt: Grupp 8 och 1970-talets feminism* (Gothenburg: Makadam Förlag, 2015).

this journey. We hope that in five years' time we—as well as you, our sisters—have made it a bit further.[21]

"Feminism" as a distinct identity and social movement ideology became a noteworthy part of the Finnish sociopolitical lexicon during the second half of the 1970s, nearly a decade later than in Sweden. This was caused by the strong presence of Marxist-Leninism, or Taistoism, in early 1970s Finland, but also in part due to the successful gender equality campaigns undertaken by the Finnish independent civic organization Association 9 (Yhdistys 9) during the second half of the 1960s.[22] Nevertheless, by 1980 the wishes of *Akkaväki*'s editorial had come true. After five years of sporadic production and a sphere of circulation that consisted primarily of existing Unioni activists, from the turn of the decade onwards *Akkaväki*'s activist media practices became more consistent, if not professional. The publication's official title was also expanded to *Akkaväki: Naisten ääni* (Hag Crew: Women's Voice), the additional subtitle referencing Unioni's prior magazine *Naisten ääni*, active between 1905 and 1949. Despite this homage, at this time the production of *Akkaväki* was taken over by the Women's Cultural Association (Naisten kulttuuriyhdistys), a more zestful, radical, and explicitly feminist group that worked in the same building as, but as a distinct entity from, Unioni. From 1988 to 1995 the magazine was named *Naisten ääni: Akkaväki* (Women's Voice: Hag Crew), signaling a move to more postmodern and artistic editorial practices and stylistic choices.[23]

During feminism's second wave, many other feminist magazines were established and disbanded in Sweden and Finland, forming periodical-based feminist counterpublics. From 1974 to 1981 the class-conscious group Women of Labor (Arbetets Kvinnor) published *Rödhättan* (Red Hats), which was initially an amateurish pamphlet before morphing into a regularly published semi-professional magazine. From 1981 to 1986 some of *Rödhättan*'s contributors moved on to write for *Kvinnotidningen Q* (Women's Magazine Q), a cultural feminist magazine embodying the punk ethos of the 1980s. In Finland too, though *Akkaväki* was the country's most notable feminist magazine, the

---

[21] "Antakaa rahani heti takaisin! Eihän tämä ollutkaan mikään oikea naistenlehti," *Akkaväki*, 1/1975, 3.

[22] See e.g. Arja Turunen, "Kapinaa ja ahtaita raameja: Suomalaisten feministien muistoja 1970- ja 1980-lukujen yhteiskunnallisesta toimintakulttuurista," *Sukupuolentutkimus–Genusforskning* 31, no. 3 (2018): 37–50; Heidi Kurvinen and Arja Turunen, "Toinen aalto uudelleen tarkasteltuna: Yhdistys 9:n rooli suomalaisen feminisminhistoriassa," *Sukupuolentutkimus–Genusforskning* 31, no. 3 (2018): 21–34.

[23] Minna Helminen, *Väkevää akkaväkeä: Naisten kulttuuriyhdistys 20 vuotta* (Helsinki: Naisten kulttuuriyhdistys, 2002), 23–77; Minna Hagner and Teija Försti, *Suffragettien sisaret* (Helsinki: Unioni Naisasialiitto, 2006), 186–89.

primarily Swedish-speaking feminist organization the Feminists (Feministit–
Feministerna) circulated its own small-scale bilingual magazine *Aikanainen–
Kvinnotid* (Time Woman–Woman Time, a bilingual title) from 1978 until 1984.
In the other Nordic countries, new women's movements produced a multitude
of magazines. From 1975 to 1984 the Danish Redstockings published *Kvinder*
(Women), a magazine aimed at presenting women's issues from a feminist
perspective to Danish women at large. In comparison, matters internal to the
Redstockings were discussed in internal circulars, produced by the movement's
local groups in larger cities like Copenhagen and Aarhus.[24] The Norwegian
feminist magazine scene was similarly split into numerous enclaves. From the
1970s until the turn of the millennium Norway's largest new women's
movement organization, the Women's Front, published an internal circular
titled *Vi er mange* (We are many) as well as the outward-facing magazine
*Kvinnefronten* (Women's Front), later named *Kvinne Journalen* (Women's
Journal). Inspired by the American magazine *Ms.*, from 1973 to 1983 popular
women's magazine *Sirene—tidssignal for kvinner og men* (*Sirene—timekeeper
for women and men*) relayed information from a feminist perspective to a
relatively large audience.[25] In Iceland, the country's Redstockings published
their magazine *Forvitin rauð* (Curious Red) from 1972 to 1982.[26]

As argued by Emma Isaksson, although *Kvinnobulletinen* was produced by
Group 8 activists, it was not an organization magazine but rather the "outward
face" of the movement.[27] *Kvinnobulletinen* can be juxtaposed with Group 8's
internal circular *Interbulletinen* (Internal Bulletin), which covered local and
national organizational affairs and was meant for the movement's existing
members. In Finland, *Akkaväki* similarly strove to reach all women in the
country instead of limited enclaves of existing activists.[28] Accordingly,
organizational affairs were excluded from the magazine's pages to avoid
giving potential members a negative picture of the Women's Cultural
Association's inner workings.[29] Both magazines were thus produced at the
grassroots level, from within the new women's movement, and by dedicated
activists, but with the clear aim of reaching women who did not have prior
commitments to the feminist cause. *Akkaväki* and *Kvinnobulletinen* featured

---

[24] Signe Arnfred, Litten Hansen and Anne Houe, *Bladet Kvinder 1975–1984* (Copenhagen:
Tiderne Skifter, 2015), 398; Dahlerup, *Rødstrømperne bind 1*, 569–70.

[25] Synnøve Skarsbø Lindtner, "Over disk som varmt hvetebrød – Sirene og den norske
populærfeminismen," in *Da det personlige ble politisk: Den nye kvinne- og mannsbevegelsen
på 1970-tallet*, ed. Hilde Danielsen (Oslo Scandinavian Academic Press, 2013), 103–52.

[26] *Forvitin rauð* available online at the Icelandic digital library, https://timarit.is.

[27] Isaksson, *Kvinnokamp*, 53–4.

[28] Helminen, *Väkevää akkaväkeä*, 25.

[29] Helminen, *Väkevää akkaväkeä*, 49.

feminist perspectives on a wide range of current sociopolitical and cultural topics. Oftentimes covering topics already in circulation within popular public discourse, the outward-facing nature of both magazines meant that they were in constant dialogue with the public sphere, seeking to influence the public discursive arena.[30] Felski's argument—that the American women's movement and the feminist counterpublic it formed never claimed to represent universal perspectives, instead offering social critiques from the standpoint of women as subjugated members of society—holds true in the cases of *Kvinnobulletinen* and *Akkaväki*. Both Nordic feminist magazines directed their messaging outward, hoping to disseminate feminist values across society at large by contesting and altering the public sphere's patriarchal discursive frameworks.[31]

As has been posited by sociologist Dieter Rucht and applied to feminist history by Kristina Schulz, for a social movement to function effectively, two components are needed: firstly, a network of groups prepared to mobilize protest, and secondly, a mass of individuals who contribute to protest activities. This translates into two distinct historical subjects of study: on one hand, an identifiable group of active members, and on the other, a mass of unidentified women who, despite their anonymity, were integral to the movement.[32] For the purpose of this chapter, the women actively involved in producing feminist magazines can be conceptualized as the former, whereas the wider readership of these magazines embodies the latter. Within the Finnish context, Solveig Bergman has fittingly interpreted the creation of feminist magazines aimed at broad national circulation as signifying an outward turn for the new women's movement.[33] This also holds true in the Swedish case. In both countries, magazines were used to convey a feminist consciousness to a broader audience, and once awareness was established, respond to this interest by providing a steady stream of information. Their emergence signaled that feminism as a social movement was coherent enough to be presented to the public at large.

---

[30] For a similar argument see Fraser, "Rethinking the Public Sphere," 67.

[31] Felski, *Beyond Feminist Aesthetics*, 167.

[32] Kristina Schulz, "The Women's Movement," in *1968 in Europe: A History of Protest and Activism, 1956–1977*, eds. Martin Klimke and Joachim Scharloth (Basingstoke: Palgrave Macmillan, 2008), 281.

[33] Solveig Bergman, *The Politics of Feminism: Autonomous Feminist Movements in Finland and West Germany from the 1960s to the 1980s* (Turku: Åbo Akademi University Press, 2002), 157.

## Financing feminist magazines

It is difficult to speak of meaningful impact without considering quantifiable data regarding a magazine's print run. Overall, the readership of Nordic feminist magazines was low in comparison to more conventional and professionally produced women's magazines in the region. Approximately 3,000 to 4,000 copies per issue of *Akkaväki* were printed from 1980 to 1982, with these figures increasing to about 5,000 over the course of the decade. Actual distribution numbers, referring to the total number of magazines sold via subscriptions and single copy sales, were much lower however, coming in at 450 in 1980, prior to peaking at 2,672 in 1983 and decreasing to approximately 300 in 1995, the year the production of the magazine was terminated.[34] Corroborating this disparity between copies printed and purchased, *Akkaväki* regularly advertised a backlog of issues for sale. The number of magazines sold most likely did not correspond to total readership, as copies were circulated between readers. Issues of *Akkaväki* were also on display in many Finnish public and university libraries.[35] In comparison, Swedish *Kvinnobulletinen* was much more widely read, reaching approximately 15,000 readers per issue during the 1970s.[36] The magazine's popularity was strong from its outset and within six months of the magazine's launch in 1971 only 400 copies remained unsold out of an initial print run of 5,000.[37] As in Finland, several Swedish public libraries subscribed to *Kvinnobulletinen*, making the magazine freely available to the public.[38]

In comparison to other Nordic feminist magazines, *Akkaväki* represents a small reader pool and *Kvinnobulletinen* a medium-to-large sized one. For example, the Danish magazine *Kvinder* had a print run of approximately 9,500 at the height of its popularity, with its general sales figures ranging from 3,000 to 7,000 copies per issue.[39] The largest print run appears to have been by the Norwegian magazine *Sirene*, which in its first year came in at approximately 35,000 magazines per issue.[40] To put these Nordic figures into perspective, in the United States the first professionally produced and commercial feminist

---

[34] Helminen, *Väkevää akkaväkeä*, 40–1.
[35] For more on the relationship between Finnish libraries and the alternative press see Risto Hannula, Kari J. Kettula and Kari Vaijärvi, *Kulttuuri- ja mielipidelehdet* (Helsinki: Kirjastopalvelu Oy, 1981), 7–8.
[36] Elgán, *Att ge sig själv makt*, 79–80.
[37] Ebba Witt-Brattström, *Å alla kära systrar! Historien om mitt sjuttiotal* (Stockholm: Nordstedt, 2010), 144–55; Eva Schmitz, "Den nya kvinnorörelsens uppkomst i Sverige från 1968," in *Kvinnorörelsen och '68: Aspekter och vittnesbörd*, ed. Elisabeth Elgán (Huddinge: Samtidshistoriska institutet, 2001), 32.
[38] "Läser Kvinnobulletinen," *Kvinnobulletinen*, 3–4/1973, 37.
[39] Arnfred et al., *Bladet Kvinder*, 389; Dahlerup, *Rødstrømperne bind I*, 571.
[40] Skarsbø Lindtner, "Over disk som varmt hvetebrød," 104.

magazine *Ms.* had an estimated circulation of 300,000 to 500,000 copies per issue and a readership of over a million.[41] Within Europe, the West German feminist magazine *Emma* increased its circulation from an initial 200,000 in early 1977 to 300,000 by its second issue, and the British *Spare Rib* had a print run of approximately 20,000 magazines per issue and an estimated readership of 100,000 due to personal circulation.[42]

What is important to note when comparing these figures is that there was no uniform way to fund a second-wave feminist magazine. The start-up costs of *Ms.* were covered by for-profit advertisers and a one-million-dollar investment by mass media conglomerate Warner Communications.[43] However, the British magazine *Spare Rib* was started on a meager 3,000 pounds. Unlike *Ms.*, which was held accountable by its investors, *Spare Rib* could freely choose the content it published.[44] As literary scholar Victoria Bazin has shown, *Spare Rib* was nonetheless caught in a paradox: "it was at least partly dependent for its survival on advertising revenue yet advertising itself was complicit in the objectification and exploitation of women, their bodies, their lives, their feelings."[45] *Kvinnobulletinen* and *Akkaväki* were similarly positioned in a paradoxical bind and caught in between, on one hand, their identities as anti-establishment publications critical of mainstream patriarchal society and, on the other hand, becoming partially reliant on state subsidies.

In 1979, almost a decade into its existence, *Kvinnobulletinen* applied for and was awarded 35,000 crowns by the Swedish government-run National Council for Cultural Affairs (Kulturrådet). The council was a public authority established in 1974 as the outcome of Swedish social democratic state policy, the aim of

---

[41] Amy Erdman Farrell, *Yours in Sisterhood: Ms Magazine and the Promise of Popular Feminism* (Chapel Hill: University of North Carolina Press, 1998), 1; Amy Farrell, "Attentive to Difference: Ms. Magazine, Coalition Building, and Sisterhood," in *Feminist Coalitions: Historical Perspectives on Second-Wave Feminism in the United States,* ed. Stephanie Gilmore (Urbana: University of Illinois Press, 2008), 60.

[42] Bailee Erickson, "'Every Woman Needs Courage:' Feminist Periodicals in 1970s West Germany," *The Graduate History Review* 2 (2010): 42–3; Laurel Forster, "Spreading the Word: Feminist print cultures and the Women's Liberation Movement," *Women's History Review* 25, no. 5 (2016): 823,

[43] Erdman Farrell, *Yours in Sisterhood,* 28.

[44] Joanne Hollows, "Spare Rib, Second-Wave Feminism and the Politics of Consumption," *Feminist Media Studies* 13, no. 2 (2013): 270–2.

[45] Victoria Bazin, "'A New Kind of Trade:' Advertising Feminism in Spare Rib," in *Re-reading Spare Rib,* ed. Angela Smith (Cham: Palgrave Macmillan, 2017), 197.

which was to promote culture and ensure its public availability.[46] This funding allowed *Kvinnobulletinen* to switch from black and white to color printing and hire a paid part-time editor. Whether a socialist anti-authoritarian organization like Group 8 should have applied for state funding was keenly debated among its members. The decision to apply for the grant was ultimately agreed on after *Kvinnobulletinen's* editorial team found out that a magazine titled *Vi Bilägare* (We Car Owners) was benefitting from the council's financial backing.[47] Ultimately, the money awarded did not match the sum applied for, therefore not allowing *Kvinnobulletinen* to reach its goal, namely becoming a monthly publication.[48]

Whereas in Sweden *Kvinnobulletinen's* editorial team had a clear vision for which funding was applied—to turn the periodical into a monthly publication—in Finland the cause and effect were seemingly reversed. Meeting external state-regulated funding requirements helped solidify a vision regarding *Akkaväki*. For most of its existence, *Akkaväki* was in part financed by 'opinion magazine support,' a state-funded grant focused on promoting circulars that relayed cultural, scientific, artistic, or social information without commercial objectives to the general public.[49] These grants were not awarded to the magazines of established organizations or societies, requiring *Akkaväki* to distance itself from the nationally well-known Unioni. Another condition for accessing the grants was that a magazine had to publish at least four issues annually. In 1980 *Akkaväki* applied for and was awarded a grant of 20,000 Finnish marks for the following year and continued to receive grants of increasing value of up to 70,000 marks annually during the second half of the 1980s. Though the size of the first grant was a disappointment—the editorial board had initially applied for 96,000 marks—securing funding was nonetheless considered a major achievement: that year alone, grants had been applied for by 73 magazines of which only 26 received funding. Telling of how reliant *Akkaväki* became on state funding, when in 1991 the Women's Cultural Association forgot to apply for funding, their magazine faced a financial crisis, which forced the editorial board to fire one of its salaried subeditors and led to the remaining subeditor quitting.[50]

---

[46] See e.g., Jenny Johannisson and Veronica Trépagny, "The (dis)location of cultural policy: two Swedish cases," accessed July 10, 2022, http://neumann.hec.ca/iccpr/PDF_Texts/Johannisson_Trepagny.pdf; Alen Doracic and Petter Edlund, "Armlängds principen och Statens kulturråd: En fallstudie om maktfördelning i svensk kulturpolitik" (Master's diss., Högskolan i Borås, 2005).

[47] Elgán, *Att ge sig själv makt*, 80.

[48] Witt-Brattström, *Å alla kära systrar!*, 150–52.

[49] Hannula, Kettula and Vaijärvi, *Kulttuuri- ja mielipidelehdet*, 3.

[50] Helminen, *Vakavaa akkaväkeä*, 36–7.

*Akkaväki* and *Kvinnobulletinen*'s acceptance of state funding could be interpreted via the lens of state feminism, where new women's movements' anti-authoritarian stances gave way to increased cooperation with the state. While this perspective indubitably helps articulate certain aspects of Nordic post-war feminist history, *Kvinnobulletinen* and *Akkaväki*'s reliance on state funding reflects a broader shift in Nordic cultural policies during the 1970s, spearheaded in Finland and Sweden by the ruling social democratic governments, which emphasized the funding of alternative culture and the inclusion of subaltern voices in the public sphere. Therefore, both magazines could hold on to their grassroots identities, with state funding regularizing the magazines' production rather than demanding (self-)censorship or the dilution of explicitly feminist content. Correspondingly, *Kvinnobulletinen* and *Akkaväki* were consistently produced based on egalitarian and communal practices. This meant upholding principles like extensive discussion and mutual agreement among the magazines' contributors and editors. As an example, according to state regulation all Finnish magazines required an editor-in-chief. The *Akkaväki* editorial team refused to abide by these regulations, instead symbolically circulating the responsibility from one activist to another only in name.[51] In Sweden questions regarding who should be responsible for producing *Kvinnobulletinen* were discussed widely, by individuals directly involved in making the magazine as well as the broader Group 8 activist base. From 1974 onwards the magazine was produced by an editorial team, led by an editor-in-chief, chosen at an annual representatives' assembly.[52] While aspects of *Kvinnobulletinen* and *Akkaväki*'s activist media practices verged on professional—both had paid subeditors on staff and some regular contributors went on to have careers as journalists—the publications predominantly relied on volunteers and free labor, with writing and editing typically taking place in the evenings and during weekends.[53] A conflict was therefore present: despite championing emancipatory and anti-authoritarian production principles, the magazines upheld a long tradition of women's unpaid intellectual and emotional labor—though in this instance for a feminist cause.

Since the late 1970s, *Akkaväki* was in part financed via funds acquired at annual Christmas markets. A holiday tradition held at Unioni's headquarters in Helsinki since 1922, the markets featured traditional handicrafts often made by elderly Finnish women.[54] Showcasing how gendered conventions and feminist innovation could covertly coexist, throughout the 1980s the Christmas markets

[51] Helminen, *Vakavaa akkaväkeä*, 32.
[52] Witt-Brattström, *Å alla kära systrar!*, 144; Elgán, *Att ge sig själv makt*, 84.
[53] Helminen, *Vakavaa akkaväkeä*, 33; Witt-Brattström, *Å alla kära systrar!*, 152.
[54] Helminen, *Väkevää akkaväkeä*, 36, 28, 79.

garnered widespread interest from festive shoppers, many of whom were most likely unaware that the profits gained from entrance fees and traditional handicraft sales were being filtered into an explicitly anti-authoritarian feminist cause.[55] During the 1980s *Akkaväki's* mainstream appeal and accessibility was further bolstered by the magazine being available for purchase from mainstream vendors like the Finnish chain store R-Kiosk (R-Kioski), which had branches across the country.[56] Despite *Akkaväki's* editorial team rejoicing in the magazine being more widely available, at the same time they interpreted this as giving in to patriarchal state pressures. In a plea urging readers to subscribe to the magazine directly, the editorial team lamented:

> When purchasing a single-issue copy, you support the patriarchy and the sexist Finnish state via 1,40 marks in sales tax, which we must pay for every single-issue copy sold. In addition, you pay 1,50–2,50 marks in sales commission to the business, from which you bought the magazine.[57]

In Sweden, *Kvinnobulletinen's* existence was dependent on the magazine being sold for profit by activists across Sweden, often to passers-by in the street. Selling an unabashedly feminist magazine to the general public could be challenging and required a careful balancing act of championing fierce activism while sticking to convention. A former member of Group 8's Gothenburg stronghold, who was a university student in the 1970s, recalled how she navigated the sexism she experienced when selling *Kvinnobulletinen* to passers-by:

> I sold *Kvinnobulletinen.* And I got so horribly provoked sometimes, because these guys and older men would come and heckle me [mimics a drunken man]: "What you want is a cock!" I was so provoked by that. [...] But these comments had me so dumbfounded, that I came up with a strategy. When I went out and sold *Kvinnobulletinen,* I wore a short coat, a pretty sweater, and I was done up. And then those arguments quickly disappeared. Because I did not want to live up to those prejudices.[58]

### A border-crossing network

In addition to creating nationally framed counterpublics, *Kvinnobulletinen* and *Akkaväki* functioned within a transnationally interconnected counterpublic

---

[55] Helminen, *Vakavaa akkaväkeä,* 79–103; Hagner and Försti, *Suffragettien sisaret,* 186.
[56] See advertisements in e.g., *Akkaväki: Naisten ääni,* 3–4/1984.
[57] "Ostitko irtonumeron?," *Akkaväki: Naisten ääni,* 1/1983, 39.
[58] Former Group 8 member, interview with author, Stockholm, Sweden, October 29, 2018.

formed by a border-crossing network of feminist magazines. In 1983, *Akkaväki* described this global counterpublic as consisting of more than 700 magazines worldwide, which "like *Akkaväki* [were] made collectively and without wages." What this global network held in common, *Akkaväki* reported, was their subaltern nature and oppositional identity vis-à-vis the patriarchal mainstream media: "Other media sources do not report on women, on women's own terms."[59] Like in Hanaholmen in 1982, a sense of transnational kinship among feminist magazine makers was fostered during international meetings. The International Feminist Book Fair, the first three of which took place in London (1984), Oslo (1986), and Montreal (1988), was a meaningful site of border-crossing knowledge transfer for Nordic and global feminists alike.[60] Based on reportage in *Kvinnobulletinen*, the magazine's closest transnational links were with its Nordic sister publications. In 1977 *Kvinnobulletinen* ran a Swedish translation of a lengthy article first published in the Danish magazine *Kvinder*, which examined the role lesbianism played within the Danish new women's movement.[61] Demonstrating national differences within the region, the Danish feminists' embrace of lesbianism provoked a homophobic outcry from *Kvinnobulletinen*'s readership. Multiple readers condemned the translated article, complaining that, unlike in Denmark, the Swedish new women's movement was not synonymous with the lesbian movement and to suggest so was misandrist.[62] In the late 1970s, *Kvinnobulletinen* showed solidarity with Finnish feminists by advertising the bilingual magazine *Aikanainen–Kvinnotid* produced by the majority Swedish-speaking organization Feminists.[63] The Norwegian magazine *Sirene* was similarly written up in *Kvinnobulletinen*, with the reviewer emphasizing that Norwegian was easy for Swedes to understand.[64] As these examples demonstrate, a significant factor connecting feminist magazines and their makers across the Nordic region was a shared linguistic heritage, with Swedish, Norwegian, and Danish being mutually intelligible. This in part explains why any mentions of the fully Finnish-language *Akkaväki* were excluded from the pages of *Kvinnobulletinen*. *Akkaväki* seems to have been aware of this linguistic hindrance: all issues published in 1980 included a summary of the magazine's content in Swedish and English.

---

[59] "Painavaa painettua," *Akkaväki: Naisten ääni*, 3/1983, 26–31.
[60] See e.g., Kaija Helo, "2nd International Feminist Book Fair," *Akkaväki: Naisten ääni*, 3/1986, 4–5; Anneli Lukka, "Villejä naisia, rohkeita kannanottoja," *Naisten ääni: Akkaväki*, 3/1988, 21–2.
[61] "En kvinna utan man är som en fisk utan cykel," *Kvinnobulletinen* 1/1977, 22–4.
[62] Ruth Bohman, "Debatt Kvinnokamp = Lesbisk kamp?," *Kvinnobulletinen*, 2/1977, 36; Marita, Monica, Ragnhild och Gunilla, "Vi måste kämpa tillsammans med män," *Kvinnobulletinen*, 3/1977, 24–5.
[63] See e.g. "Recensioner," *Kvinnobulletinen* 2/1979, 37; "Recensioner," *Kvinnobulletinen*, 2/1980, 12.
[64] "Recensioner," *Kvinnobulletinen*, 4/1974, 30.

Whereas *Kvinnobulletinen*'s transnational networks were focused on the Nordic region, *Akkaväki* was in dialogue with a broader range of transnational influences. It was significantly inspired by the West German feminist circular *Emma*, occasionally even printing direct translations of German articles.[65] Showcasing the extent to which Nordic feminist news nevertheless took precedence, in 1984 *Akkaväki* published a translated article originally featured in *Emma*, the topic of which was not the German-speaking world but rather a women's self-help center in Sweden.[66] Inspiration from the Anglophone world was also prevalent on the pages of *Akkaväki*, particularly within the magazine's theory-focused centerfolds. These centerfolds featured academic texts by Finnish and foreign feminist thinkers and were the main outlet for international scholarly feminist writing in Finland throughout the 1980s, especially prior to the launch of the Finnish women's studies journal *Naistutkimus–Kvinnoforskning* (Women's Studies) in 1988. The centerfolds' texts were typically translations of work by key feminist academics, most often American and British scholars like Ann Oakley, Catharine A. MacKinnon, and Adrienne Rich. A member of the *Akkaväki* editorial team, who was responsible for much of this translation work, described the process as exhilarating and fulfilling:

> We translated and published texts by Ann Oakley and Adrienne Rich completely without permission. I was very excited and very satisfied whenever we managed to introduce new thoughts and theories in Finland. Women's studies was still in its infancy, so there was no other way to read this stuff in Finland.[67]

The practice of translating articles and circulating them transnationally was an established part of second-wave feminist activist media practices.[68] This was made possible by the oppositional counterpublic that these media practices formed, which rejected hierarchical and profit-based conventions in favor of communal and anti-authoritarian approaches. A regular contributor to *Akkaväki*, who worked as a paid subeditor for the magazine from 1988 to 1990 prior to shifting into professional journalism, reflected on these dynamics as follows:

---

[65] See e.g., Cornelia Kazis, "Ilman häpeää ja pelkoa," trans. Riitta Liimatainen, *Akkaväki: Naisten ääni*, 3/1983, 20–21; Marja Paavilainen, "Oi Emma Emma," *Akkaväki: Naisten ääni*, 5/1985, 36–8.

[66] Mette Bergh, "Noita-asema," transl. Helena Auvinen, *Akkaväki: Naisten ääni*, 3–4/1984, 22–3.

[67] Former *Akkaväki* editorial team member, interview with author, Skype, November 9, 2017.

[68] See Maud Bracke, Julia C. Bullock, Penelope Morris and Kristina Schulz, eds., *Translating Feminism: Interdisciplinary Approaches to Text, Place and Agency (1945–2000)* (Cham: Palgrave, 2021).

Copyright was not given a second thought. Or, well, it was understood that this was not allowed and even the *Naisten ääni* logo [...] is from Swedish feminists somewhere. [...] But there was no negative feedback or demands, so we could go on doing it [translating and reprinting material from other feminist magazines]. But it was, of course, a time prior to the internet. And Finland being peripheral and the small circulation numbers, so was it worth it to recruit some lawyer? And it [international magazines blaming *Akkaväki* for borrowing content] would not have matched the ideology of the other feminist organizations.[69]

As these examples demonstrate, the transnational networks to which *Akkaväki* and *Kvinnobulletinen* understood themselves as belonging, and which guided the magazines' media practices, were based on tangible border-crossing exchanges but also imaginaries of a global sisterhood. From a comparative perspective, while in Finland *Akkaväki* utilized this imagined global community of feminist magazines to provide examples of similar activism abroad and therefore justify its own presence within the Finnish media landscape, the Swedish *Kvinnobulletinen* predominantly focused on reportage that accounted for nationally demarcated differences in feminist ideology and praxis, at times seeking to set Swedish feminism distinctly apart from its transnational counterparts.[70]

## Conclusion

The main function of feminist magazines was to spread the word of feminism.[71] In Finland, *Akkaväki*'s editorial team tested a variety of promotional methods, from taking out expensive adverts in the country's main newspaper *Helsingin Sanomat* to plastering stickers with the magazine's logo onto the walls of women's public toilets.[72] Across Sweden, *Kvinnobulletinen*'s readers were urged to both read the periodical and act as its promoters by demanding that local department stores, newsagents, and bookstores stock the magazine.[73] As these concluding examples suggest, and as I have argued throughout this chapter, these two Nordic magazines are best interpreted as subaltern counterpublics, which focused on elevating women's voices within patriarchal

---

[69] Former *Akkaväki* editorial team member, interview with author, Helsinki, Finland November 4, 2017.
[70] For more on imagined communities and the new women's movements in the Nordic region see Yoken, "Nordic Transnational Feminist Activism," 30–1, 158–59.
[71] For a similar argument see Forster, "Spreading the Word."
[72] Helminen, *Väkevää akkaväkeä*, 36.
[73] See e.g., archival documents housed in the Jönköping County Popular Movement Archive (Jönköping läns folkrörelsearkiv): Grupp 8 i Jönköping. E:1 Korrespondens mm 1973–1976.

society. *Akkaväki* and *Kvinnobulletinen* were in constant dialogue with the public sphere, despite the magazines developing in opposition to how women were represented in it. In material terms too, though the magazines' activist media practices were distinctly anti-authoritarian, *Kvinnobulletinen* and *Akkaväki* chose to rely at least in part on state funding. The media landscape in which feminist activists produced these magazines therefore tells a distinctly Nordic story, where social democratic governments passed cultural policies aimed at supporting and proliferating subaltern voices represented in the alternative press.

In her foundational text, Nancy Fraser described counterpublics as being formed of "subordinate *social* groups."[74] In retrospective accounts, activists who belonged to *Akkaväki* and *Kvinnobulletinen*'s editorial teams have described magazine making as an intensely sociable and thoroughly communal experience, marked by hours of volunteer labor, and resulting in fierce disagreements and meaningful friendships.[75] With this chapter I wish to make an intervention in the existing historiography surrounding Nordic feminism's second wave, arguing that the region's feminist magazines should not be studied solely for their contents, or as readily accessible conduits of the region's new women's movements' historical narratives. Instead, I posit that the activist media practices involved in producing and distributing feminist magazines— the ideological and practical choices editorial teams made and how these choices affected the circulation of feminism as a sociopolitical force—are historical phenomena deserving of analysis in their own right. Returning to Fraser's work, it can be argued that the activists responsible for making feminist magazines formed a distinct subsection of the feminist counterpublic in the Nordic region, functioning simultaneously at the local, national, and transnational levels.

The production of new women's movement magazines in the Nordic region spanned from the early 1970s into the 1990s, challenging the timeline typically associated with second wave feminism and blurring the artificial borders used to demarcate between feminism's waves. It is however important to remember that the activists producing and distributing feminist magazines changed over time, and with these changes came alterations to the magazines' contents and appearances. A focus on activist media practices must therefore pay heightened attention to nuanced change over time, rather than approach the multi-year print run of any given magazine as a static or all-encapsulating snapshot.

---

[74] Fraser, "Rethinking the Public Sphere," 67.
[75] See e.g., Helminen, *Väkevää akkaväkeä*, 31–6; Witt-Brattström, *Å alla kära systrar!*, 144–53.

# Transnational encounters and conflicts

Chapter 7

# Post-war Americanization and Finnish cigarette television advertising

Jukka Kortti

*University of Helsinki, Finland*

**Abstract:** Americanism and the spread of television were among the most important phenomena in the Post-War Europe. Of all the products, tobacco, especially cigarettes, are one of the most American influenced advertising product categories in the history of advertising. This chapter studies Finnish Post-War Americanization through the lens of television cigarette advertising. It shows how businesspeople soaked up the American ideas of modernism in advertising, even in such a periphery region as Finland was in the post-WW II decades. The chapter asks how American ideas of modernization were represented in advertising and marketing, and how the Finns adapted them in the context of their own post-war culture and society.

**Keywords**: modernization, Americanization, television, advertising, cigarettes

\*\*\*

Perhaps the most important advertisers in the first years of Finnish television were the tobacco companies. With their large amount of capital, they were imposingly engaged in television advertising and continued to expand their presence until the public demand for legislative action began to restrict the advertising of tobacco on television in the mid-1960s. A total ban on Finnish tobacco advertising on television came into effect in 1970. Around the same time, American cigarette companies also agreed to put an end to TV advertising in the US.

The tobacco industry had been a significant player throughout advertising and marketing history. Moreover, most of the globally well-known tobacco brands, such as Marlboro, are American, and make use of mythic national images of the Wild West, for example. American ideas about marketing, and the use of

Americanism as a referent system[1] for advertising, had a strong influence on Finnish television commercials. Cigarette advertising is perhaps one of the best examples of this. The advertising campaigns of tobacco companies were a kind of marketing school for Finnish advertising professionals in the 1950s and 1960s.

This chapter studies Finnish Post-War Americanization through the lens of television cigarette advertising. It shows how businesspeople soaked up the American ideas of modernism in advertising, even in such a periphery region as Finland was in the post-WW II decades. The chapter asks how American ideas of modernization were represented in advertising and marketing, and how the Finns adapted them in the context of their own post-war culture and society.

Finnish television started as a commercial enterprise and included advertising right from the start. Hence, Finnish advertisers, including the tobacco industry, had better opportunities for modern advertising than other Nordic countries, which did not have television advertising until the 1980s. In Sweden, for instance, "Americanization" and American commercial television meant something vulgar, in poor taste, and harmful to the Swedish welfare state ideal, and the polar opposite of the Swedish (public service) broadcasting.[2] Therefore, Finnish advertising agencies had the most effective advertising medium of the era among their fellow Nordic countries through their utilization of American-influenced campaigns.

### Marshall plan of ideas

Finnish advertising professionals had regularly visited the United States since the 1920s—and broadcasting professionals had also done so after World War II. The style and effects of their advertising, the use of interview studies and psychology, and the core idea of marketing came from the United States. The books of the most important American advertising executives of the 1950s and 1960s, such as Rosser Reeves, were translated into Finnish. In practice, the most important sources were American magazines such as *Esquire, Life, Ladies' Home Journal*, and *Harper's Bazaar*.[3] Most of the new generation advertising people in the 1960s had lived their youth in the 1950s; they were the first in

---

[1] Referent systems are clearly ideological systems, and draw their significance from areas outside advertising. See Judith Williamson, *Decoding Advertisements: Ideology and Meaning in Advertisements* (London Boyers, 1998 [1978]), 17, 19.

[2] Tove Thorslund, *Do You Have a TV? Negotiating Swedish Public Service through 1950s Programming, Americanization and Domesticity* (Stockholm: Stockholm University, 2018), 128–29.

[3] Visa Heinonen, "Kolme 'mainosmestaria' ja modernin mainonnan alku Suomessa," in *Keulakuvia ja peränpitäjiä: Vanhan ja uuden yhteiskunnan rajalla,* eds. Riitta Oittinen and Marjatta Rahikainen (Helsinki: SHS, 2000); Visa Heinonen and Hannu Konttinen, *Nyt Uutta Suomessa: Suomalaisen mainonnan historia* (Helsinki: Mainostajien Liitto, 2001), 153–61.

Finland to taste chewing gum and Coca Cola, listen to jazz, and later to rock'n'roll, and to watch American short films (cartoons, newsreels, etc.) in movie theatres.

As American Tom O'Dell noted in his account of the Americanization of Sweden, Americanization and modernity are often closely linked phenomena. Americanization can be perceived as a modern process, and consumption is one of the primary structures through which it is constructed as such.[4] America has been viewed as the fulfillment of utopian promises that European culture had failed to deliver.[5]

The cultural Americanization of Europe had begun already in the interwar years. However, it was especially after World War II that American 'cultural imperialism' took a stronghold of post-war Western Europe through the media.[6] We must remember that, for Europeans, including the Nordic countries,[7] America is not only an actual topographic area, a political nation, and an economic system, but also very much a philosophical idea—a fetish and a myth.[8]

---

[4] Tom O'Dell, *Culture Unbound: Americanization and Everyday Life in Sweden* (Lund: Nordic Academic Press, 1997).

[5] Mike-Frank G. Epitropoulus and Victor Roudometof, "Introduction: America and Europe Fragile Objects of Discourse," in *American Culture in Europe: Interdisciplinary Perspectives*, eds. Mike-Frank G. Epitropoulus and Victor Roudometof (London Praeger, 1998), 4.

[6] See, e.g., Alexander Stephan, *The Americanization of Europe: Culture, Diplomacy, and Anti-Americanism after 1945* (New York: Berghahn Books, 2006); Reinhold Wagnleitner, *Coca-Colonization and the Cold War. The Cultural Mission of the United States in Austria after the Second War*, trans. Diana M. Wolf (Chapel Hill and London: The University of North Carolina Press, 1994); Heide Fehrenbach and Uta G. Poiger, eds., *Transactions, Transgressions, Transformations: American Culture in Western Europe and Japan* (New York and Oxford: Berghahn Books, 2000); Kristin Ross, *Fast Cars, Clean Bodies: Decolonization and the Reordering of French culture* (Cambridge, MA: The MIT Press, 1997); Rob Kroes, *If You've Seen One, You've Seen the Mall: Europeans and American Mass Culture* (Urbana and Chicago: University of Illinois Press, 1996); Visa Heinonen, Jukka Kortti and Mika Pantzar, "How Lifestyle Products Became Rooted in the Finnish Consumer Market – Domestication of Jeans, Chewing Gum, Sunglasses and Cigarettes," *National Consumer Research Centre working papers* 80/2003 (Helsinki: National Consumer Research Centre, 2003).

[7] About the Americanization of Scandinavia, see Mikael Nilsson, *The Battle for Hearts and Minds in the High North* (New York: Brill, 2016); Poul Houe and Sven Hakon Rossel, eds., *Images of America in Scandinavia* (Amsterdam: Atlanta, 1998); Tom O'Dell, *Culture Unbound: Americanization and Everyday Life in Sweden* (Lund: Nordic Academic Press, 1997); Rolf Lundén and Erik Åsard, eds., *Networks of Americanization: Aspects of the American Influence in Sweden* (Uppsala: Uppsala University, 1992).

[8] Birgitta Steene, "The Swedish Image of America," in *Images of America in Scandinavia*, eds. Poul Houe and Sven Hakon Rossel (Amsterdam: Atlanta, 1998), 145.

Accordingly, in analyzing the television commercials, I use a modified version of the semiotic myth system created by the French structuralist Roland Barthes.[9] Briefly, the aim is to identify the specific modernization ideologies, worldviews, and mentalities that have been coded by certain symbols and discourses into the commercials. These connotations have created myths associated with some consumer goods or services, giving them a new meaning. Identifying why and how specific myths were attached to specific commodities is the focal point of the analysis. The study is concerned with both the signifiers (*the form*) and the signs: the commodities advertised by commercials and the marketing presentations created around them. However, the signified (*the concept*), which includes all of the connotations associated with a commodity, is placed in particular focus. These connotations not only provide information about the socio- and cultural-historical changes of the era, but also about the effect of American-based modernization ideologies during the rapid changes in Finnish society that took place in the 1960s.

Altogether, the Americanization of Finland did not take place through an influx of physical artifacts so much as through ideas and cultural goods. Most products, including cigarettes that were consumed in Finland in the 1960s were also produced in Finland. In many cases, American products, such as cars, were either too big or too expensive for the Finnish consumer market. In addition, the rather small Finnish market was not very attractive to American companies. The transaction costs, import fees, costs of packing, freight, and so on were simply too high. Although Finland was the only western country that participated in World War II that did not receive a post-war Marshall Plan Aid package, Finland received instead "the Marshall Plan of ideas."[10] America was idolized in the 1950s and 1960s just because it seemed to be a place in which things were better, faster, and more effective.

The ideology of American modernization not only held a promise of a better life through its progressiveness, but also reflected "a worldview through which America's strategic needs and political options were articulated, evaluated, and understood," as Michael E. Latham notes in his study on American social sciences and "nation building" in the Kennedy Era.[11] Indeed, media and consumption were not the only areas of culture and society used to transfer the American way of life and hopefully prevent countries from falling into communism in Europe. For instance, the wide-reaching and carefully planned

---

[9] Ronald Barthes, *Mythologies* (London: Paladin Books, 1973).

[10] Marja Alaketola-Tuominen, *Jokapojan amerikanperintö: Yhdysvaltalaisia kulttuuriv-aikutteita Suomessa toisen maailmansodan jälkeen* (Helsinki; Gaudeamus, 1989), 21.

[11] Michael E. Latham, *Modernization as Ideology: American Social Science and "Nation Building" in the Kennedy Era* (Chapel Hill and London: The University of North Carolina Press, 2000), 8.

American educational policy of the time included exchange programs (the Fulbright programme, the Rockefeller Foundation, and the Ford Foundation) as a type of *public diplomacy*.[12]

The American scholarship programs were the central tool in transmitting the ideas of American social sciences into the Nordic countries. Although they were the "slow media" of public diplomacy—with advertising, films, television programs, and magazines being the "fast media"—American social sciences had a major impact on the development of the Nordic welfare states during their fast-moving reformative years.[13]

Nevertheless, the Cold War battle over hearts and minds was very much about the media. In Finland, it also involved the introduction and establishment of television. The Soviet television programs were transmitted from Estonia through the Tallinn TV station, and people could watch its programs in Southern Finland. The Tallinn television service constituted a serious problem for Finland, as it offered the Soviet Union an excellent medium of propaganda. In addition to the programs, it was also a case of technology and a Cold War battle for broadcasting space. The Soviets wanted to sell their TV system to Finland. The American RCA won, however, mainly because they offered their transmission system at half the price. Also, the Finnish businesspeople—and those in the technology department of Yleisradio as well—wanted the Western system. It was then clear that the Soviets had fallen behind.

In the early days of Finnish television, the Americans practiced their wartime "psychological warfare" especially through the USIS[14] (United States Information Service), which supplied a wealth of American film programs to Finnish television companies, including Yleisradio.[15] In this chapter, however,

---

[12] See e.g., Mark Sovey and Hamilton Cravens, eds., *Cold War Social Science: Knowledge Production, Liberal Democracy, and Human Nature* (New York: Palgrave Macmillan, 2012); Christopher Simpson, ed., *Universities and Empire: Money and Politics in the Social Sciences during the Cold War* (New York: The New Press, 1998).

[13] Jukka Kortti, "Slow media under cross pressures: US educational diplomacy in the Nordic countries during the Cold War," in A *Nordic Model of Propaganda and Persuasion*, eds. Fredrik Norén, Emil Stjernholm and Claire Thomas. (London: Palgrave Macmillan, 2022).

[14] The US historians speak more about the USIA (United States Information Agency), and the USIS referred to the USIA's office in Finland

[15] See Raimo Salokangas, "The Finnish Broadcasting Company and the Changing Finnish Society, 1949–1966," in *Yleisradio 1926–1996: A History of Broadcasting in Finland*, ed. Rauno Endén (Helsinki: SKS, 1996), 133–34; Jukka Kortti, "Television Creating Finnish Consumer Mentality in the 1960s," in *Finnish Consumption: Emerging Consumer Society between East and West*, eds. Visa Heinonen and Matti Peltonen (Helsinki: SKS, 2013), 154–76; Heidi Keinonen, "Early Commercial Television in Finland: Balancing between East and West," *Media History* 18, no 4 (2012): 177–89.

I focus on how the ideas of American advertising were influencing the early of Finnish television.

## Sponsored by Amer Cigarettes

The very first Finnish public television broadcast featuring advertising was produced in early 1956. It was sponsored by Amer Tupakka, a Finnish tobacco company. This initial broadcast was produced by the associations of engineers and students, who had established their own TV station a year before that. The story of this TV station, TES-TV, later Tesvisio, ended in 1964, when Yleisradio bought it after Tesvisio encountered an economic crisis.[16]

National broadcasting company Yleisradio started television broadcasting in the autumn of 1957. From the very first day, it included commercials. Based on the proposal by the advertising and businesspeople, the administrative board of Yleisradio decided to found a separate company that would be independent of Yleisradio and would be owned by advertisers, advertising agencies, and film production companies. The new company was called Oy Mainos-TV Reklam Ab (nowadays known as channel MTV3, the third oldest commercial television company in Europe, owned by Telia Company). The pattern for this system came from Britain, where ITV (Independent Television) was founded as a commercial TV company a couple of years before—in competition with the BBC.[17]

The subsequent changes in Finnish cigarette advertising thus tell us not only about the evolving regulations and development of the advertising industry, but also about the first years of television broadcasting in general. The Finnish tobacco company Amer (nowadays known as Amer Sports, a sports equipment company) was, for example, the most important sponsor of Tesvision. The Golden Age of American television in the 1950s and the early 1960s was also "golden" for American cigarette advertising as well.

The 1960s, especially the first years of the decade, was a significant period for the Finnish tobacco industry. It was the time when Finnish smokers turned to smoking American-style filter cigarettes. In the 1960s, the share of American-style filter cigarettes was only 15%, but by 1963 it had already reached 60%.[18] The "American-style" was also manifested in the brand names. Every new Finnish cigarette brand had an English name, such as *Boston, Milton, Strong,*

---

[16] Jukka Kortti, *Modernisaatiomurroksen kaupalliset merkit: 60-luvun suomalainen televisiomainonta* (Helsinki: SKS, 2003), 22–31.

[17] However, the Finnish version differed from the British one, especially in one particular sense. Mainos-TV did not have its own channel, but leased its broadcasting time from Yleisradio. This system was unique in the whole world—and was certainly not trouble-free.

[18] Reijo Kurkela, *Tupakka tupakkalain jälkeen* (Helsinki: Tilastokeskus, 1987), 73–4, 78–9.

etc.[19] The marketing of actual American cigarette brands in Finland also started at the turn of the 1960s.

At the same time when the Finnish tobacco industry was enjoying its heyday, with access to significant financial resources, a new advertising medium was born: television. Like the advertising professionals, the very American-influenced Finnish tobacco industry was also well aware of the power of this new medium for marketing, right from the beginning of Finnish television. The main Finnish tobacco companies were able to partner with the best advertising agencies, because the agencies were also handling their other advertising media, media planning, marketing ideas, and creativity in general.

The whole advertising business in Finland went through a generational change during the 1960s. This older generation of white-coated, pipe-smoking advertising artists, who considered especially suggestive advertising to be an oddity, was soon replaced by dynamic young people. These new young minds followed the current trends, and were committed to a belief in progress according to the perspective of the 1960s. Creativity was the basis for all modern advertising in the 1960s, such that the core "idea" of campaigns was the guiding principle for everything. Teams of copywriters and art directors working together became a general phenomenon during the 1960s. Indeed, this small Nordic capitalist country in the shadow of the Soviet Union had its "creative revolution" in American-style advertising in the 1960s,[20] and tobacco companies were among the best sponsors of such creativity.

Amer sponsored the very first public broadcasting in Finland in 1956. The show was called the "Boston Show;" *Boston* was a new Finnish cigarette brand introduced in the previous year by Amer. Among other things there was a Boston orchestra (Boston-orkesteri) playing in the studio. "Boston show" was also the

---

[19] The same phenomenon can be found in other European countries as well during this period. For instance, the Danish-manufactured brand *Holiday*, which was "an America blend of tobacco produced by American machines under control of American experts, proclaimed: 'It's OK, it's a Holiday.'" Nils Arne Sorensen and Klaus Petersen, "Ameri-Dames and Pro-American Anti-Americanism in Denmark after 1945," in *The Americanization: Culture, Diplomacy, and Anti-Americanism after 1945*, ed. Alexander Stephan (New York and Oxford: Berghahn Books, 2007), 127.

[20] The creative revolution refers to the swift development of American advertising during the 1960s. In addition to core ideas with strategic force becoming the basis for advertising campaigns, copywriters and art directors started working as teams to carry out these ideas. During the later 1960s, they often consisted of new (baby boom) generation professionals who applied the counterculture symbolism of the 1960s. Regarding the "creative revolution," see for example Stephen R. Fox, *The Mirror Makers: A History of American Advertising and Its Creators* (New York: Morrow, 1984), 218–71. A good account of this development is the TV serial drama *Mad Men* (AMC, 2007–2015).

title of one of the early entertainment shows. *Life* cigarettes, a brand of another Finnish tobacco company Suomen tupakka (Tobacco Finland), also sponsored one of the early shows. This kind of broadcast sponsoring by tobacco companies had started already back in the late 1920s, when American cigarette brands such as *Lucky Strikes* had their own music shows and orchestras on radio.[21]

Like American big cigarette brands—*Camel, Lucky Strike,* and *Chesterfield*—in the United States from the 1940s to the 1960s,[22] Finnish brands, mostly owned by Amer, were the main sponsors of many television shows. For example, Amer sponsored the first Finnish live broadcast aired from the Finnish National Opera, the ballet *Swan Lake,* in January 1957. The following year, Amer sponsored the quiz show *Tupla tai kuitti* (Double or Quit) with its cigarette brand Milton (losers of the show got a carton of Miltons!). As in the USA in the 1950s, sponsored quiz shows were mostly produced by advertising agencies in Finland. The quiz show scandals, in which the advertisers fixed the shows for their advertising purposes, provided important motivation for getting the advertisers out of such programming in the US, and to move to the so-called magazine format, i.e., funding through television spots, at the turn of the 1960s. In Finland, such sponsoring ended in the mid-1960s, when Mainos-TV took over the creation and production of all of its programs.

The sponsor model, which was the basis of the whole television business in the "Golden Age of television" (1940s and 1950s) in America,[23] was also a remarkable feature of the first years of Finnish commercial television. After all, Finland was the first to introduce sponsored programs in Europe (soon followed by countries such as Austria and West Germany) and the very American-influenced tobacco industry was at the vanguard of the business. There were many individuals in Finnish business life who were aware of the potential of television for advertising. Beginning in the early 1950s, Finnish advertising and trade magazines published many articles about television. These advertising people also visited the United States, and understood what this new medium meant for advertising.

### From animation to lifestyle

Sponsored programs were often live shows, and were not recorded, so it is not possible to watch them nowadays. But the Finnish cigarette spots are still there for us to watch.[24]

---

[21] Fox, *Mirror Makers,* 154.

[22] See Shaw and Alan, "Cigarettes," 314–15.

[23] See for example Lawrence R. Samuel, *Brought to You By: Postwar Television and the American Dream* (Austin: University of Texas Press, 2001), 3–149; Fox, *Mirror Makers,* 210–17.

[24] In my extensive study, I analyzed 21 cigarette spots from 1957 to 1970. The films were primarily collected from the collections of The Finnish Film Archive and advertising

Animated commercials and cartoons were a second major genre, which arose after "Broadway-like musical extravaganza" appeared in American film advertising during the 1950s.[25] Those genres were often mixed, since the fantasy figures were usually moving to the beat of the soundtrack in the animated commercials and cartoons. A typical example of this kind of advertising film is *Muriel Cigars*' black-and-white cartoon commercial *Sexy Cigar*, made in 1951 (Lennen & Newell, Inc.), where a cigar couple is singing and dancing to the musical style. The lady cigar, purring in the Mae West style, says the famous line in a sexy voice: "Why don't you pick me up and smoke me some time?"

You can find musical influences in the Finnish film advertising of the 1950s as well. This decade was the heyday of the Finnish film industry. In 1952, the number of films produced per capita in Finland was the highest in the world.[26] "Finnish Hollywood" produced entertainment, comedies, musicals, and farces. In the early 1950s, one in every four films was a musical. As the moviegoers were a first-rate target group for advertisers and the Finns seemed to want to be entertained, music had a significant role in the advertising films of the time as well.[27]

A typical advertising film[28] from that era is the color film *Boston Baari* (Boston bar, SEK) for *Boston* cigarettes, made in 1958. Couples are shown dancing and smoking cigarettes in a musical-style artificial bar setting. The film also includes animated sequences where the cigarettes are moving to the beat of the soundtrack. The same kind of animation was used in American cigarette commercials, e.g. in the pioneering black-and-white commercial *Barn Dance* for Lucky Strike cigarettes made in 1950 (N.W Ayer & Son), where the cigarettes are dancing to the beat of the jingle—an advertising music piece made in a catchy, repetitious manner. The Finnish black-and-white commercial in *Boston "Osto"* (Boston purchase, SEK, 1965) is almost identical to the Lucky Strike spot.

---

agency SEK & Grey, which was then named SEK, one of the biggest agencies in Finland in the 1960s (and still today). The American spots are mostly from the collections of The Television Advertising and Culture Archive at Brooklyn College (the Celia Nachatovitz Diamant "Classic Television Commercials" collection and the Ted Bates collection), the Museum of Television & Radio in New York, and 'Classic Cigarettes Volume 1' by Video Resources New York Inc. (Museum of Television and Radio as an advisor).

[25] Samuel, *Brought to You By*, 24.

[26] Kari Uusitalo, "Suomalainen elokuvatuotanto 1948–1952: Taustaa ja tosiasioita," in *Suomen kansallisfilmografia 1948–1952, osa 4*, chief ed. Kari Uusitalo (Helsinki: Edita and Suomen elokuva-arkisto, 1992), 21.

[27] Kaarina Kilpiö, "The Use of Music in Early Finnish Cinema and TV advertising," in *Advertising Research in the Nordic Countries*, eds. Lotte Yssing Hansen and Flemming Hansen (Copenhagen: Samfundslitteratur, 2001), 71–2.

[28] Not really a commercial or a spot, because it was made for movie theatres before the era of television.

Boston "Osto" was not an exception. Just as in the black-and-white *Winston Tastes Good* spot made in the late 1950s (William Esty Inc.), "where the letters and shapes metamorphose pleasantly against the flowing choral background, and the solid bands at the top and bottom of the Winston package design serve percussively to score the clapping on the soundtrack," as Lincoln Diamant puts it,[29] the letters metamorphose in the black-and-white *Boston Metsästäjä* (Boston Hunter, SEK, 1965) and in the black-and-white *Bristol-TV* (SEK, 1965). Bristol was another cigarette brand of the Amer company.

One of the most famous animated American cigarette commercials of the era is S*moking Penguin* (Ted Bates, Inc., 1954), advertising Kool Cigarettes. The black-and-white commercial combines animation and live film footage. The cartoon character "Willie the Penguin" is walking on a bed of hot coals and skates on ice, while a stream is flowing through a winter landscape in the live footage of the film. Kool was the first successful menthol cigarette by Brown & Williamson. The cartoon penguin was introduced already in 1934. In 1950s, Willie jumped into the TV medium as Kool's spokesman.[30]

The first Finnish menthol cigarette brand was *Meil,* launched by Amer in 1959. The color commercial *Menthol-Meil* (SEK, 1967) shows scenes from an airport, an Alpine skiing resort, and a sailing club. A man dressed in a suit and a hat is lighting a cigarette and then smoking and smiling to the camera in a close-up. The narrator says: "A new wind is blowing across the world..." In the following sequence, a woman dressed in skiing clothes is smoking on a wintry mountain set. Narrator: "You can feel the fresh aroma of menthol cigarettes." In the last sequence, a man dressed in a white V-neck sweater and a white scarf is smoking on a sailing dock. Narrator: "And, besides complete tobacco pleasure, it provides—freshness." The last picture contains a pack of Menthol-Meil cigarettes on a clear, icy kind of glass.

Let us take a closer look at this commercial. Nature metaphors, such as the freshness of ice and winter in both the Kool and Menthol-Meil spots discussed above, had already been popular in advertising since the early twentieth century. Moreover, the concepts of leisure time, luxury, and wealth have been encoded into the Menthol Meil spot through the different scenes. These codes may not sound so glamorous today, but Finland was still a poor post-war country in the beginning of the 1960s, and only a few had an opportunity to experience alpine skiing (unlike cross-country skiing, which was a national sport back then) or sailing; they were considered to be the recreational activities of the elite. Also, air travel, especially international flights, was a rather rare activity among common people in Finland in the early 1960s. Thus, the

---

[29] Lincoln Diamant, *Television's Classic Commercials: The Golden Years, 1948–58* (New York: Hastings House, 1971), 124.
[30] Shaw and Alan, "Cigarettes," 313.

gentleman in the airport looks more like a successful businessman. The advertiser wanted to encode images of a modern, international lifestyle. The line "There's a new wind blowing" illustrates a fascination with modern times.

The increasing personalization and use of images in advertising was crystallized in the idea of lifestyle advertising, which found its way into Finnish advertising in the late 1960s.[31] As Leiss, Kline and Jhally, who have studied the evolutions of advertising, put it, television has "powerful visual methods of storytelling and the matrix of consumption styles it portrays."[32]

### Seeking modern success

The 'modern lifestyle' was a dominant referent system for Finnish cigarette commercials in the early 1960s. Modern success is the specific focus of the *Bristol-Speaker* (SEK, 1961) spot. Although lifestyle advertising often implies suggestive, subconscious elements, this commercial does not leave much room for such subtlety. The spot starts with the narrator talking to the camera:

> Why does a man like you smoke Bristol? A man seeks success. That's why he chooses Bristol. Bristol carries the sign of success. Bristol is so successful, that you can get it at the old price but in a new, modern package. It's longer and more stylish.

The setting of the first scene is a modern city, creating the image of a modern urban milieu. The next scene shows the set in actual size, with a woman posing in front of it. Closer to the camera, a man holds a pack of Bristol cigarettes in his hand, lights a cigarette, and inhales the smoke. Narrator: "Get to know the success. Pay less—and say: Thanks... but I prefer Bristol." The connotations of a modern way of life are quite directly encoded into the product, and the "modern" package is also emphasized.

The characters and the set are clumsy pastiches of post-war Hollywood movies. Movies were (and are) important media in representing smoking. American films were widely shown during the post-war decades all over Western Europe, and the product placement of American cigarette brands certainly increased the smoking of filter cigarettes among Finnish smokers.

After the interwar period, smoking became an essential part of the personal glamour of many film stars, such as James Dean, Humphrey Bogart, Marlene

---

[31] See Heinonen et.al., "How Lifestyle Products Became Rooted in the Finnish Consumer Market."

[32] William Leiss, Stephen Kline and Sut Jhally, *Social Communication in Advertising: Persons, Products and Images of Well-Being* (London and New York: Routledge, 1997), 262.

Dietrich, Mae West, Bette Davis, Lauren Bacall, Rita Hayworth, and Maureen O'Hara. In addition to actors and actresses, sport and music celebrities and other entertainers acted as product personalization for cigarettes after the 1920s. Hollywood studios had established extensive relationships with advertisers, and had proven their willingness to allow the introduction of external commercial discourses into their apparently autonomous narratives long before the 1950s.[33]

Hollywood's commercial messages blurred the boundaries between narrative and advertising discourses.[34] More than a window on the world American movies have been "the shop window."[35] Finland was not an exception to this effect. However, the period of using celebrities in cigarette commercials was quite short, lasting from the late 1950s until the early 1960s. This was, first of all, due to increasing restrictions on cigarette advertising, but using entertainers in advertising was also a trend of that time.

### Do it in the American way

Most distinctly, American influences in Finnish cigarette advertising can be found in the Marlboro commercials. Marlboro by Philip Morris was targeting women in the 1920s, but because of the unsatisfactory sales it was successfully repositioned as a brand for men by the advertising agency Leo Burnett Company in the 1950s. The famous Marlboro cowboy was introduced in 1954. During the early years, however, the cowboy was only one of the ways to encode masculinity into the lifestyle advertising of the brand. Among other things, the new "Settle back" campaign was designed to undo the damage of the articles published in *Reader's Digest* magazine in 1957, which ranked the full-flavored Marlboro stronger than some plain tipped brands in terms of tar and nicotine. In order to restore the image of the brand, the campaign encoded celebrities and relaxed settings into the Marlboro brand.[36]

Amer started manufacturing Marlboro in Finland in 1961. The commercial made in the following year, *Marlboro-laituri* (Marlboro jetty, Markkinointi Viherjuuri, 1962) included the famous American jingle "The Marlboro Song" in the soundtrack. The scene of the commercial is a jetty by a lake or sea. Water skis are resting against the railing, and there is a transistor radio on the table.

---

[33] Jay Newell, Charles T. Salmon and Susan Chang, "The Hidden History of Product Placement," *Journal of Broadcasting & Electronic Media* 50, no. 4 (2006): 575–94.

[34] Ross, *Fast Cars, Clean Bodies*, 90–1.

[35] See Anne Friedberg, *Window Shopping: Cinema and the Postmodern* (London: University of California Press, 1994).

[36] Paul Rutherford, *The New Icons? The Art of Television Advertising* (Toronto: Toronto University Press, 1994), 39.

The camera zooms back, and we see a woman lying in a chair, singing in lip-synch (in English). While singing, the woman opens a pack of Marlboro. She takes her eyes off the pack and looks up to the lake where a man, tanned and dressed in white, is waving at her from a boat. He drives to the jetty, jumps off the boat and approaches the woman and kisses her shoulder, while she hides the pack of Marlboros behind her back. He takes a cigarette from the pack she is holding, lights it, inhales, blows the smoke and lies down on the jetty ("Why not settle back and enjoy a full-flavored smoke?," as the lyrics to The Marlboro Song go). Attentive viewers might notice the Philip Morris logo tattooed on the back of his hand. In the last picture, text (in Finnish) announces "with taste" and (in English): "The filter cigarette with <u>unfiltered</u> taste."

The tattoo was a part of Marlboro's "masculinity campaign" by Leo Burnett—together with images of cowboys and the idea of changing the package from a mild white design to a bold red in an assertive V-shaped pattern. The cowboy character was supplemented with a variety of other rugged, mature types. The tattoo was to suggest toughness and a romantic past—to create a myth of mystery and intrigue around the product.[37] Most Finns probably did not understand the symbolism of the tattoo. That is why a columnist in the Finnish advertising trade journal *Mainosuutiset* decided to enlighten Finns:

> Marlboro has taken a symbol from a faraway subject, tattooing. That symbol has a barbarous kind of reputation for us, but is a common masculine, even respectful description of a sailor amongst the Anglo-Saxon sailing peoples. The symbolism hits the bulls-eye, because this cigarette includes "the salty flavor of sea" and the image of times when "the ships were made of wood and the men of iron."[38] Let's see, how Finnish smokers are going to take it.[39]

Scenes like this were popular in American cigarette commercials in the 1950s and 1960s. For example, a commercial for Parliament cigarettes features a couple in a sailing boat, and a couple is water-skiing in an *Oasis* cigarette commercial. Like the Menthol Meil analyzed above, Oasis was a menthol cigarette advertised with the line: "Freshest Taste in Smoking."[40] Especially during the 1960s, when cigarette advertisers wanted to convince the viewers

---

[37] Fox, *Mirror Makers*, 223; Rutherford, *The New Icons?*, 39.
[38] The popular line from Finnish song *Laivat puuta, miehet rautaa*, introduced by singer/actor/sportsman Tapio Rautavaara in 1952.
[39] Vilkkusilmä, "TV: Tuote ja tunnukset," *Mainosuutiset* 3/1962, 7.
[40] The source for these commercials is *Classic Cigarette Commercials Volume 1* by Video Resources New York Inc. Unfortunately there is no information about the years and agencies on the VHS cassettes.

that cigarettes were not dangerous, those kinds of visual elements increased. Young, athletic-looking adults engaged in vigorous activities and surrounded by pristine environments were featuring in very life-stylish cigarette visuals.[41]

To be sure, the previous *Marlboro laituri* spot differs from other Finnish tobacco commercials of the era. This tells us about the precise instructions provided by Philip Morris for the Finns in their Marlboro advertising. Although Amer licensed Marlboro, the advertising agency was not SEK (as it was for the other Amer Brands), but Markkinointi Viherjuuri. The demand to use a different agency came from Philip Morris, because the parent company wanted to have a different agency than the other Amer brands, which were the competitors of Marlboro.[42] Modern (American) marketing called for a unique selling proposition (USP), the famous marketing strategy introduced by American advertising guru Rosser Reeves for television advertising during the 1950s.[43]

This did not automatically mean that the international companies held total control over the marketing of their subsidiaries; however, the giant tobacco company Philip Morris already had a strong control over the campaigns of their local manufactures in those days.

Neither was this the last time when Philip Morris intervened in Marlboro advertising in Finland, although Markkinointi Viherjuuri was quite free to handle their Marlboro advertising during the rest of the 1960s. In 1969, Amer and Viherjuuri introduced a competition to choose the "Finnish Marlboro Man." The competition was very popular, having over 2600 pictures sent from ordinary Finnish men. Five men were chosen, and people voted for a sheet-metal worker to become the Finnish Marlboro Man. He was a tough-looking, masculine man who drove the recently introduced Swedish car Saab 96 that was manufactured in Finland. The print ad also stated that the new Marlboro man would be seen in many contexts and on many occasions.

However, that was about the only time the Finns ever saw their Finnish Marlboro Man. In the following year, the American marketing people from Philip Morris came to Finland and said that this was not working. A Finnish urban man, who drove the first Finnish-made car, had to give way to the rugged outdoor Marlboro cowboy, who was introduced fifteen years before by Leo Burnett. Although this new cowboy campaign appeared on American television in late 1963, the campaign was not an immediate success.[44]

---

[41] Shaw and Alan, "Cigarettes," 315.

[42] Interview of advertizing art director Hannu Konttinen June 4, 2001.

[43] Fox, *Mirror Makers*, 187–88.

[44] Rutherford, *The New Icons?*, 39–40.

Finnish advertising people tried to resist the idea, saying that this kind of childish western myth would not work in Finland,[45] although the popularity of the western myth in the movies, on TV, and in popular literature was also a trend in Finland, just as in America, in the 1950s and 1960s. For instance, the American TV series *Bonanza* and *The Virginian* were very famous in Finland during the 1960s. However, the marketing people of Philip Morris argued that because it seemed that tobacco advertising was going to be banned, it was better to build a truly global brand all over the world. The images of the cowboy campaign were also easy to transform into print.

And the Americans were right. The tobacco industry was in the vanguard of global branding in the late 1960s, and Finnish advertising people had to give way to multinational marketing strategies. After the total advertising ban was introduced in many countries, the Marlboro cowboy showed its strength and became one of the longest-running successes in advertising history, a cultural icon. Merely one picture of a riding cowboy was enough to get the advertising message through.

The Marlboro cowboy is a classic example of a product personalization, when the person is the product. In this version of a personalized format, the person conveys a range of attributes to be associated with the product, like ruggedness and masculinity with Marlboro.[46] When the images of the Wild West are transferred to the world of cigarettes, they work, according to semiotics, as signifiers for the signified. The product substitutes for the mythical scene, which is meant to signify attributes such as adventure, masculinity, freedom, etc.[47]

### The Smoking Frontier Spirit under the shadow of a ban

However, the Marlboro cowboy was never seen on Finnish television, because tobacco advertising on television was banned in 1970. Even before that, tobacco advertising on television had to be produced under strict restrictions, which forced advertisers to create many kinds of often innovative solutions.

A bill to decrease smoking was introduced in the Finnish Parliament already in the mid-1950s. Especially in the early 1960s, political statements supporting a ban on cigarette advertising in television increased. The press supported the plan vigorously, because it wanted to capture all of the substantial advertising money of the tobacco companies. After the negotiations between the TV

---

[45] Konttinen interview. There were doubters in the agency, and in the company in America too. They feared that the campaign was too macho and too limited. Rutherford, *The New Icons?*, 40.

[46] See Leiss et al, *Social Communication in Advertising*, 254.

[47] Gillian Dyer, *Advertising as Communication* (London: Methuen, 1982), 123–24.

companies and the tobacco industry in 1963, the latter preferred to withdraw from television advertising. Tobacco companies became worried that the whole industry would take on a bad image.[48]

However, tobacco companies came back to television in the beginning of 1964. But now, cigarette advertising in television included many of restrictions. Tobacco commercials were not allowed to broadcast in children's and sport programs. Only one tobacco commercial was allowed to broadcast per night, and it had to be after nine o'clock. The restricted airtime was divided between the tobacco companies.[49]

But the most important aspect of producing tobacco advertising for television were the restrictions concerning what can be shown in the commercials. Humans were not allowed to show in the spots, with the exception of only one (male) arm. Or, if there were people in a commercial, they had to be in an outdoor scene, and doing nothing related to the product. Conversations and discussions were also not allowed in the commercials.

These restrictions naturally challenged the advertising people to invent new, creative solutions in the latter part of the 1960s. Due to the restrictions, cigarette advertising had to concentrate on male smokers.[50] This is why you could say that a strong emphasis on masculinity dominated Finnish cigarette commercials in the late 1960s. Also, the creativity in Finnish cigarette advertising really came to fruition in those last years of tobacco advertising on television.

Although the Marlboro cowboy came a bit late to conquer the Finnish airways, a modern version of the cigarette cowboy appeared on Finnish television screens. In order to challenge the "official" Finnish "men's cigarette" brand North State by Suomen Tupakka, and to target male smokers who preferred strong cigarettes, the main competitor of Suomen Tupakka, Amer, introduced the brand Strong in the late 1960s. The *Strong "rekkamies"* (truck driver) spot made in 1968 (SEK) starts with a scene of an approaching truck. Then comes a cut to the driver's hand as it changes the gear of the truck. After that, the hand takes a cigarette from a pack of Strong and a lighter, lightening the cigarette (off screen). The hand puts the lighter back beside another pack of Strong. The smoking hand switches back to the gear stick, and then to the car radio and turns the radio on. Fast bebop jazz starts playing in the soundtrack.

---

[48] Kortti, *Modernisaatiomurroksen kaupalliset merkit*, 333–35.

[49] Pentti Hanski, *Pöllön siivin: MTV:n vuodet 1955–1984*, ed. Markku Onttonen (Helsinki: Otava, 2001), 117.

[50] The Finnish brands that were clearly targeting women appeared in the 1970s. *Virginia Slim* by Philip Morris was introduced in 1968, and Finnish brands referred to the women's liberation movement in their advertising. However, due to restrictions, campaigns were forced to concentrate on print advertising.

The last scene shows the truck driving along the wintry highway at night. The slogan goes (freely translated): "The men who go ahead, who do things and see things, prefer a strong smoke. Filter Strong 1:84. Night and day."[51]

The connotations are clear. The truck driver, the setting, and the announcement tell whom the product targeted. The commercial uses a modern version of the lonesome cowboy—the myth of a masculine profession. Strong is the cigarette brand of the mobile, masculine professionals.

There is no doubt that the Strong campaign was influenced by Marlboro advertising. As mentioned before, the first connotations of masculinity in the Marlboro commercials go way back to the mid-1950s. The first "macho" commercial was a black-and-white *Marlboro "Smoker"* from 1955 (Leo Burnett, Inc.). In the documentary-style live-action film, a "real man" works with a sports car engine. The narrator: "This is a man who smokes Marlboro Cigarettes. What kind of a man is he?" The man: "I'm a guy who likes to work on my car. I like to take it apart and put it together. I get to working on it, and I forget where I am…what time it is. I even forget to eat." The narrator: "You don't forget to smoke, though." The man: "I always smoke when I work. They go together." As Lincoln Diamant puts it:

> This was the first of a vast group of competitive cigarette commercials that succeeded in equating masculine virility with puffing, and probably did as much for U.S. lung cancer specialists as it did for U.S. tobacco companies. The "Marlboro Man" epitomized this glamorous, independent approach—male actors swathed in a heavy dose of reality and documentary lighting. It was certainly a change-of-pace campaign for what had once been considered "a woman's cigarette."[52]

A man who smokes a masculine cigarette brand is an independent traveler of his own road, either a cowboy or a car driver disappearing into the horizon. As consumer scholars Visa Heinonen and Mika Pantzar have suggested, the strong pioneering spirit of the settlers in the American West was equally evident among Finnish peasants clearing their own wilderness. The American values of freedom and democracy were well suited to Finland, where no royal court or strong noble class ever existed, unlike in so many other European countries. Finnish society had strong peasant roots and an egalitarian tradition. In both countries, the progressive tone in the building of the nation may be related to a sort of "new

---

[51] "Miehet, jotka menevät ja tekevät, vetävät ne väkevät. Filter Strong 1:84. Night and day."
[52] Diamant, *Television's Classic Commercials*, 118–19.

frontier" ideology.[53] Perhaps the underlying concept of Finnish cigarette advertising in the 1960s can be seen as a big cowboy heading into the West.

## Conclusions: You need to step forward

Economic growth in Finland was particularly rapid in the 1960s—at least compared with other Scandinavian countries. Before the 1950s, Finland was the least developed country among the Nordic countries, but by the early 1970s it had caught up to the typical form of most industrialized societies in the world.[54] For example, the average annual rates of real national product growth by country were 5% in Finland in the 1960s and about 3,3% in Sweden, Denmark, and Norway.[55] The gross domestic product at factor cost increase was sevenfold in Finland in the period 1956–1973.

Accordingly, Finland was one of the fastest-developing industrial countries in the world during the 1960s. Enhancing urbanization and internationalization were the main goals of Finnish politicians and businessmen. Finland became, to use the phrase by John Kenneth Galbraith,[56] an "affluent society" in the fast lane. As one *Boston 100* (SEK, 1960) cigarette commercial states: "You need to step forward."

Media sociologist Michael Schudson argues that the tobacco industry is an example of an industry that increased demand, not through the intrinsic superiority of its product, but through advertising.[57] Advertising constantly plays a role in changing the nature of that demand.[58] And the demand in tobacco advertising relied predominantly on the ideology of American modernism.

America had become the symbol of modernity in post-war Europe. America meant wealth, a comfortable standard of living, freedom, and a peaceful life—

---

[53] Visa Heinonen and Mika Pantzar, "Little America: The Modernization of the Finnish Consumer Society in the 1950s and 1960s," in *Americanisation in 20th Century Europe: Business, Culture, Politics, Vol.2*, eds. Mathias Kipping and Nick Tiratsoo (Centre d'Histoire de l'Europe du Nord-Ouest, Université Charles de Gaulle Lille 3, 2002).

[54] See for example Dieter Senghaas, *The European Experience: A Historical Critique of Development Theory* (Leamington Spa/Dover and New Hampshire: Berg Publishers, 1985), 71–80.

[55] Gerold Ambrosius and William H. Hubbard, *A Social and Economic History of Twentieth-Century Europe* (London: Harvard University Press, 1989), 144.

[56] John K. Galbraith, *The Affluent Society* (London: Hamish Hamilton, 1958).

[57] Michael Schudson, *Advertising, the Uneasy Persuasion: Its Dubious Impact on American Society* (New York: Basic Books, 1984), 178–208.

[58] See Eric H. Shaw and Alan Stuart, "Cigarettes," in *The Advertising Age: Encyclopedia of Advertising. Vol 1*, eds. John McDonough and Karen Egolf (New York and London: Fitzroy Dearborn, 2003), 313.

happiness, which would be realized in consumption. America meant "the American dream." Most of these American features are also the attributes of modernism. The tobacco industry has used the images of glitter, luxury, wealth, success, romance, pride, individuality, relaxation, adventure, danger, action, freedom, pleasure, happiness, fellowship, friendship, style, sportiness, and youth as their coding categories for advertising—the modern myths that advertising makes it natural and self-evident to pursue.

In many ways, these American attributes conflict with the ideal of Nordic social democracy, as the Norwegian-born cultural philosopher Steinar Bryn has observed. Whereas America means individualism, self-realization, profit-orientation, freedom, etc., social democracy values community orientation, social responsivity, people orientation, and equality. But Bryn also shows how these Norwegian values have changed from the 1960s to the 1990s, moving towards the American values.[59]

This is obviously true in "late modern times," but the situation was different during the formative years of the Nordic welfare states. The strict restrictions, and the later total ban, on tobacco advertising can also be seen as a sign of a paternalistic society. Finnish society went through modernization in its entirety. The late 1950s and 1960s were also a period when Finland took big steps towards joining the Scandinavian welfare society. In a manner of speaking, the country caught up with the other Nordic countries in a remarkably short time in this sector of society as well. It was moving towards being a "planned society." This means, briefly, that disturbances and problems in society could be best resolved through scientific planning and organizing.

After all, "Americanization is not linear narrative of Europe becoming just like America, but rather a complex tale of how Europe has incorporated elements of the American model and redefined both them and the European contexts into which they were brought," as Mary Nolan states in her account of German imaginings of America.[60]

Cigarette advertising is a good example of this process. Despite the use of strong, often mythical, American imagery, the commercials were distinctively native adaptations of that imaginary. This likewise applies to other forms of American popular culture adopted in Europe during the 1950s and the 1960s.

---

[59] Steinar Bryn, "The Americanization of the Global Village: A Case Study of Norway," in *Networks of Americanization: Aspects of the American Influence in Sweden*, eds. Rolf Lundén and Erik Åsard (Uppsala: Uppsala University, 1992), 22, 33.
[60] Mary Nolan, "America in the German imaginations," in *Trasantions, Transgressions, Transformations: American Culture in Western Europe and Japan*, eds. Heide Ferenbach, and Uta G. Poiger (New York: Berghahn Books, 2000), 10.

For instance, the Nordic countries had their own Elvis Presley—a national version of the iconic rock-and-roll singer—and they could also have adopted others from other European countries.[61]

Although American modernization ideologies shaped Western Europe profoundly in the post-war years, there were many national peculiarities in individual European countries, including the Nordic countries, and in their individual media systems.

---

[61] See e.g., Bertel Nygaard, "Mediating Rock and Roll: Tommy Steele in Denmark, 1957–8," *Cultural History* 11, no. 1 (2022).

Chapter 8

# "We want to live. We want peace": The peace movement in the Finnish and Swedish print media, 1980–1984

Heidi Kurvinen

*University of Turku, Finland*

**Abstract:** After a decade of détente, the accelerating arms race between the United States and the Soviet Union intensified the Cold War tension from the late 1970s onwards. This resulted in mass campaigns against nuclear weapons around the Global North. In this chapter, the peace movement will be approached through reporting of Finnish and Swedish print media between 1980 and 1984. It will be argued that the Nordic news coverage shared common denominators that were not bound to national contexts, including an interest in major peace marches. At the same time, local contexts had an impact on the ways in which journalists and interviewees commented on the peace movement. The data consists of digital print media texts that are analyzed by using contextual close reading. Particular emphasis will be placed on the cultural denominators that explain the differences and similarities found in the coverage.

**Keywords:** Cold War, peace movement, journalism, print media, Finland, Sweden

\*\*\*

They traveled by train, car, ferry and private bus, by bike and on foot. Over two million people marched [for peace] all over Western Europe yesterday.[1]

The excerpt above is from an article about European peace marches, published in the Swedish tabloid *Aftonbladet* in October 1983. It illustrates the newsworthiness of transnational peace organizing, and it indicates the media's importance in reporting on the movement as part of the political landscape of the early 1980s. The accelerating arms race between the two

---

[1] Åke Malm and Rolf Svensson, "2 miljoner på marsch i Europa," *Aftonbladet*, October 23, 1983, 9.

global superpowers, the United States and the Soviet Union, had been intensifying tensions between East and West since the late 1970s. In the autumn of 1983, the European organizing was at its peak when approximately five million people protested against the plans of the North Atlantic Treaty Organization (NATO) to place intermediate nuclear munitions in Great Britain, the Netherlands, Belgium, Italy and West Germany by the end of that year.[2]

People's fear of nuclear war was most intense in countries that were directly influenced by the balancing act between the two powers. However, the Cold War also had an impact on countries at the margins of global politics, including in the Nordic region, and the mass media played a key role in this.[3] The media

---

[2] E.g. Anton Öhman, "Peace Actions and Mainstream Media: Framing Nuclear Disarmament Protests in Welfare Sweden," in *Social Movements in 1980s Sweden*, eds. Helena Hill and Andrés Brink Pinto (Cham: Palgrave Macmillan, 2023), 167–68, 172; Laura Branciforte, "The women's peace camp at Comiso, 1983: Transnational feminism and the anti-nuclear movement," *Women's History Review* 31, no. 2 (2022): 316–17; Alice Holmes Cooper, "Media framing and social movement mobilization: German peace protest against INF missiles, the Gulf War, and NATO peace enforcement in Bosnia," *European Journal of Political Research* 41 (2002): 38, 42–3, 50–1; Christoph Becker-Schaum et al., "Introduction: The Nuclear Crisis, NATO's Double-Track Decision, and the Peace Movement of the 1980s," in *The Nuclear Crisis: The Arms Race, Cold War Anxiety, and the German Peace Movement of the 1980s*, ed. Christoph Becker-Schaum et al. (New York and Oxford: Berghahn Books, 2016); Sasha Roseneil, "The Global Common: The Global, Local and Personal; Dynamics of the Women's Peace Movement of the 1980s," in *The Limits of Globalization*, ed. Alan Scott. Second edition (London and New York: Routledge, 2003), 56–7; Astrid Mignon Kirchhof, "Spanning the Globe: West German Support for the Australian Anti-Nuclear Movement," *Historical Social Research* 39, no. 1 (2014): 264–66; Jonathan Strauss, "The Australian Nuclear Disarmament Movement in the 1980s," in *Issues on War & Peace: Proceedings of the 14th Biennial Labour History Conference*, eds. Phillip Deery and Julie Kimber (Melbourne: Australian Society for the Study of Labour History, 2015), 39–50; Kathrin Fahlenbrach and Laura Stapane, "Visual and Media Strategies of the Peace Movement," in *The Nuclear Crisis: The Arms Race, Cold War Anxiety, and the German Peace Movement of the 1980s*, ed. Christoph Becker-Schaum et al. (New York and Oxford: Berghahn Books, 2016); Kim Salomon, "The Peace Movement – An Anti-Establishment Movement," *Journal of Peace Research* 23, no. 2 (1986): 115–17.

[3] Henrik G. Bastiansen and Rolf Werenskjold, "Mapping Nordic Media and the Cold War," in *Nordic Media and the Cold War*, eds. Henrik G. Bastiansen and Rolf Werenskjold (Gothenburg: Nordicom, 2015); Henrik G. Bastiansen, Martin Klimke and Rolf Werenskjold, "Introduction: Mapping the Role of the Media in the Late Cold War Methodological and Transnational Perspectives," in *Media and the Cold War in the 1980s: Between Star Wars and Glasnost*, eds. Henrik G. Bastiansen, Martin Klimke and Rolf Werenskjold (Cham: Palgrave Macmillan, 2019), 4–6; Tapio Juntunen, "'We Just Got to Keep Harping On About It': Anti-Nuclearism and the Role of Sub-Regional Arms Control Initiatives in the Nordic Countries During the Second Cold War," in *The INF Treaty of 1987: A Reappraisal*, eds.

provided an arena for the ideological struggles of the Cold War, with developments in global politics framed slightly differently in different countries.[4] This was complemented by the "ideological work" of the media—to use Stuart Hall's conceptualization—which encouraged a preferred understanding of the world by constructing the news agenda and offering the framings through which it should be interpreted.[5]

In this chapter, I focus not on the balance between the Cold War powers but on the grassroots organizing it created: the peace movement against nuclear weapons. I will analyze how the movement and its most visible form of protest, i.e. peace marches, were reported on in Finnish and Swedish print media between 1980 and 1984.[6] Adopting a transcultural approach, the chapter argues that collective organizing for world peace during this period was a "cultural thickening" that connected people around the world.[7] In terms of Nordic media, this meant that news coverage shared common denominators that were not bound to national contexts, including an interest in major peace marches. At the same time, local contexts had an impact on the ways in which journalists and interviewees commented on the movement. I will demonstrate this by examining the similarities and differences in the news coverage. These discrepancies will be explained by the countries' respective positions in the

---

Philipp Gassert, Tim Geiger and Hermann Wentker (Göttingen: Vandenhoeck & Ruprecht GmbH & Co., 2020), 216–17.

[4] About the cultural turn in Cold War Studies see Johanna Rainio-Niemi, *The Ideological Cold War: The Politics of Neutrality in Austria and Finland* (London and New York: Routledge, 2014), 10–2; Annette Vowinckel, Marcus Payk and Thomas Lindenberger, "European Cold War Culture(s)? An Introduction," in *Cold War Cultures: Perspectives on Eastern and Western European Societies*, ed. Annette Vowinckel et al. (New York: Berghahn Books, 2012), 5.

[5] Stuart Hall, "Culture, the media and the ideological effect," in *Mass Communication and Society*, eds. James Curran, Michael Gurevitch and Janet Woollacott (Beverly Hills: SAGE, 1979), 340–42.

[6] The timeframe has been selected based on the historical developments in the armament race. The tension increased in the late 1979 due to the Soviet Union's invasion in Afghanistan on December 24. NATO's plan of placing intermediate nuclear munitions in Europe made 1983 a culmination point in the collective peace organizing. See e.g. Juntunen, "We Just Got to Keep Harping On About It," 215; Holmes Cooper, "Media framing," 42–3. The selected period is supported by the share of digitized media texts that reveal an increase in reporting relating to the anti-nuclear movement until 1983 after which it started to decline. Similar interpretation has been made by Öhman in his study. See, Öhman, "Peace Actions and Mainstream Media," 172.

[7] Andreas Hepp and Nick Couldry, "What should comparative media research be comparing? Towards a transcultural approach to 'media cultures,'" in *Internationalizing Media Studies*, ed. Daya Kishan Thussu (London: Routledge, 2009), 32–47.

global political landscape and their differing journalism cultures. Hence, the arguments presented in this chapter resonate with the results of prior comparative studies on professional journalism and news values.[8] The chapter will be concluded with a discussion of culturally bound understandings of political agency, which influenced the reporting of children's role in peace organizing in the two countries.

I collected my research data from digitized newspaper and magazine archives, using culturally specific variations of search terms related to the peace movement.[9] Due to the limitations of the digitized collections at the time of this study, the data is neither comparable nor representative. First, the digital interface of the National Library of Finland (NLF) comprised only a small sample of the newspapers and magazines published in Finland during the period under study.[10] Second, the digital archive of *Helsingin Sanomat*, Finland's biggest national newspaper, had limited search functions, and for this reason, it offered less sophisticated opportunities for data collection than the NLF's digital archive. Third, the National Library of Sweden had digitized only the country's biggest newspapers, leaving Swedish magazines and local newspapers unavailable for my research. However, these limitations did not hinder my analysis because my focus is on neither quantitative comparison nor newspapers' political leanings. Instead, I view media texts as an "instrument of the society," to use Lisa Gitelman's concept.[11] The texts I analyze offer an insight into the cultural climate of Finland and Sweden during a period when collective organizing for world peace brought masses of people together in demonstrations

---

[8] About journalism cultures and comparative studies on professional journalism see e.g. Thomas Hanitzsch, "Deconstructing Journalism Culture: Toward a Universal Theory," *Communication Theory* 17, no. 4 (2007): 367–71. About news values e.g. Johan Galtung and Mari Ruge, "The Structure of Foreign News: The Presentation of the Congo, Cuba and Cyprus Crises in Four Norwegian Newspapers," *Journal of International Peace Research*, no. 2 (1965): 64–90; Tony Harcup and Deirdre O'Neill, "What is News? Galtung and Ruge Revisited," *Journalism Studies* 2, no. 2 (2001): 261–80; Tony Harcup and Deirdre O'Neill, "What is News? News values revisited (again)," *Journalism Studies* 18, no. 12 (2017): 1470–488.

[9] For instance, in Finnish the keywords such as 'rauhanviikko' (peace week), 'rauhanpäivä' (peace day), 'rauhanmarssi' (peace march), 'rauhankulkue' (peace train) and 'rauhanjuna' (peace train) offered a rich material whereas in Swedish better search words turned out to be 'fredståg' (peace train), 'fredsdemonstration' (demonstration for peace) and 'fredsaktion' (peace action).

[10] For example, the leading Finnish-language national daily, *Helsingin Sanomat*, or any of the Finnish-language newspapers with left-wing leanings were not digitally available through the NLF when the data was collected. Additionally, the availability of Swedish-language newspapers was much better than the Finnish-language ones.

[11] Lisa Gitelman, *Always Already New: Media, History, and the Data of Culture* (Cambridge, MA: MIT Press, 2006).

and other activities around the world. I analyze the data by using contextual close reading,[12] emphasizing the cultural denominators that explain the differences and similarities found in the coverage.[13]

## Heightening interest in 1981

The 1970s and 1980s witnessed a new wave of globalization, which resulted in a more transnational nature of social change organizing. Simultaneously, the accelerating circulation of mediated knowledge accentuated the influence of public opinion in processes that crossed national borders.[14] Read in this context it becomes understandable that the ideological dimensions of the Cold War conflict globally fostered a modified interest in pacifism: an ideology with its roots in the eighteenth century. It was accompanied with activism that arose from other social movements, such as the women's movement and the green movement, which combined their understanding of world peace with the ideological basis of their own. The different strands were unified by mass campaigns against nuclear weapons creating an ideological vacuum that framed people's lived experiences around the world.[15] Peace marches organized during the annual United Nations (UN) Disarmament Week, launched in 1979, were the most visible part of this early 1980s activism.[16]

---

[12] E.g. Hannu Salmi, *What is Digital History?* (Cambridge and Medford: Polity Press, 2021).

[13] A similar kind of an approach is used in my forthcoming book titled *Feminism in Finnish Print Media, 1968–1985.*

[14] Akira Iriye, *Global Community: The Role of International Organizations in the Making of the Contemporary World* (Berkeley: University of California Press, 2002), 113–56; Emmanuel Mourlon-Druol, "'Managing from the Top': Globalisation and the Rise of Regular Summitry, Mid-1970s–early 1980s," *Diplomacy & Statecraft* 23, no. 4 (2012): 680–81; Juntunen, "We Just Got to Keep Harping On About It," 215–16.

[15] Salomon, "The Peace Movement," 125; Martin Ceadel, "Pacifism and pacificism," in *The Cambridge History of Twentieth-Century Political Thought*, eds. Terence Ball and Rickhard Bellamy (Cambridge: Cambridge University Press, 2008), 475–76, 481–82; Iriye, *Global Community*, 160–61; Lawrence S. Wittner, "The Forgotten Years of the World Nuclear Disarmament Movement, 1975–78," *Journal of Peace Research* 40, no. 4 (2003): 438–39, 451–52.

[16] Aleksander N. Kalyadin, "Role of Non-Governmental Organizations in UN Activities for Peace and Disarmament," *Bulletin of Peace Proposals* 18:3 (1987): 394–96; Jette Baagø Klockmann, "Remembrance Diplomacy by the Mayors of Hiroshima and Nagasaki in the UN, 1976–2015," *The International History Review* 40, no. 3 (2018): 527–28.

The threat of a new world war was constantly present, including in the neutral countries of Finland and Sweden.[17] This allowed the peace movement around the world to bring together a wide spectrum of people with diverse backgrounds, ranging from traditional peace organizations to trade unions, professional groups and churches,[18] and this included the establishment of variety of peace groups that also fostered Nordic collaboration.[19] Some of the Nordic groups, such as Journalists for peace saw working actively to prevent the nuclear war as their shared ethical responsibility.[20] Nonetheless, Swedes' and Finns' experiences were shaped by the two countries' respective geopolitical positions,[21] which also influenced the press coverage of the peace movement.[22]

In Finland, the early discussions of the strengthening peace movement often used the rhetoric of the movement's power to connect people of different political persuasions.[23] Eila Jokela, a retired journalist and former editor-in-chief of the popular women's magazine *Kotiliesi*, commented on activities during the first UN Disarmament Week in Finland in 1981:

---

[17] Vowinckel et al., "European Cold War Culture(s)," 1–2; Rainio-Niemi, *The Ideological Cold War*, 3–4, 6, 12–3; Bastiansen, Klimke and Werenskjold, "Introduction;" Cecilia Åse, "Ship of Shame: Gender and Nation in Narratives of the 1981 Soviet Submarine Crisis in Sweden," *Journal of Cold War Studies* 18, no.1 (2016): 118; Marie Cronqvist, "Survival in the Welfare Cocoon: The Culture of Civil Defense in Cold War Sweden," in *Cold War Cultures: Perspectives on Eastern and Western European Societies*, ed. Annette Vowinckel et al. (New York: Berghahn Books, 2012), 197–98.

[18] Becker-Schaum et al., "Introduction," 9–10; Strauss, "The Australian Nuclear Disarmament Movement."

[19] Jon Grepstad, "The Peace Movement in the Nordic Countries," *International Peace Research Newsletter*, no. 4 (1982): 14; Niels Jorgen Haagerup, "The Nordic Peace Movements," in *European Peace Movements and the Future of the Western Alliance*, eds. Walter Laqueur and Robert Hunter (New Brunswick, N.J.: Transaction, 1988); Irene Andersson, "Kolleger! Det är dags att handla nu! Lärare för freds bildande och yrkesetikens betydelse, 1982–1984," in *En historiker korsar sitt spår: En vänbok till Roger Johansson om att lära sig av historien och lära ut historia*, eds. Katarina Blennow, Pål Brunnström and David Örbring (Malmö: Malmö university, 2019), 215.

[20] Andersson, "Kolleger!," 210–11. See also "Toimittajat tukemaan rauhantyötä," *Etelä-Suomen Sanomat*, March 19, 1982, 9; "Journalister för fred: Ingen kan vara neutral inför kärnvapenhotet," *Västra Nyland*, June 23, 1982, 1, 6; "Santti: Väestönsuojelu luo turvallisuutta," *Etelä-Suomen Sanomat*, October 28, 1982, 13; "Journalister samlas till fredskongress," *Österbottningen*, October 11, 1983, 5.

[21] Juntunen, "We Just Got to Keep Harping On About It," 235.

[22] National differences in news coverage of the peace movements have also been noticed in previous studies. See, e.g. Öhman, "Peace Actions and Mainstream Media," 165–66.

[23] E.g. Sirpa Rasimus, "Rauhanliike näkee nyt idänkin aseiden uhkan," *Etelä-Suomen Sanomat*, November 25, 1981, 15.

The image of Senate Square was unforgettable: over 30,000 participants. [...] Those tens of thousands of people were not on the move against the Soviet Union or the United States. Instead, they were against nuclear weapons and the arms race and in favor of general disarmament.[24]

Jokela's text captures the early signs of the mass organizing in Finland and a widening of the ideological spectrum of the peace movement's actions, as was noted by *Suomen Kuvalehti*, a weekly magazine with a conservative tone.[25] As more and more Finnish people joined in the peace actions, the movement became a newsworthy topic in and of itself. In October 1981, the marches brought together thousands of people around the country, and the coverage was framed by their news value: it was the first time that signs of a mass movement had been seen in Finland.[26]

Signs of awakening interest in the peace movement were also visible in Sweden, as *Dagens Nyheter* indicated in a 1981 article about a demonstration in Stockholm: "It was a short demonstration march from Kungsträdgården to Norra Latin. Approximately 5,000 people participated. Many of those watching from the pavement joined the march."[27] The widening base of peace organizing was the main framing in Sweden. However, the journalistic gaze on local organizing was initially more critical in Sweden than in Finland. For instance, *Dagens Nyheter* quoted a German protestor, according to whom the Swedish movement was surprisingly small compared with those in other countries: "Isn't there more interest in peace in Sweden? In Bonn, there were 30,000 of us. Here, it is only a couple of hundred. And the peace meeting in Stockholm a couple of days ago attracted only 84 participants."[28] This criticism targeted the Swedish people in general, whom the interviewee portrayed as less active than people in Western Europe. By including the quote in the news, the reporter seems to suggest that the so-called 'Swedish middle way' of the Cold War era

---

[24] Eila Jokela, "Elämän puolesta," *Uusi Suomi*, November 7, 1981, 2.

[25] Leena Häyrinen, "On isänmaallista edistää rauhaa," *Suomen Kuvalehti*, no. 51–52, 1981, 10–4.

[26] E.g. "Rauhanmarssista tuli yleisömenestys," *Etelä-Suomen Sanomat*, October 29, 1981, 12; "120 000 marssi rauhan puolesta," *Länsi-Savo*, October 29, 1981, 11; "Ennätysmäärä rauhanmarssijoita: 120 000 vaati jäähyväisiä aseille," *Helsingin Sanomat*, October 29, 1981, 14; "Ge livet en chans," *Folktidningen Ny Tid*, November 5, 1981, 1, 15; "Då 120 000 marcherade för fred," *Arbetartidningen Enhet*, November 6, 1981, 8.

[27] Birgitta Nyblom, "5 000 i fredsmarch: Det är ett svek att tiga," *Dagens Nyheter*, October 25, 1981, 32.

[28] Kjell Löfberg, "Örebro: Gatuteater, allsång," *Dagens Nyheter*, October 25, 1981, 32.

that completed the geopolitical neutrality with pacificism and embedded it in the Swedish national identity had passivated citizens in their peace quest.[29]

Actually, the 1981 submarine crisis, in which a Soviet submarine became stranded in Swedish waters on October 27, would heighten the fear of nuclear war in Sweden,[30] and this had an effect on the scale of grassroots organizing. According to Tapio Litmanen, a total of approximately 200,000 people participated in various peace marches in Finland during the UN Disarmament Weeks between 1981 and 1984.[31] By comparison, as many as 100,000 people joined a single peace protest in Gothenburg in May of 1982.[32] Although the Gothenburg march was part of an all Nordic peace meeting demanding a nuclear free region, the initiative was launched and organized by local peace groups demonstrating a clear difference in the activity of organizing in Finland and Sweden.[33] In fact, the peace movement was collectively nominated as the "Swede of the year" in 1983 and compared to other European movements— including the Finnish one—its media portrayal was immensely positive, as Anton Öhman has pointed out.[34]

---

[29] The idea of the Swedish middle way derives back to the 1930s and it has been given different meanings in different historical contexts. E.g. Carl Marklund, "The Social Laboratory, the Middle Way and the Swedish Model: Three frames for the image of Sweden," *Scandinavian Journal of History* 34, no. 3 (2009): 274; Emma Rosengren, *Gendering Nuclear Disarmament: Identity and Disarmament in Sweden during the Cold War* (Stockholm: Stockholm university, 2020), 60–1.

[30] Rosengren, *Gendering Nuclear Disarmament*, 137–41; Åse, "Ship of Shame."

[31] Tapio Litmanen, "International Anti-Nuclear Movements in Finland, France and the United States," *Peace Research* 30, no. 4 (1998): 6. The demonstrations had their peak in 1983 when approximately 200 000 people participated in peace marches around Finland. In 1982, the number had been slightly lower and the interest towards the marches diminished considerably in 1984. See e.g. Esa Kero, "Rauha hei!," *Helsingin Sanomat*, October 31, 1982, 26; "200 000 ihmistä marssi Suomessa rauhan puolesta: Mikkelin rauhankulkueessa ennätykselliset 2 000 ihmistä," *Länsi-Savo*, October 27, 1983, 1, 4; "Yli 200 000 rauhanmarssilla," *Etelä-Suomen Sanomat*, October 27, 1983, 1.

[32] Håkan Thörn, "Nya sociala rörelser, globalisering och den sociologiska eurocentrismen," *Sociologisk Forskning*, no. 2 (2003): 4. About the news coverage e.g. Margareta Artsman, "100 000 i manifestationen mot kärnvapen i Europa," *Svenska Dagbladet*, May 16, 1982.

[33] Katsuya Kodama, *Peace on the move: A sociological survey of the members of Swedish peace organizations.* (Stockholm: Almqvist & Wiksell International, 1990), 48; Anna-Lisa Björneberg, "Internationella kvinnoförbundet för fred och frihet: Göteborgskretsen," in *"Så här kan vi inte ha det!": Fem kvinnoorganisationer i Göteborg: 100 års ideellt arbete, när samhället svek*, ed. Anna-Lisa Björneberg et al. (Gothenburg: Göteborgskvinnor i rörelser, 2019), 76–8; Öhman, "Peace Actions and Mainstream Media," 178–80.

[34] Öhman, "Peace Actions and Mainstream Media," 165–66. See also June Roos, "Årets svensk: Fredsrörelsen!," *Aftonbladet*, September 3, 1983; Ulf Nilsson, "PR-slaget om kärnvapen har börjat," *Expressen*, January 6, 1983.

Arguably, the two countries' respective geopolitical positions explain the differences in the selected framings. Finland was more vulnerable to Soviet politics, which made the peace organizing a heated question in domestic politics.[35] Particularly, the traditional peace organizing, which was allegedly in the hands of the extreme political left, caused agitation in the political right. Corresponding with Sharon D. Stones' findings of the Toronto press,[36] the peace movement was, thus, distinctively connoted with communism in newspapers that had right-wing leanings.[37] Resulting from this, newspapers across the political spectrum emphasized the broad nature of the 1980s mass organizing, as was mentioned earlier. Simultaneously, the topic bore potential tensions that increased its newsworthiness[38] an example of which is the debate of the significance—or not—of the 10 days travel of the so-called peace train organized by Finnish artists in 1982.[39]

In Sweden, the peace organizing was more connected to the overall popularization of alternative movements and, as such,[40] the all-encompassing nature of the domestic demonstrations did not have as a significant purpose in the news coverage as it had in Finland. Even when Swedish journalists acknowledged how the quest for peace resonated with increasing numbers of citizens, their main interest was in a demonstration's message rather than its power to connect people across political divides.[41] In some articles, journalists went as far as openly criticized the idea that the anti-nuclear movement had allegedly permeated the whole of society.[42] More often the articles, however,

---

[35] Litmanen, "International Anti-Nuclear Movements," 3–6.

[36] Sharon D. Stones, "The Peace Movement and Toronto Newspapers," *Canadian Journal of Communication* 14, no. 1 (1989): 65–8.

[37] E.g. Esko Salminen, "Prof. L.A. Puntila: Kolmas maailmansota mahdoton ajatus," *Uusi Suomi*, September 1, 1979, 13; Antti Blåfield, "Tavoitteet ovat samat, keinoista kiistellään: Kenelle kuuluu yksinoikeus rauhaan," *Suomen Kuvalehti*, no. 51–52 (1980), 12–3; Ismo Airinen, "Stalinistit eivät johda Rauhanpuolustajia," *Uusi Suomi*, October 25, 1981, 4 (letter-to-the-editor); Timo Lipponen, "Pääsihteeri Jorma Hentilä: Rauha ei ole kenenkään yksinoikeus. 'Neuvostoliittoakin on voitava arvostella,'" *Uusi Suomi*, October 3, 1982, 16–7.

[38] E.g. Galtung and Ruge, "The Structure of Foreign News," 64–90; Harcup and O'Neill, "What is News? Galtung and Ruge Revisited," 261–80; Harcup and O'Neill, "What is News? News values revisited (again)," 1470–488.

[39] E.g. "Rauhanjuna höyryää," *Uusi Suomi*, April 13, 1982, 2 (editorial); Vesa-Pekka Koljonen, "Päivästä päivään," *Helsingin Sanomat*, April 19, 1982, 15; "Kiskot kolkkaa rauhaa, rau-haa: Sanoma saavutti Lahden," *Etelä-Suomen Sanomat*, April 25, 1982, 3; Jarmo Hakanen, "Jukka Tarkka: Toisinajatteleva tohtori," *Apu*, no. 18 (1982), 30–1.

[40] About Katsuya Kodoma's argumentation see, Öhman, "Peace Actions and Mainstream Media," 168.

[41] Staffan Larsson, "De marchade för fred och rättvisa," *Expressen*, May 17, 1982.

[42] E.g. Björn Vinberg, "I går var vi 70 000 duvor," *Expressen*, May 16, 1982, 32.

revealed the sympathies of the journalists toward the quest for peace, showing traces of advocacy journalism. These news items were aimed at motivating enlightened citizens to act as a united front.[43] Reporting on the peace movement was, thus, also influenced by national journalism cultures that seemed to allow more diverse and sometimes contradictory voices in Sweden than in Finland. They also explain the ways in which the connection of the local organizing and the transnational movement were presented in the studied countries, as I will now show.

### Different ways of framing the transnational movement

The peace movement was inherently transnational but activist practices actualized in local contexts.[44] This interconnection between the global and local is present in the Nordic news coverage but, interestingly, Finnish and Swedish journalists approached it in different ways.

The Swedish press emphasized the movement's transnational nature by accompanying news items and columns about local demonstrations with accounts of vast demonstrations in other European cities.[45] An early example is an article published in *Expressen* in 1981. The article included three major images that showed the differences in size among demonstrations in Stockholm, London and Rome. The main text emphasized the shared global experience: "The slogans were the same in London, Rome and Stockholm and all the other cities: Stop the nuclear weapons. We want to live. We want peace."[46] The connection between the Swedish demonstrations and the transnational movement was strengthened by the revelation that one of the speakers in Stockholm had been Bernard Benson author of *The Peace Book*, a popular book aimed at children. Benson's presence linked Swedes to the transnational chain

---

[43] Rasmus Rønlev, "Aktivistisk journalistik med måde: Når journalister hyldes for at tilskrive sociale bevægelser retorisk handlekraft," *Rhetorica Scandinavica* 27, no. 86 (2023): 122–40; Declan Fahy, "Objectivity, False Balance, and Advocacy in News Coverage of Climate Change," in *Oxford Research Encyclopedia of Climate Science* (Oxford: Oxford University Press, 2017); Öhman "Peace Actions and Mainstream Media," 173–76, 184.

[44] E.g. Kirchhof, "Spanning the Globe," 254–57, 264–70; Branciforte, "The women's peace camp."

[45] E.g. "Fredsdagen," *Expressen*, October 25, 1982; "Fredsrörelsen: Ett mäktigt vapen," *Expressen*, January 16, 1983; "För fredens skull," *Expressen*, October 22, 1983; "Firade FN-dagen med fredsprogram; Eva Bruno, Fredsaktivister i ambassadsblockad: 224 greps av polisen," *Göteborgs-Posten*, October 25, 1983, 12.

[46] "Överallt marscherade man för freden," *Expressen*, October 25, 1981, 7.

of grassroots organizing that had actualized around the world since the book's publication in 1980.[47]

The interconnectedness between domestic and transnational demonstrations was also emphasized in 1983 when the leading morning paper *Dagens Nyheter* published a short article about a demonstration in Stockholm. It reported that 50,000 people had gathered at Norra Bantorget and formed a human chain—a transnational protest form in itself—between the US and Soviet embassies. Interestingly, the article was not the main story on the page.[48] Instead, the lead article described the demonstrations in West Germany while smaller articles appeared on the same page about demonstrations in London, Rome, New York, Vienna and Prague.[49] As proximity is one of the criteria that increases the newsworthiness of an event, a different page structure would have made more sense from the point of view of craft practice.[50] Previous research has also shown that it was symbolic actions such as human chains that maintained the movement's media visibility.[51] Hence, the explanation for the transnational emphasis needs to be found in the framing cues, to use Öhman's reasoning. By connecting the Swedish protests with similar demonstrations in other European cities, these relatable news items offered motivation for readers to act, and aligned Swedish neutrality with the aims of the transnational peace movement.[52]

In Finland, too, the peace movement's transnational nature was mentioned when journalists described collective organizing for world peace in general.[53] For instance, sociologist Erik Allardt, interviewed in *Helsingin Sanomat* in 1982, pointed out the role of television in the transnational circulation of activist practices:

---

[47] E.g. "Faktabetonat hos Schildts," *Hufvudstadsbladet*, September 10, 1981, 3; Birgitta Boucht, "Vi vill leva!," *Hufvudstadsbladet*, October 25, 1981, 3; "Bensonin Rauhankirja suomeksi," *Uusi Suom*, June 19, 1982, 12. The book was translated in Swedish in 1981 and it also reached Finnish-Swedish audience. The Finnish translation appeared in 1982.

[48] Dag Bjerke, "Palme övertalades att hålla kort fredstal," *Svenska Dagbladet*, October 23, 1983, 5. See also "Fredståg mot Öst och Väst," *Svenska Dagbladet*, October 23, 1983, 1.

[49] Thomas Lundin, "Västtyska fredsvecka fick kraftfull final;" Ingmar Lindmarker, "Karnevalsyra i London-tåg;" Gustav von Platen, "Splittrad marsch i Paris;" "Halv-miljon i Rom-protest;" "Felande länkar i New York;" "100 000 deltog i marsch i Wien;" "Fredsprotest stoppad i Prag," *Svenska Dagbladet*, October 23, 1983, 5.

[50] Galtung and Ruge, "The Structure of Foreign News;" Harcup and O'Neill, "What is News?"

[51] Fahlenbrasch and Stapane, "Visual and Media Strategies," 222–23.

[52] Öhman, "Peace Actions and Mainstream Media," 174, 177–78.

[53] Matti Klemola, "Sodan pelko marssittaa Eurooppaa," *Helsingin Sanomat*, December 20, 1981, 29; "200 000 ihmistä marssi Suomessa rauhan puolesta: Mikkelin rauhankulkueessa ennätykselliset 2 000 ihmistä," *Länsi-Savo* October 27, 1983, 4.

[...] people who marched in Helsinki on Wednesday might have seen on television the previous Sunday how people in Stockholm had formed a human chain from the Soviet embassy to the US one. This is how people learn, how they find models for their behavior and gain the courage to act in a similar way.[54]

Interestingly, however, huge demonstrations abroad did not receive the same visibility as they did in Sweden: the Finnish media seem to have missed the transnational potential of the coverage. Instead, Finnish papers represented the peace movement from a specifically local vantage point. Reporting focused on local marches and demonstrations in other parts of Finland, although journalists did briefly point out the UN-issued slogans for each year's march.[55] Separate articles about foreign demonstrations appeared, but they were not connected to the Finnish organizing, and they usually did not include any images, unlike the reports on Finnish marches.[56]

This can partly be explained by craft practices. Unlike the Swedish marches, the Finnish marches did not take place on the same days as demonstrations in

---

[54] Matti Klemola, "Rauhanliikkeessä piilee arvaamaton voima," *Helsingin Sanomat*, October 31, 1982, 25.

[55] E.g. "Ennätysmäärä rauhanmarssijoita: 120 000 vaati jäähyväisiä aseille," *Helsingin Sanomat*, October 29, 1981, 14; "Ge livet en chans," *Folktidningen Ny Tid*, November 5, 1981, 1, 15; "Då 120 000 marcherade för fred," *Arbetartidningen Enhet*, November 6, 1981, 8; "Sade haittasi rauhanmarssia: Tuhansia marssijoita ja katselijoita Lahdessa," *Etelä-Suomen Sanomat*, October 28, 1982, 13; "Miljoonia askeleita rauhan puolesta," *Helsingin Sanomat*, October 28, 1982, 8; "Över 200 000 tågade i Finland, *Vasabladet*, October 27, 1983, 1, 11; "'Jorden hotas – den borde botas!'" *Åbo Underrättelser*, October 25, 1984, 1, 11; "Mikko Juva Loviisassa: Rauhanliikkeen oltava realistinen," *Etelä-Suomen Sanomat*, October 27, 1983, 12; "Yli 200 000 rauhanmarssilla," *Etelä-Suomen Sanomat*, October 27, 1983, 1; "Lähes 400 hankolaista mukana rauhankulkueessa," *Hangon Lehti*, October 27, 1984, 17.

[56] E.g. Pentti Sadeniemi, "L-Saksan historian suurin rauhanmielenosoitus Bonnissa," *Helsingin Sanomat*, October 11, 1981, 38; "250 000 i Bonn mot kärnvapen," *Vasabladet*, October 11, 1981, 1, 9; "Valtava marssi," *Länsi-Savo*, October 11, 1981, 1; "Mielenosoittajat vaativat ydinaseetonta Pohjolaa," *Etelä-Suomen Sanomat*, October 11, 1981, 14; "Sadattuhannet marssivat ydinaseita vastaan," *Etelä-Suomen Sanomat*, October 25, 1981, 17; "Rauhanmarssit keräsivät tuhansia mielenosoittajia," *Uusi Suomi*, October 26, 1981, 10; "Europa tågade för fred," *Vasabladet*, October 23, 1983, 1, 12; "Hela Västeuropa på fötter: Enorm protestaktion möter eurorobotarna," *Borgåbladet*, October 22, 1983, 1; "Euroopan rauhanmarssit keräsivät kaksi miljoonaa osanottajaa," *Etelä-Suomen Sanomat*, October 23, 1981, 13.

other countries.[57] The different timing of the protests, thus, separated the news from one another. Furthermore, most Finnish newsrooms relied on international news agencies in their reporting on foreign demonstrations whereas local gatherings were followed by their own reporters. This corresponds with smaller Swedish newspapers, which—unlike *Dagens Nyheter* and other national dailies—did not have their own correspondents in big European cities to report directly on foreign demonstrations but focused instead on local actions.[58] An additional explanation can be found in the conservative reporting of foreign news and the Cold War, which continued to define Finnish journalism in the early 1980s.[59]

Ultimately, however, the main reason for the differences between the Finnish and Swedish coverage may concern different understandings of the relevance of local people's collective organizing for world peace: there seems to have been a stronger need to emphasize national differences in Finland than in Sweden. For example, the awakening of the anti-nuclear movement in other countries sparked a discussion of the ways in which such demonstrations suited—or did not suit—the Finnish mentality. Articles pointed out Finland's unique position in world politics, and a particular kind of Finnishness was placed at the center of local peace organizing.[60] Foreign demonstrations were also used to contrast with the movement in Finland: they showed that Finnish organizing was peaceful in nature and brought people from different backgrounds together. A prominent example is a comment made by a journalist in *Suomen Kuvalehti* in 1983: "Peace Week has caused some rather unpeaceful fights between protestors and police in West Germany. Here, the peace movement's action week will be held next week—much more peacefully, of course."[61] There are obvious reasons for this framing that emphasized the restlessness of German protestors: the shared experience of nuclear fear was a result of global

---

[57] E.g. Vesa Santavuori, "Suurmielenosoitus rauhan puolesta Tukholmassa," *Helsingin Sanomat*, October 25, 1982, 21; Lauri Karén, "Rauhanliike ei ole Ranskaa heilauttanut," *Helsingin Sanomat*, October 22, 1983, 25; Pentti Sadeniemi, "Rauhanliikkeen tempaus vaisu," *Helsingin Sanomat*, October 22, 1983, 25; "Marsseilla nähdään sosialisteja," *Helsingin Sanomat*, October 22, 1983, 25.

[58] E.g. "25 000 'byggde bro' – Vi förklarar fred mot krig," *Göteborgs-Posten*, October 23, 1983, 15.

[59] Juha Herkman, "The Structural Transformation of The Democratic Corporatist Model: The Case of Finland," *Javnost – The Public: Journal of the European Institute for Communication and Culture* 16, no. 4 (2009): 73–90.

[60] E.g. "Rauhanpuolustajien puheenjohtaja Paavo Rintala: SKP:n riidat vaikuttavat," *Suomen Kuvalehti*, no. 51–52 (1980), 14–5; Hannu Savola, "Marssi ei edistä rauhaa," *Suomen Kuvalehti*, no. 10 (1983), 28–30.

[61] Arja Piispa, "Rauhan vuoksi marssitaan keskiviikkona," *Apu*, no. 42 (1983), 40.

developments that had led millions of people to join peace marches around the world. However, the fear was more present in countries such as West Germany, which was on the front line of the planned missile program.[62]

Whereas foreign demonstrators occasionally received affective interpretations in Finnish media texts, local protestors were presented as committed and conformity-seeking as can be seen in *Uusi Suomi*'s quote: "Despite a few painted faces and the Latin rhythms played by some musicians, the demonstrators marched for peace with rather stern faces."[63] The seriousness of the peace quest was particularly evident in the debate of the 1982 peace train. The effort was depicted in a lively and nearly joyful manner but,[64] according to the critique, its significance was questionable since it did not promote the peace work in a proper, i.e. serious, manner.[65] The disparity between the affective framing of foreign demonstrations and the calm protests in Finland becomes particularly clear if we use the Swedish data as a point of contrast. While the majority of Swedish articles represented the demonstrations' upbeat and peaceful nature,[66] people's nuclear fears were also discussed in the local context.[67] The coverage often zoomed in the opinions of a common Swede and as such, the peace protests were presented as a shared experience of the people.[68]

A possible explanation for the differences in connecting the local organizing with the transnational one can be found in the political traditions of the two countries. Neutrality was part of Swedish identity; hence, peace organizing could be woven into the country's position in world politics. Sweden actively promoted détente between the two poles of the Cold War, and it was engaged in disarmament; both positions had emerged from the country's foreign-policy

---

[62] Roseneil, "The Global Common," 57, 61; Holmes Cooper, "Media framing," 50–2.

[63] "'Kivaa elämää ei saa pamauttaa,'" *Uusi Suomi*, October 27, 1983, 8.

[64] Markus Jokela, "Sata taiteilijaa kymmenen päivän kiertueella: Rauhanjuna puksutti ensimmäisen etappinsa," *Helsingin Sanomat*, April 17, 1982, 16; Mattiesko Hytönen, "Tarkoin seurattu juna," *Helsingin Sanomat*, April 18, 1982, 29.

[65] *Uusi Suomi*, April 13, 1982, 2 (editorial); Martti Valkonen, "Narsisseja rauhanjunalle," *Uusi Suomi*, April 21, 1982, 2; "Kiskot kolkkaa rau-haa, rau-haa: Sanoma saavutti Lahden," *Etelä-Suomen Sanomat*, April 25, 1982, 3; Jarmo Hakanen, "Jukka Tarkka: Toisinajatteleva tohtori," *Apu*, no. 18 (1982), 30–1.

[66] E.g. Gert Malmberg, "Tusentals på fredsmöte i Göteborg," *Göteborgs-Posten*, October 23, 1983, 14; Tiuu Gräslund, "Samba för freden," *Expressen*, October 26, 1984, 20. See also Öhman, "Peace Actions and Mainstream Media," 176–78, 180.

[67] Harald Hamrin, "Efter ubåtsaffärerna: Fredsrörelsen växer," *Dagens Nyheter*, May 8, 1983, 10. See also Annika Hultén, "Slåss för livet: 'Man måste bli livrädd för att börja kämpa,'" *Aftonbladet*, May 23, 1983, 25.

[68] Öhman, "Peace Actions and Mainstream Media," 180–81.

tradition of non-alignment and neutrality.[69] In Finland, neutrality was a more pragmatic choice.[70] Consequently, the Finnish peace movement was tied up with the country's geopolitical position, and this placed the Finnish movement at a distance from protestors in other countries. The press coverage suggested that this was due to self-censorship in relation to the Soviet Union. Journalist Martti Valkonen captured the essence of Finnish organizing when pointing out that the peace work was done in the shadows:

> The work for peace, if anything, should withstand the daylight. The purpose of a peace march that is held in the darkness of a weekday evening [as happened in Finland, unlike other European countries, where demonstrations took place on Sunday afternoons] seems mostly to be to scare its participants.[71]

Another factor that clearly distinguishes Swedish and Finnish articles is the role played by children in the portrayal of the movement. Arguably, this was a result of the two countries' different cultural understandings of children's political agency, as I will show next.

### Child-specific voices and adults' protectionist anxiety

"Of course, children can act on behalf of the quest for peace. They can demonstrate, for example."[72] This *Dagens Nyheter* caption accompanied an image of schoolchildren holding placards. Similar images appeared in both countries, resonating with the overall iconography of the peace movement, in which children, women and the elderly took center stage.[73] However, the Swedish press gave children a more active role in the movement than did the Finnish press. For example, the tabloid *Aftonbladet* portrayed children as active agents in a two-page article about a press conference on a peace action organized by schoolchildren in 1982. The article included quotes from children about

[69] Åse, "Ship of Shame," 117; Bo Strath, "Neutralitet som självförstålse," in *Den svenska framgångssagan?*, eds. Kurt Almqvist and Kaj Glans (Stockholm: Bokforlaget Fisher, 2001), 195.
[70] Rainio-Niemi, *The Ideological Cold War.*
[71] Martti Valkonen, "Rauha kestää päivänvalon," *Uusi Suomi*, November 2, 1982, 2.
[72] Kerstin Vinterhed, "Vad kan barn göra för freden?," *Dagens Nyheter*, February 27, 1983, 11.
[73] Öhman, "Peace Actions and Mainstream Media," 181.

their ideas for peace organizing: Magnus, Peter and Erika, for example, said their plan was to "demonstrate and write poems to end war."[74]

Children's active agency was supported by major campaigns in Swedish schools, which encouraged children to participate in peace organizing by making their own demands. In early 1980s Finland, peace education was similarly embedded in the curriculum, and school classes took part in various events related to the peace movement.[75] In 1982, the local newspaper *Länsi-Savo* remarked on the young participants in a peace march: "It was striking that so many young people were active in both Pieksämäki and Mikkeli. The local school organized a spontaneous peace demonstration in Puumala. The students did a short peace march in the village center."[76] As this quote indicates, the schoolchildren's participation was noted from a journalist's eyewitness perspective. Although the article was accompanied by a picture of two small children in pushchairs holding up a peace symbol, the children's own voices were not to be heard. Similarly, in 1983, another article in *Länsi-Savo* used an image of demonstrators with small children and holding a placard with the words: "My child is alive, how long?"[77] The articles thus acknowledged the peace movement's cross-generational nature,[78] but they were unable to embrace the active agency of young children.

---

[74] Marianne Hühne, "För vår skull, sluta kriga! Barnen som ska ta över och sköta jorden' kallade till presskonferens," *Aftonbladet*, October 22, 1982, 24–5. About articles that include children's active agency see also Pia Nordström, "Vi vill ha fred!," *Expressen*, May 11, 1981, 20; "'Tjuvstart i fredsmarchen,'" *Göteborgs-Posten*, May 12, 1982, 7; Ingegerd Ekstrand, "Idag tågar 4000 barn genom Stockholm," *Aftonbladet*, October 22, 1982, 24–5; "Inför internationella nedrustningsdagen: 6 000 elever gav freden en chans," *Dagens Nyheter*, October 23, 1982; "En kedja för freden," *Svenska Dagbladet*, October 25, 1982, 1; Thomas Lerner, "De sjöng för freden," *Dagens Nyheter*, October 28, 1982, 144; "Det borde all världens statsmän se," *GT*, September 1, 1983, 14; Bo Engzell, "2000 skolbarn i samling för fred," *Dagens Nyheter*, December 10, 1983, 22; "'Fåglar' frös för freden," *Göteborgs-Posten*, April 12, 1984, 60.
[75] Andersson, "Kolleger!;" Bengt Thelin, "Early tendencies of peace education in Sweden," *Peabody Journal of Education* 71, no. 3 (1996): 95–110; Åke Bjerstedt, *"Peace Education" – "Friedenserzihung" – "Education de la Paix": Fredsorienterande aktiviteter i skolan i olika länder vid 1980-talet mitt* (Lund: Lund university, 1986).
[76] "Puumalassa spontaani rauhanmarssi: Mikkelin ja Pieksämäen nuoret aktiivisia," *Länsi-Savo*, October 28, 1982, 3. See also "Taiteilijoiden suurtyö: Rauhanjuna matkaan," *Länsi-Savo*, April 16, 1982, 8; Kristiina Alapuro, "Rauhan asema," *Suomen Kuvalehti*, no. 17 (1982), 6–9.
[77] *Länsi-Savo*, 27.10.1983, 4. See also "Sade haittasi rauhanmarssia: Tuhansia marssijoita ja katselijoita Lahdessa," *Etelä-Suomen Sanomat*, October 28, 1982, 13.
[78] Fahlenbrach and Stapane, "Visual and Media Strategies," 223–24.

Even children's fear was framed by adults' point of view in Finland. Eila Jokela depicted adults' anxieties in *Uusi Suomi* in 1982: "Over the autumn, I have noticed that many children have started to be afraid. I have listened to their discussions of nuclear war and missiles on trams and buses. Their little faces are filled with the anxious expressions of adults."[79] Adult anxieties thus overruled a more child-specific perspective, which would have highlighted different aspects of the children's fears. Some commentators have claimed that although this kind of protectionist anxiety about children is widespread in Western countries, in Nordic countries it is children's autonomy, rather than adults' anxieties about their vulnerability, that takes center stage.[80] My Finnish data contradicts this claim. Some Finnish texts even used children's fear as a political tool to criticize the left-wing leaning peace movement, as can be seen in the following quote from the leading bourgeois daily *Uusi Suomi*:

> The most unfortunate side effect of the peace movement is the use of war and particularly the horrors of nuclear war to intimidate children. [...] They have been so successful with this sadistic way of making children anxious that the results scare even the perpetrators themselves.[81]

The quote visualizes young children that are almost paralyzed by the fear caused by adults. In terms of older children, there were a few texts that presented a more dynamic consequence of the fear.[82] In October 1983, for example, *Länsi-Savo*'s youth section devoted a whole page to peace related texts and images. One image showed two schoolboys, one of whom, thirteen-year-old Rauno, had made posters for an upcoming march "so that there would not be those wars," as the caption quoted him saying.[83] Likewise, in 1983 *Uusi Suomi* quoted a placard held by an eleven-year-old demonstrator: "Guns away."[84] The texts portrayed children who used their fear to get active in the peace quest.

[79] Eila Jokela, "Uuden vuoden kortteja," *Uusi Suomi*, December 31, 1982, 2. See also "Kiskot kolkkaa rau-haa, rau-haa: Sanoma saavutti Lahden," *Etelä-Suomen Sanomat*, April 25, 1982, 3.
[80] Katya Johanson, "Culture for or by the child? 'Children's culture' and cultural policy," *Poetics* 38 (2010): 387–88.
[81] Pentti Poukka, "Vettä kaikille," *Uusi Suomi*, October 29, 1983, 2.
[82] Lena Nyreen, "Annorlunda fredsmarsch i Vanda: Också skoleleverna med i fredsfronten," *Arbetartidningen Enhet*, November 6, 1981, 8.
[83] *Länsi-Savo*, October 16, 1983, 12.
[84] "'Kivaa elämää ei saa pamauttaa,'" *Uusi Suomi*, October 27, 1983, 8.

Children's fear was also recognized in Swedish papers,[85] but instead of the protectionist anxieties of adults, Swedish coverage presented fear as the main framing for children's active engagement with the movement.[86] This more child-centered approach can be explained by the Swedish understanding of children's place in wider media culture. In Sweden, journalists had raised the question of children's culture in newspapers as early as the 1950s. This approach had been further encouraged by the left-leaning societal climate of the late 1960s, which had called for more acknowledgment of children's culture, i.e., the inclusion of child-specific viewpoints in mainstream media.[87] Children's perspective was similarly central in the Swedish peace education of the 1980s.[88] Both aspects fostered the coverage of children's active engagement in the early 1980s peace movement and impacted the way in which journalists encouraged active citizenship via positively framed protest coverage.[89]

The left-wing orientation of cultural discussions also characterized 1970s Finland, but the understanding of children's culture seems to have differed somewhat. The Finnish notion of children's culture resembled the socialist realism of the East,[90] and as a result, journalists regarded children's political agency from adult-centered viewpoints. For example, media education was integrated into the curriculum as early as the 1970s, while the Committee for Children's Culture suggested the censorship of foreign comics in particular.[91] This ethos resulted in a journalism that discussed children's ideas about serious issues such as environmentalism, but without acknowledging their active role in actions for societal change. The Finnish reliance on the adult perspective can also be seen as an indication of craft practices that valued experts' opinions

---

[85] "Kärnvapenkriget det är eleverna mest rädda för," *GT*, November 7, 1984.

[86] E.g. Lars Epstein, "Inför internationella nedrustningsdagen: 6000 eleven gav freden en chans," *Dagens Nyheter*, October 23, 1982; "De sjöng för freden," *Dagens Nyheter*, October 28, 1982, 144; Bo Engzell, "2000 skolbarn i samling för fred," *Dagens Nyheter*, December 10, 1983, 22.

[87] Marie Cronqvist, "From Socialist Hero to Capitalist Icon: The Cultural Transfer of the East German Children's Television Programme Unser-Sandmännchen to Sweden in the Early 1970s," *Historical Journal of Film, Radio and Television* 41, no. 2 (2021): 378–93. About Scandinavian discussions of children's media see Helle Strandgaard Jensen, *From Superman to Social Realism: Children's media and Scandinavian childhood* (Amsterdam: John Benjamin's Publishing Company, 2017).

[88] Andersson, "Kolleger!," 211.

[89] Öhman, "Peace Actions and Mainstream Media," 183–86.

[90] Johanson, "Culture for or by the child?," 392.

[91] Merja Heikkinen, "Government policy and definitions of art: The case of comics," *International Journal of Cultural Policy* 14, no. 1 (2008): 83.

over the voices of ordinary people.[92] The same practices were in use in all newsrooms, regardless of country, but the coverage of the peace movement suggests that there was more room for child-specific viewpoints in Sweden than in Finland.[93] More clearly, the Finnish press mostly excluded children's voices from texts that depicted protest actions, whereas the Swedish coverage managed to recognize the ways in which children and adults conducted activism side by side, without obscuring child-specific viewpoints

## Conclusion

The fear of nuclear war shaped people's experiences in the early 1980s, especially in Europe. Tens of thousands of people around the world joined peace marches to make a change. Collective fear was in the air too for those who stayed at home and received information about the peace demonstrations through the mass media.

In this chapter, I have focused on print media coverage of collective peace organizing in two neighboring countries, Finland and Sweden, which ostensibly occupied similar positions in world politics: both were neutral countries. In practice, Finland's geopolitical position made it more vulnerable to Soviet pressure, while the 1981 submarine crisis put the danger on Sweden's doorstep. Both factors had an impact on collective organizing, but news coverage was also influenced by national journalism cultures. This meant that the meanings of peace activism were negotiated in local contexts, even though collective organizing was a phenomenon that crossed national borders. Consequently, the respective countries' geopolitical positions, as well as their understandings of children's societal role, had an effect on the ways in which peace marches in general and children's activism in particular were presented. While Swedes appeared as active participants in wider European peace organizing, Finland was presented as a more passive and isolated nation where the peace movement's transnationalism was adopted only partially and in ways that suited the nation's position in world politics. In this way, news items and other articles helped to create a mental representation of citizens' role in transnational peace organizing. Consequently, journalists had the power to extend or limit the imaginable futures of local peace organizing, and they often did so in subtle ways.

---

92 Heidi Kurvinen, "Children and the Mediated Experiences of the Welfare State: The International Year of the Child (1979) in the Finnish Public Sphere," in *Experiencing Society and the Lived Welfare State*, ed. Pertti Haapala et al. (Cham: Palgrave Macmillan, 2023).

93 The adult viewpoint is present in some of the Swedish texts. E.g. Annika Olsson, "NUFF kämpar för fred: Ge inte barnen krigsleksaker," *Dagens Nyheter*, October 23, 1980, 16; "Ann Margret Dahlquist-Ljunberg svarar Margareta Garpe: Det är dag att lära barnen fredens heroism!," *Expressen*, March 14, 1983, 5; Harald Hamrin, "Efter ubåttsaffärerna: Fredsrörelsen växer," *Dagens Nyheter*, May 8, 1983, 10; "Här kommer fjällbyskolan. De går för freden," *Göteborgs-Posten*, November 10, 1983, 4.

Chapter 9

# In our image: The revolution in Eastern Europe in two Norwegian newspapers

Birgitte Kjos Fonn

*Oslo Metropolitan University, Norway*

**Abstract:** In November 1989 the Berlin Wall, the foremost symbol of the East–West division, fell. The following months saw a chain of reforms, conflicts and change in many Eastern European countries. People took to the streets and tried to break free from dictatorship, repression and surveillance; it was dramatic and full of historic moments, events that also represented the opening of the more abstract 'Iron Curtain'—a massive international revolution. Four months later, East Germany held its first, and only, democratic election, leading to a reuniting of the two Germanys the following autumn. This chapter is a study of how this defining period towards the end of the Cold War was interpreted in two influential Norwegian newspapers. In Norway, as elsewhere, the media was full of joy and celebration for the events. I aim to show the most important frames by which the coverage was characterized, and also suggest how these were shaped by international news flows, national interests, changing journalistic norms and emerging ideological currents.

**Keywords:** Berlin Wall, Norwegian media, journalism history, neoliberalism, economic journalism

\*\*\*

On 9 November 1989, East German authorities were forced to open the Berlin Wall—the foremost symbol of the East–West division since 1961. Shortly after, East German citizens began dismantling the wall, which acted as a tremendous demonstration of popular power against the rulers. The event also represented the opening of the more abstract "Iron Curtain"—a massive international revolution. The following months saw a chain of reforms, conflicts and change in many Eastern European countries. People took to the streets and tried to break free from dictatorship, repression and surveillance; it was dramatic and full of historic moments. In March 1990, communist East Germany held its first, and only, democratic election, leading to a reuniting of the two Germanys the following autumn.

This chapter is a study of how this defining period towards the end of the Cold War was interpreted in two influential Norwegian newspapers. In Norway, as elsewhere, the media was full of joy and celebration for the freeing of the population of the Eastern Bloc.[1] More than 30 years later, however, it is important to obtain a more nuanced view of this period; indeed, almost from the moment the first stone was removed from the Wall, other frames began emerging. In this chapter, I aim to show the most important frames by which the coverage was characterized, and suggest how these were shaped by emerging ideological currents, supported by national interests, international news flows and changing journalistic norms.

## Background and corpus

I have chosen to study two newspapers with different editorial approaches: *Aftenposten* and *Dagbladet*. These newspapers were among Norway's most influential, but with different political and editorial traditions. One was broadsheet and one tabloid, and they had very different profiles, also with regard to international news. They therefore represented journalistic diversity in an age when the print newspaper was still an important source of information and shaper of public opinion.[2]

The study is set in a period of change: Through the post-war era Norway combined the successful building up of a welfare state with being an open economy with extensive trade relations abroad. When a general wave of belief in a more pure market liberalism flushed in over Western Europe around 1980, Norway—as many other Western countries—carried through a set of economic reforms, with deregulation of many economic sectors and increased internationalization as a result. The emerging belief in the "market," and a parallel feeling that the "old" solutions no longer worked, influenced both the right and left side of politics. Underlying this belief was a more subtle understanding that the West was about to win the "battle of hearts and minds" between the East and West, that had been going on all through the Cold War.

The studied period is also loosely framed by a gradual dissolving of the Norwegian party press, in particular from the 1980s. A former party press needed to find a new fundament in an emerging, predominantly commercial media landscape. This had at least two implications: not only did *the idea of the market* play an increasingly important role in both politics and the public

---

[1] As for example shown by Henrik G. Bastiansen in his study of the weeks surrounding the fall of the Berlin Wall in television, radio and four Norwegian newspapers: Henrik G. Bastiansen, "Da Berlinmuren falt: En komparativ studie av presse, radio og TV i 1989," *Mediehistorisk Tidsskrift* 15, no. 1 (2018): 34–90.

[2] They are still among the top national papers, online and in print.

sphere, and thereby also in the media, but the press also needed to give increased attention to their *reader market.*

This was the case also for the two newspapers chosen here. In the 1980s, the broadsheet *Aftenposten* (The Evening Post), rid itself of its formal connection with the conservative party ("The Right"), but retained its political views in editorials and commentaries. *Dagbladet* (The Daily Paper) was a social-liberal, left-leaning "boulevard paper" already from the 1930s, that had a close relationship with the social-liberal party ("The Left") until the 1970s.

Of specific concern for this period of change in the media landscape was the general expansion of the business press. In both Europe and the United States, the business press has often been associated with neo-conservative or neo-liberal movements, and is said to have played a particularly important role in spreading free market ideas.[3] In this period, it expanded both in terms of readership and number of new outlets.

Furthermore, the business press asserted considerable influence on the general interest press, also in the Nordic countries. A Nordic comparative study documents its influence both on the general media context and on the general production of public knowledge, ideology and meaning in the decades up to the turn of the millennium.[4] The study identified a double movement: an increase in (and increasingly powerful) business media, also with more general-interest coverage, and an increase in business journalism in general-interest media—with a specific focus on the promises of "the market." This journalism was no longer directed only at the business community, but also at ordinary readers, as more and more people became active market actors, as for example in a more market-oriented housing sector, but also as shareowners. The authors of the Nordic study also argue that these developments in the media landscape had such a profound effect that they should be included in the modern history of these countries.[5]

The Cold War has been studied quite extensively, and a few of these studies also examine the relationship between the Cold War and the media—also in the

---

[3] See for example Wayne Parsons' early account of the business press in the United Kingdom and the United States: Wayne Parsons, *The power of the financial press: Journalism and economic opinion in Britain and America* (Cheltenham: Edward Elgar, 1989).

[4] Peter Kjær and Tore Slaatta, eds., *Mediating Business* (Copenhagen: Copenhagen Business School, 2007).

[5] Kjær and Slatta, *Mediating Business*, 35–6.

Nordic countries.[6] The interplay between foreign journalism regarding the Cold War, and the emerging market ideology towards its end, has been given little attention. A couple of contributions however indicate that there were interesting changes also to foreign news in these decades: A Danish study for example detected considerably more business angles in foreign news reporting around the turn of the century.[7] My own study of international content in Norwegian newspapers between 1975 and 2005, based on the same general-interest outlets as in this chapter, shows how business news became an exceedingly important part of the foreign/international news reporting in Norway in this period.[8]

The fall of the Berlin Wall was a concrete event, taking place on the ground where people lived their lives and hoped (and feared) for their futures, but its important symbolic function as a "farewell to communism" also had ideological implications and consequently implications for journalism about economic and political affairs. My aim in this chapter is to study this moment in history, when the international order that had characterized the Cold War was falling apart, to gain more insight into how the situation was being seen by the media.

Another way of adjusting to the new expectations of the readers—and contributing to shaping them —was to focus more on *the personal*. This was a trait that had been described in media studies at least since the 1960s,[9] but in this period, the media in both the Nordic countries and elsewhere was increasingly characterized by more "human touch" and reportage, including

---

[6] E.g. Henrik G. Bastiansen and Rolf Werenskjold, eds., *Nordic Media and the Cold War* (Gothenburg: Nordicom, 2015); Henrik G. Bastiansen, Martin Klimke and Rolf Werenskjold, eds., *Media and the Cold War in the 1980s* (New York and London: Palgrave, 2018); Bastiansen, "Da Berlinmuren falt;" Rolf Werenskjold, *That's The Way It Is? Medienes rolle i proteståret 1968* (Oslo: University of Oslo, 2011); Birgitte Kjos Fonn, *Orientering: Rebellenes avis* (Oslo: Pax, 2011).

[7] Hans Henrik Holm, "The Effect of Globalization on Media Structures and Norms: Globalization and the Choice of foreign news," in *News in a Globalized Society*, ed. Stig Hjarvard (Gothenburg: Nordicom, 2001), 113–47.

[8] Birgitte Kjos Fonn, "Nye måter å dekke Vesten på: En studie av internasjonalt stoff i to norske aviser 1975–2005," *Mediehistorisk Tidsskrift* 19, no. 1–2 (2022): 178–202.

[9] "Personification" was for example a point in Johan Galtung and Mari Holmboe Ruge's "The Structure of Foreign News. The Presentation of the Congo, Cuba and Cyprus Crises in Four Norwegian Newspapers," *Journal of Peace Research* no 1. (1965), 64–91. The article also contains other points of interest to the findings in my chapter, for example, its identification of "cultural proximity" and "reference to elite nations" as important factors in foreign news. There were methodological unclarities in Galtung and Ruge's seminal article that makes comparison with later material difficult, but it was nevertheless a collection of very interesting observations of how foreign news is structured.

the more personal aspects of elite persons.[10] This trait was also detectable in foreign news.[11]

The newspapers chosen for this study changed in different directions and at a different pace. As a tabloid from 1983, *Dagbladet* was placing more weight on personalization, large photos etc., whereas *Aftenposten* assumed tabloid features in a more gradual way; and did not assume a tabloid *format* until 2003. Their economic coverage was also different. *Aftenposten* had traditionally included business pages, but was increasingly influenced by the new ways and more heavy market coverage of the emerging business press.[12] *Dagbladet* seems to have been less influenced by these trends, but as the new century dawned, introduced more "modern" business coverage of various kinds.[13]

### Corpus

The chapter is, first, based on a quantitative study of foreign news in both newspapers in the last decade up to the revolutions in Eastern Europe, including four issues a year per paper in 1975, 1980 and 1985 (from front page stories to short notes). A part of this specific data set has been published in my earlier study that deals with international news in a more longitudinal perspective.[14] For this chapter, the material up to the latter part of the 1980s has been expanded with the aim to specifically assess the coverage of the countries behind the Iron Curtain and their relationship to the outside world.

The second, and for this chapter most important, data set is concerned with the coverage of Eastern Europe in 1989–1990. I specifically followed the dramatic periods from 10 to 20 November 1989 and from 12 to 19 March 1990.

---

[10] See for example Birgitte Kjos Fonn, Harald Hornmoen, Nathalie Hyde-Clarke and Yngve Benestad Hågvar, eds., *Individual Exposure and Subjectivity in Journalism* (Oslo: Cappelen Damm Akademisk, 2017).

[11] Fonn, "Nye måter å dekke Vesten på;" Holm, "The Effect of Globalization on Media Structures and Norms."

[12] See also Kjær and Slaatta, *Mediating Business*.

[13] Fonn, "Nye måter å dekke Vesten på;" Martin Eide and Christine Myrvang, *Alltid foran skjermen: Dagbladet og det digitale skiftet* (Oslo: Universitetsforlaget, 2018). A case study of the two newspapers' coverage of the international stock market crash in 1987 shows that though *Dagbladet* displayed more scepticism towards the promises of deregulated markets in their editorials and op-eds, they were already using similar sources from the business community in their news reporting as *Aftenposten*—and in that way furthered the same kinds of solutions and worldviews. Birgitte Kjos Fonn, "Denne gangen er det annerledes: En studie av børskrakket i 1987 i to norske aviser," in Birgitte Kjos Fonn, Ellen Lexerød Hovlid and Birgit Røe Mathisen, eds., *Presse, profesjon og politikk: Festskrift til Paul Bjerke* (Oslo: Cappelen Damm Akademisk, 2022), 209–36.

[14] Fonn, "Nye måter å dekke Vesten på."

The latter was the week of the first and only democratic election of the German Democratic Republic, the GDR (East Germany), up to when the results became public. I also collected two issues a month per paper between November 1989 and the first half of March 1990, to obtain an impression of how the region was being covered between these two major events. All articles of relevance to the development in Eastern Europe were registered, and prominent examples close-read. The weeks under study in November and March 1989–1990 resulted in 38 issues, and 14 issues from the sample between those periods, in all 52 issues. In this sample, editorials, debate and commentaries were included.

## Foreign news in different forms

When we study foreign or international news, it is useful to make a distinction between its different forms. There is on the one hand the 'classical' *foreign news*: news taking place in a foreign country. This may be a story about an election or a new government. Another type is news about *international relations*, for example, stories about conflicts between countries. A third category is *foreign affairs news*: news that involves the foreign relations of the country in which the paper is published—such as Norway's relations with Moscow, London, Washington or Stockholm. *Foreign affairs* is of course a kind of international relations, but as news institutions often have a particular focus on their own country's foreign affairs, it is useful to regard this as a separate category. All these different forms contribute to our perception of the reality that surrounds us.[15]

As international news is not only about "high politics" and the political elites, each of these categories also has a civil society aspect. There are considerable differences between covering high politics—the words and deeds of governments, politicians and other people with power—and reporting from events and lived life "on the ground:" depicting the lives and opinions of, for example, the voter, the baker, the butcher, the representative of a non-governmental organization, or even the local politician. Naturally, different types may appear in one and the same piece of news. But these differences, and the balance between them, have considerable influence on the message that the public receives regarding important events and developments in the world.[16] This framework indicates the different frames that international news can have, as is demonstrated in table 9.1.

---

[15] Fonn, "Nye måter å dekke Vesten på."
[16] Ibid.

**Table 9.1.** International news by societal level, type of events and type of relationships. Based on Fonn, "Nye måter å dekke Vesten på," 191.

| | Foreign news | International relations | Foreign affairs news |
|---|---|---|---|
| Political elite level | Elite level abroad, e.g., national elections, high-level political power struggles, state administration, other official bodies or persons, political decisions ranging from security policy to economics. | Relations between countries (and national actors as in point 1) or between countries and international organizations, or within international organizations. Also major international developments that can be attributed to decisions or developments at this level. | Relations between the country where the news outlet is published, with foreign countries, regions or international organizations at the elite level. The location of the news can be domestic. |
| Civil society level | Civil society level abroad, e.g., lower-level power struggles, guerrilla wars, riots, demonstrations, or events and developments among individuals, households, organizations, businesses. Also stories about the effect of political decisions on individuals, households, organizations and businesses. | International relations at civil society level. Examples: the relationship between civil society and other countries and/or the international level. It can be individuals or organizations—on both sides. Also includes trends affecting civil society in multiple countries/regions (such as trade, drought, women's liberation). | The relations of the country where the news outlet is published with foreign countries/international organizations, at civil society level. Relations between national organizations in the publishing country and other nations or similar actors in other nations are included here, as is the relationship between the publishing country's citizens and other nations/regions and/or their actors. The location of the news can be domestic. |

Foreign or international news differs from domestic news in important respects. The dependence on written and second-hand sources is often much higher in foreign news than in domestic journalism. Good coverage on the ground is more difficult to attain when events take place abroad. This is among the traits that traditionally have led to a high politics dominance in foreign news. It may however also be more difficult to secure interviews with people of power.

This was particularly apparent in the countries behind the Iron Curtain, as it was challenging to work in this region during the Cold War—for language reasons, reasons of censorship etc. Major outlets took pride in having correspondents in Moscow, but in Norway, only *Aftenposten* and the Norwegian Broadcasting Corporation (NRK) achieved this. On the other hand, the Norwegian network of foreign correspondents was at its peak in the period from 1975–1994, with *Aftenposten* on top: by 1990, it had a total of 10 offices around the world, Moscow and a special Eastern Europe correspondent included. *Dagbladet* had fewer correspondents in this period—indeed, only two, in London and New York—but actively used stringers and freelancers, also in Eastern Europe.[17] Most papers at the time also used the Norwegian News Agency (NTB), whose foreign news service was dominated by international news agencies like Reuters, United Press International (UPI) and Associated Press (AP). These agencies were West based, but often had people in the East Bloc, most notably Moscow. The major newspapers had furthermore direct access to such bureaus, and television used footage from the same sources. Finally, the Norwegian News Agency had exchange arrangements with Swedish, Danish and Finnish news agencies and their correspondents, also in Moscow.

Despite a certain presence behind the Iron Curtain, the repression of the citizens there both with regard to free speech and its press made these Western outlets and sources all the more important. The full effect of a presence there would therefore likely not be attained, and the news was often based either on open Western sources or on anonymous "diplomatic sources." This may be why I found a relatively low amount of coverage of the East Bloc before the 1990s. Approximately one in six articles about international issues on the whole (Norwegian foreign affairs included) was about the East Bloc, whereas only 5% came from the Eastern European countries outside the Soviet Union.[18] This number—not surprisingly—increased as the region started to change. In the corpus covering the whole period from 1975 to 2005, over 10% came from Eastern Europe.

---

[17] Werenskjold, *That's The Way It Is?*, 277, 249. See also Jan Fredrik Hovden and Rolf Werenskjold, "The Cold War Reporters: The Norwegian Foreign-News Journalists and Foreign-News Correspondents, 1945–1995," in *Media and the Cold War in the 1980s*, eds. Henrik G. Bastiansen, Martin Klimke and Rolf Werenskjold (New York and London: Palgrave, 2019), 189–221.

[18] Op-eds and commentaries were not included in this study, so the total Eastern European coverage on the pages was likely higher. On the other hand, the main reason for writing commentaries about a topic is often also that it is in the news.

Over the years, there was also a general rise in all kinds of international news pertaining to the civil society.[19] Only by comparing 1975 and 1985—in other words, a distance of no more than a decade—we see a fundamental change in the direction of more civil society angles, in both newspapers. In 1975, a majority of articles were still about the elite level, ten years later civil society angles could be found in a small majority. This development can probably be seen in connection with the increasing use of reportage and personification in news (although this was not the only reason). The main point is, however, that as many Eastern European countries began opening up in the 1980s, it was reasonable to expect increased coverage of civil society issues in the East Bloc.

### From "the people" to "the market"

The remarkable international event on 9 November 1989 led to widespread celebration. The newspapers brought forth their most powerful descriptions, e.g. "Boundless joy and celebration in Berlin," or "Day of hope"[20] and "Freedom celebration in Berlin."[21] Other media had similar formulations, as shown by Henrik Bastiansen in his in-depth study of four newspapers, television and radio in Norway in the two weeks preceding and following 9 November: for instance, "The Joy is Boundless," or "Last Night The Berlin Wall opened: The Whole of Germany Rejoices."[22]

In the first days after the Wall fell, the newspapers were rife with notions like democracy, freedom and human rights. Victory for the people of East Germany was a main theme in both text and illustrations: Bastiansen writes that the papers were "particularly engaged with the popular masses and ordinary people."[23] These events not only opened the Wall—or the future for Eastern Europeans who finally faced the opportunity to live free lives—it also opened a new field of sources for the media. As one East German citizen expressed it when talking to *Dagbladet*, they had been bullied by the Stasi for 40 years: But "(n)ow we dare to talk."[24]

As demonstrated, the celebration of the people's victory was tremendous, but the interest also soon waned, in all outlets. This is also an important point in Bastiansen's study, which only goes up to 15 November 1989, by which point the coverage had dropped considerably.

---

[19] As shown in Fonn, "Nye måter å dekke Vesten på."
[20] *Ap* (*Aftenposten*), November 11, 1989, front page title and editorial.
[21] *Db* (*Dagbladet*), November 11, 1989, front page title.
[22] *VG* (another Norwegian newspaper) November 11, 1989 and NRK (Norwegian Broadcasting Company) November 10, 1989, cited in Bastiansen, "Da Berlinmuren falt," 51, 76.
[23] Bastiansen, "Da Berlinmuren falt," 53
[24] Håkon Lund, "Framtida ikke lenger grå," *Db*, November 16, 1989, 16–7.

We will now take a closer look at the frames relating to the liberation processes in the relevant East Bloc countries. It is important to be aware that in my sample from November 1989 to March 1990 about one quarter of all articles are primarily about the developments in the Soviet Union. While this is an interesting topic on its own, I have concentrated on the nations that tried to leave the Soviet domain, including the Baltic States—such as Lithuania. Despite that it differed from many other Eastern countries by actually being part of the Soviet Union, the development there resembled that of the other Eastern European states. When it came to the rest of the Soviet Union's fate—those states that would later become a part of the Russia-led Commonwealth of Independent States (CIS)—it was at this stage more unclear. This also means that I have not gone further into the coverage of the enduring drama around Soviet General Secretary Mikhail Gorbachev.

I detected four important frames relating to these processes throughout the four months from November to March. These are a) the people's revolt, b) the leaders, c) the East as seen from the West (in particular, from Western Europe and d) Eastern Europe as a market. Finally, I will give a short account of how the election in the GDR was covered.

As the intervals in my study vary (one and a half weeks in November and one week in March, and twice a month between these weeks), it does not make sense to give specific figures, the important thing is that all these were prominent frames in the coverage. [25]

It is also important to note that almost two thirds of the articles studied are found in *Aftenposten*, as the broadsheet quite simply had more pages and more articles than the tabloid *Dagbladet*. This, of course, contributed to shaping the coverage in differing ways in the two outlets, as did a notable difference with respect to titles, images and frames.

### The people's revolt

Despite the fact that new frames appeared, the people's revolt did not disappear. *Aftenposten* and *Dagbladet* mostly covered the same events that took place on the ground. This was of course due to the drama of the situation, but likely also to the agenda of the news agencies, as both outlets followed this agenda fairly closely: demonstrations in Lithuania the one day, in Czechoslovakia the next. The same event, however, could result in a main foreign news story in one paper and a short note in another.

Both sent teams of reporters to some of the countries as the revolts evolved, and also used their own correspondent or stringer resources. In some cases, ordinary citizens were important sources, and the papers' own photographers contributed with original photos from the field. *Dagbladet* however seems to

---

[25] These were the prominent frames; there are also articles with other, individual frames.

have had an advantage at this stage in its tabloid and personalized approach to news—it seemingly had a more developed tradition for interviewing "ordinary people" or depicting life on the ground. On 18 November, *Dagbladet* for example published full-page reportages from Berlin and Prague where the citizens played the main part.[26] Another notable example included Romania: In late December 1989, the Romanian dictator Nicolae Ceaușescu and his wife were executed. *Dagbladet* (who often only had a couple of foreign news pages), published no fewer than 14 news articles on nine pages about Romania on 27 December 1989, the majority of which had a civil society frame, focusing on the popular revolution and citing ordinary citizens. A major reportage from Bitterfeld, south of Berlin, in *Dagbladet* in March 1990 is also worth mentioning. This was Europe's most polluted city and thus unsuitable for children to grow up in, and the reportage gave a heartbreaking impression.[27] These examples represent an interesting contrast to content from news agencies, or for that matter many articles from *Aftenposten*'s own staff, in which the citizens would more often appear as a "faceless" mass. *Aftenposten* however to an extent compensated for having less human touch by publishing columns in which (former) Eastern European dissidents wrote about democracy, human rights and freedom of speech.[28]

### The leaders

Despite the fact that the "people" were a powerful force in the Eastern European events, there was no way around the leaders. The words and deeds of the top leaders—high politics—are of course the type of news to which it is easiest to get access, as it constantly streams out of news agencies. The Eastern European leaders had a reputation of being enemies of the people, but during the revolts, new leaders who were believed to *represent* the people appeared: for example, Ion Iliescu in Bucuresti, Vaclav Havel in Prague and Vytautas Landsbergis in Vilnius. These were often examples of *foreign news* rooted in developments in the Eastern countries themselves, but still with a high politics approach.

Western leaders also had their fair share of the coverage regarding Eastern Europe in *international relations* stories—such as the involvement of US President George Bush or US Defence Minister Dick Cheney in the events.[29] *Foreign affairs news* was also an arena where the leaders played important roles, as when the Norwegian prime minister discussed German re-unification

---

[26] Håkon Lund and Einar Hagvaag, "Øst-Europas nye ansikt," *Db*, November 18, 1989, 4–5.
[27] Håkon Lund, "Disse barna vokser opp i Europas mest forurensede by"/"Flykter fra byen," *Db*, March 15, 1990, 23–5.
[28] E.g. György Konrád, "Europa smittes av frihet," *Ap*, November 10, 1990, 44; and Milan Simecka, "Tsjekkoslovakiske eventyr," *Ap*, January 24, 1990, 44.
[29] Per Egil Hegge, "USA vil skjære ned på forsvarsutgiftene," *Ap*, November 20, 1989, 8; Per Egil Hegge, "Havel: Vi ber ikke om pengestøtte," *Ap*, February 21, 1990, 8.

with the US president—and decided that they agreed on what they wanted.[30] All these are natural topics for news, but it contributes to an impression that the Eastern people's revolt was often seen from above, from the viewpoint of high politics, and it was also, to a degree, seen from the viewpoint of the West.

The use of both high politics and Western angles was less prominent in *Dagbladet* than *Aftenposten*. The difference between the two can also be illustrated by *Dagbladet's* more personalized coverage even when high politics were concerned. On 10 January 1990, the Czechoslovakian president Vaclav Havel's upcoming visit to Norway that spring was announced. *Aftenposten's* short article had a typical high politics frame, but mentioned a few personal facts about Havel. The tabloid did the same, but it also largely interpreted this as a "celebrities story"—about Havel's popularity, and how he lived and worked.[31]

### The East seen from the West—in particular the EEC

Among the examples of the East, as seen from the West, the effect of the events on (Western) Europe was the most important, in particular regarding the European Economic Community—the EEC (later the European Union, the EU). Both papers gave their theme pages names like "The New Europe" or "A Changing Europe," which, of course, was an apt way of interpreting the events. But upon closer investigation, the notion "Europe" often tended to be synonymous with the EEC.

The fall of the Wall almost seamlessly slid into the question of the future of the EEC. There is reason to believe that this was in part a result of how the international news agenda was translated and interpreted in Norwegian media: the future of the EEC was likely what the international community—understood as political leaders, other powerful people and institutions and the international media themselves—regarded as the important issue. In other words, the high politics of international relations was a prominent aspect of the coverage.

The question of a German re-unification was also very much treated as an EEC question. Some even took on the character of a celebration of the EEC's part in the liberation process. *Aftenposten's* Brussels correspondent opened a news ingress about plans for a European "Marshall help" for the East by stating that "A strong EEC has contributed to Eastern Europe's democratization process." The Eastern Europe coverage of that day was referred to on the front page, with the title "Brotherhood and EEC Aid."[32]

---

[30] Morten Fyhn, "Syse tar opp tysk samling," *Ap*, February 21, 1990, 7.
[31] Bente Egjar Engesland, "Havel kommer til Norge i mai," *Ap*, January 10, 1990, 6; and Ingolf Håkon Teigene, "Så vanskelig å være president i dette landet," *Db*, January 10, 1990, 19.
[32] Per Nordrum, "Massiv EF-bistand til Øst-Europa," *Ap*, November 20, 1989, 8.

The developments in Eastern Europe were also often interpreted as *foreign affairs news*, and in that, about Norway's relationship with the EEC. Already in the 1960s, there had been considerable differences of opinion about whether Norway should join the organization. There were more pro-EEC opinions and positive views on the European common market among the national elites (including the press) and on the political right, whereas there was increased resistance on the "grassroots" and on the left. In 1972, a membership referendum split the nation in two and ended with a small majority for staying out. When the Berlin Wall fell almost two decades later, Norway was in the process of joining the planned European Economic Area (EEA).[33] The fallen Wall, however, offered new opportunities for Norwegian politicians and commentators to re-open the EEC question. Both outlets published interviews and opinions that used the events in Eastern Europe as a point of departure for furthering their views on Norway and the EEC—including the waging of internal conflicts in Norwegian political parties.[34]

The EEC debate in 1989–1990 centered around the balance between Norway's influence in Europe and its sovereignty, and whether to accept the community's more and more pronounced pro-market policies. These debates were often intertwined, and the events in Eastern Europe played directly into them. In a number of articles of all kinds, the liberation process was interpreted as a danger that Norway would 'miss the boat.' One politician expressed fear that the former communist state Hungary would become an EEC member before Norway,[35] while a later defense minister wrote an op-ed saying that as a result of the recent events in Eastern Europe, Norway risked becoming an outsider in Europe if they did not join the EEC.[36] An *Aftenposten* commentator warned that the EEC would now be increasingly occupied with the developments in the East, and that Norway could simply forget the hope of a common, decisive body with the EEC (regarding the EEA).[37] *Dagbladet*, for its part, interviewed a *former* EEC commission head, who offered assurance that Norway would not be the EEC member that would be most difficult to integrate, given the recent developments in the East—but also that the EEC would not become "the united

---

[33] Eventually, a new referendum again ended with a small majority for staying out in 1994.
[34] E.g. An-Magrit Austenå, "Ap uten visjoner for Øst-Europa" and "Syse må se østover," both *Db*, November 16, 1989, 6; "EF og vi," *Ap*, December 27, 1989, 2 (editorial); Hanne Gamnes, "Jagland: -93 kan bli EF-valg," *Ap*, February 21, 1990, 6, and "EFTA-løpet fullføres," *Db*, March 14, 1990, 2 (editorial).
[35] Austenå, "Ap uten visjoner for Øst-Europa."
[36] Johan Jørgen Holst, "Vi kan bli europeisk utkant," *Ap*, November 16, 1989, 2. Similar arguments from the same commentator were reiterated later in *Ap*: "Vårt fremtidige Europa," February 21, 1990, 2 and "Nato og det nye Europa," March 19, 1990, 2.
[37] Per Nordrum, "Glem et felles beslutningsorgan!," *Ap*, January 24, 1990, 2.

states of Europe" (in other words, the participating states would not have to cede much sovereignty) in the foreseeable future.[38]

### Eastern Europe as a market

The last frame is the one in which East Germany and other liberating Eastern European states were simply understood *as a market.* It might have been difficult to celebrate the end of decades of dictatorship and repression without celebrating democracy, but political freedom, free elections and a market economy could also be juxtaposed, as in this *Aftenposten* editorial the day after the Wall fell: "one country after another are moving in the direction of what for decades has been the sole brand of the reviled West—political freedom and market economy."[39]

Whereas *Dagbladet* had more human touch in their stories, *Aftenposten's* most prominent civil society angle was business news. Five days after the Wall fell, we learned that "The (Norwegian) Export Council (was) proposing to Hungary."[40] After nine days, one front-page story was published with the title "The Business Sector in the Starting Pit: Race Towards New Markets." The fear of missing the boat for Norwegian actors was just as pronounced in the business coverage as in the EEC coverage (and could be two sides of the same coin). *Aftenposten* wrote that the East was "'in'[41] in the business world," and that Norwegian business needed to get ready for it as soon as possible.[42] The events also made *Aftenposten* describe the GDR as a possible new *Wirtschaftwunder,* just as West Germany had been for years.[43]

Business news of course gives an opportunity to see the events from the Easterners' perspective, as it will often typically be civil society stories, but as we see, the concern here primarily lies with Norwegian business. One interesting business source however represented not only Eastern European business, but even Eastern European "big capital:" *Aftenposten* devoted almost an entire broadsheet page to what they (admiringly) called a Czech "super-capitalist"—the vice president of Skoda, Miroslav Mikes. "Our future lies in going back to the system of the past," Mikes stated—to the situation before

---

[38] Ingolf Håkon Teigene, "EF blir ikke et 'forent Europa,'" *Db*, February 21, 1990, 6.

[39] "Vestlig ansvar i øst," *Ap*, November 10, 1989, 2 (editorial).

[40] Ragnhild Moy, "Eksportrådet frir til Ungarn," *Ap*, November 14, 1989, 6.

[41] I.e. modern, hot.

[42] Kai Ove Evensen, "Kappløp mot nye markeder," *Ap*, November 18, 1989, 5.

[43] Nils Morten Udgaard, "DDR ligner mer og mer på Vesten," *Ap*, November 18, 1989, 4.

World War II when Skoda was a privately owned company with a major share of foreign owners.[44]

Mikes also underlined his ideology for the future: that the state should never interfere with business. But when commenting on the fact that the Czechoslovakian government had warned that the transition to a market economy would lead to increased prices and unemployment, he articulated it in the following way: "The unemployment should be the government's problem."[45]

### The election

The last part of this paper is a short case study of East Germany's first—and last—democratic election, which took place in March 1990: an event that I think illustrates many of the points above. At stake was not only who was going to run the country, but what kind of country it would be, including the pace and style of a possible re-unification.

The question of German re-unification was raised from the start, as in *Aftenposten*'s editorial on 10 November 1989:

> This is a question all parties have tried to speak softly about for a long time, but that now inevitably comes to the fore, and that reaches far beyond today's two German states. At the end of the day, this is a question about the whole of Europe's future.[46]

At this stage, many commentators and experts still deemed a re-unification impossible, at least in the short or medium term—the major question concerned what kind of transition the GDR wanted and needed. It had yet not been decided as to whether the GDR should opt for "socialism with a human face" or the more market-liberal West German model. *Aftenposten*'s commentator, however, had already made up his mind on 18 November 1989. Judging from the changes that had taken place in one week, he came to the conclusion that the GDR was on its way to becoming a state that "looks more and more like the West:"

> When the GDR moves towards more democracy [...] the result can be nothing but an East German state that will be a mirror image of the West German one—and a part of a common German area in the middle of Europe.[47]

---

[44] The communists seized power in Czechoslovakia in 1948, in a coup supported by the Soviet Union.

[45] Morten Fyhn, "Tsjekkisk superkapitalist," *Ap*, January 24, 1990, 15.

[46] "Vestlig ansvar i øst," editorial.

[47] Udgaard, "DDR ligner mer og mer på Vesten."

German re-unification was thereafter the topic of editorials, op-eds, weekend analyses and reportages all through the months studied.

When the election was nearing, most doubts about whether the two Germanys would be reunited were removed—almost no political actor remained against re-unification. The more urgent question was what re-unification meant. Was it a question of uniting the two parties on equal terms, or of West Germany (called the Federal Republic of Germany, FRG) "swallowing" the GDR?

This was the main dividing line between the two main opponents in the election: the Social Democrats (SPD) and the conservative Alliance that also included the Christian Democrats (CDU), the party of the West German Chancellor Helmut Kohl. The Social Democrats wanted a slower approach and one that secured more equality between the two Germanys; and it was of course also based on social democratic politics, whereas the Alliance wanted the GDR to re-join what was at the time West Germany.[48]

One important aspect of the coverage of the election in East Germany was how it was centered around West Germany. This was even more conspicuous as several news reports at the same time pointed to the fact that Western politicians had literally taken over and "colonized" the election, with campaign machinery that was far more powerful than that of their Eastern counterparts.[49] But this acknowledgment, which was also cited in the international press, did not prevent the outlets from confirming this Western angle by placing Helmut Kohl in the main role. The occurrence of Eastern politicians in my corpus was surprisingly low.

A notable exception was an interview with the new (post-Wall) GDR leader Hans Modrow in *Aftenposten* a few days ahead of the election. *Aftenposten's* main question to Modrow was why the GDR did not privatize property as Hungary and Poland had done. Modrow answered that the GDR would both retain some as state property and leave some to the market, as in Austria and France—with "a market economy that is both social and ecological" as the goal. Half of the article had the form of a commentary. In the last paragraph, the journalist took on the task of explaining to the readers what the people of the GDR really wanted, as Volkswagen was about to start producing Polo in the East, and Opel and Mercedes were next in line: "This is tangible—and what really makes an impression on the voters of the East."[50]

---

[48] Which was possible due to Article 23 in the West German constitution.

[49] E.g. Nils Morten Udgaard, "Vestlig driv over DDRs valgkamp," *Ap*, March 12, 1990, 12; Jon-Hjalmar Smith, "Rask samling etter DDR-valget," *Db*, March 13, 1990, 16; and "Helmut, Helmut," *Db*, March 15, 1990, 21.

[50] Nils Morten Udgaard, "DDR foran skjebnevalg," *Ap*, March 15, 1990, 12.

But what did the East German voters want? It is difficult, in this corpus, to find information about what the voters really wanted, and there is little information about the alternatives to Kohl's policies. An interesting reportage was published in *Aftenposten* on 12 March 1990. It transpires from this article that the voters had been worried that a re-unification would lead to unemployment and a steep increase in mortgages. However, according to *Aftenposten*, a few anonymous voters had "no panic," as Kohl had assured them that the West German security net would take care of them. Aside from one open source—an engineer who stated, "We have lost our self-confidence, and that is the only thing we cannot buy with D-marks"—Kohl and another CDU representative were the main sources.[51] In that respect, this article was quite typical.

At this point, the difference between the CDU-led Alliance and SPD was 30 versus 34%. The Alliance, however, was steadily growing. In retrospect, we know that the conservative Alliance won the election, that Germany was re-united under the West German umbrella, and that Kohl continued as chancellor for the next eight years. But less than a week before the election on Sunday 18 March, the Social Democrats were still ahead of the conservative alliance.[52]

We also know in retrospect that many Eastern European countries chose a more "pure" capitalism than e.g. the Nordic countries, and also that the GDR chose the social-economic model of West Germany. In other words, the expectations in *Aftenposten* turned out to be correct. But the voters present in the coverage were few, both before and after the election tide turned. To the extent that the sample from these two major papers is representative, the Norwegian public knew little of the changes that took place among the public over the course of those days. The interesting question therefore concerns what information the actors in the Norwegian press (i.e., journalists, columnists and interviewees) had about what the people wanted: except for overthrowing their dictators and living free lives in democracies. It is reasonable to suspect that the speculations about what the East German people wanted were partly based on elite sources, and may also have included an element of wishful thinking that turned out to come true.

Despite being the outlet with the most ambitious coverage from the ground, the presence of voters was also relatively low in *Dagbladet*, and the choice of sources could seem fairly accidental. On 17 March, *Dagbladet* for example interviewed three citizens who planned to vote for the Alliance—which also turned out to be the election winners—but it appears from the article that they had met the three "outside a butcher's." However, *Dagbladet*'s reportages from

---

[51] Udgaard, "Vestlig driv over DDRs valgkamp."
[52] Udgaard, "Vestlig driv over DDRs valgkamp."

the polluted Bitterfeld, which had appeared two days earlier, contained no fewer than 10 important civil society sources—politicians, parents, doctors and children—although the stories did not specifically touch upon the election.[53] Even more than in the eventful week in November, the coverage seemed to be governed by the common news agenda, where high politics and international relations were the main questions and European political and business interests were also important. The definition of the interests of "the people" of Eastern Europe seems largely to have been left to other forces.

Seven months later, in October 1990, Germany was re-united after 29 years. Less than one and a half years later, the Soviet Union dissolved. And with that, the communist era was over. Through the 1990s and 2000s, the focus on the market became a significant feature in both newspapers, also as foreign news was concerned, but still with a marked difference between the two. The tabloid *Dagbladet* decreased its foreign news coverage in the years to come (but would rapidly send reporting teams abroad whenever major international events broke), but increased its focus on personal and consumer economy, issues that in the twenty-first century also could contain international aspects. As *Aftenposten* eventually changed to a tabloid format, its foreign coverage became increasingly more civil society oriented, and international business news played an important part in that process.[54]

### Concluding remarks

In this chapter, I have analyzed the dramatic events in 1989–1990 via samples from two Norwegian newspapers. When studying these events over a longer perspective than just the days around the dismantling of the Wall, and looking for more frames than the established "people's victory," we see that high politics continued to dominate, and, in interesting ways, that Western European interests and also business interests, contributed to shaping the coverage of the fallen Wall. The events in 1989–1990 took place in a period where a pro-market ideology had become increasingly stronger in many Western countries, and the citizens of the Eastern European countries were not only interpreted as people who now deserved their freedom, but also as important market actors and markets for the West.

The relationship between East and West Germany was a main issue from the beginning, and the boundaries between this relationship and the future of the European Economic Community were blurred almost from day one. We also see how the events in Eastern Europe were interpreted in a Norwegian context,

---

[53] Lund, "Disse barna vokser opp i Europas mest forurensede by;" "Flykter fra byen."
[54] Fonn, "Nye måter å dekke Vesten på."

with the combination of promises for the future and fear of missing the boat for both politicians and businesses.

As we have seen, news with civil society angles were on the rise in this period. It is however also important to notice how differing focuses in the conservative broadsheet and the liberal tabloid could give different impressions of similar developments. Despite this, in this historically unique drama, one would have expected more coverage of those people that were most affected by the change. Though the popular revolts were one of the main frames, representatives of civil society often appeared as a faceless mass or as rather random quotes. The relative lack of voices from the ground may have contributed to an interpretation of the fallen Wall in the image of what was at that time "the West"—and as a question of what was in the interest of the West.

# Bibliography

## Original Sources

### Archival source

Aleksandra Gripenberg's Collection, the Archives on Literature and Cultural History of the Finnish Literature Society.

Archives of Suomen Naisyhdistys (Finnish Women's Association) within the Helsinki City Archives.

The Finnish Film Archive (National Audiovisual Institute), Helsinki.

Museum of Television & Radio, New York City.

The Television Advertising and Culture Archive at Brooklyn College (the Celia Nachatovitz Diamant "Classic Television Commercials" collection and the Ted Bates collection), New York City.

### Published texts

Europaeus, D. E. D. *Kirjoituksia Suomen kansan tärkeimmistä asioista suurimmaksi osaksi syrjä-sensuureista paenneita, 1 nidos: Onko Suomen kansa voimihinsa päästettävä vain eikö?* Helsinki, 1862.

Gripenberg, Aleksandra. *Naisasian kehitys eri maissa I.* Porvoo: Werner Söderström Osakeyhtiö, 1905.

Gripenberg, Aleksandra. *Naisasian kehitys eri maissa II.* Porvoo: Werner Söderström Osakeyhtiö, 1906.

Gripenberg, Aleksandra. *Naisasian kehitys eri maissa III.* Porvoo: Werner Söderström Osakeyhtiö, 1908.

Kivi, Aleksis. *Seitsemän veljestä.* Helsinki: SKS, 1870.

Palme, Olof. SAP Congress 1981, book 2/CD.

Perussuomalaiset rp., Periaateohjelma, 19 October 2018, https://www.fsd.tuni.fi/pohtiva/ohjelmalistat/PS/ (accessed 13 October 2021).

Sohlman, August. *Det unga Finland: En kulturhistorisk betraktelse.* Stockholm: C. M. Thimgren, 1855.

Yrjö Yrjö-Koskinen, *Nuijasota. Sen syyt ja tapaukset. Jälkimmäinen osa.* Turku, 1859.

### Newspapers and magazines

*Aftenposten* 1975, 1980, 1985
*Aftonbladet* 1979–1984
*Ajan Suunta* from the 1930s
*Akkaväki* from the 1970s
*Akkaväki: Naisten ääni* from the 1980s
*Apu* 1979–1984

*Arbetartidningen Enhet* 1979–1984
*Astra* from the 1920s and 1930s
*Borgåbladet* 1979–1984
*Dagbladet* 1975, 1980, 1985
*Dagens Nyheter* 1979–1984
*Eeva* from the 1930s
*Emäntälehti* from the 1920s and 1930s
*Etelä-Suomen Sanomat* 1979–1984
*Expressen* 1979–1984
*Folktidningen Ny Tid* 1979–1984
*Frihet* 1980, 1982, 1984, 1987, 1989 and 1990
*GT* 1979–1984
*Göteborgs-Posten* 1979–1984
*Hangon Lehti* 1979–1984
*Helsingin Sanomat* 1979–1984
*Helsingin Uutiset* from the 1850s and 1860s
*Hopeapeili* from the 1930s
*Hufvudstadsbladet* 1979–1984
*Kauneudenhoitolehti* from the 1930s
*Koti ja Yhteiskunta* from the 1880s, 1890s and 1900s
*Kotiliesi* from the 1920s and 1930s
*Kvinnobulletinen* from the 1970s, 1980s and 1990s
*Länsi-Savo* 1979–1984
*Mainosuutiset* 1962
*Morgonbris* 1981, 1983, 1985, 1987, 1989 and 1990
*Naisten Ääni* from the 1920s and 1930s
*Päivätär* from the 1850s and 1860s
*Sanan-Lennätin* from the 1850s and 1860s
*Sanomia Turusta* from the 1850s and 1860s
*Suomen Julkisia Sanomia* from the 1850s and 1860s
*Suomen Kuvalehti* 1979–1984
*Suomen Nainen* from the 1920s and 1930s
*Suomen Uutiset* from 2014 onwards
*Suometar* from the 1850s and 1860s
*Svenska Dagbladet* 1979–1984
*Toveritar* from the 1920s
*Tvärdrag* 1983, 1984, 1986, 1987, 1989 and 1990
*Työläis- ja talonpoikaisnaisten lehti* from the 1920s
*Uusi Suometar* from the 1850s and 1860s
*Uusi Suomi* 1979–1984
*Vasabladet* 1979–1984
*Västra Nyland* 1979–1984

*Åbo Underrättelser* 1979–1984
*Österbottningen* 1979–1984
*Yle uutiset* from 2012 and 2020

## Research literature

Abbot, H. Porter. *The Cambridge Introduction to Narrative*. Second edition. Cambridge: Cambridge University Press, 2008.

Ahl, Helene, Karin Berglund, Katarina Pettersson, and Malin Tillmar. "From feminism to FemInc.ism: On the uneasy relationship between feminism, entrepreneurship and the Nordic welfare state." *International Entrepreneurship and Management Journal* 12 (2016): 369–392.

Aikasalo, Päivi. *Alli Wiherheimo. Uranaisen sydän*. Helsinki: Otava, 2004.

Alaketola-Tuominen, Marja. *Jokapojan amerikanperintö. Yhdysvaltalaisia kulttuurivaikutteita Suomessa toisen maailmansodan jälkeen*. Helsinki: Gaudeamus, 1989.

Allern, Sigurd. "When Journalists Frame the News," in *Media and Revolt. Strategies and Performances from the 1960s to the Present*, edited by Kathrin Fahlenbrach, Erling Sivertsen and Rolf Werenskjold, 91–106. Oxford: Berghahn Books, 2014.

Althusser, Louis. *Positions, 1964–1975*. Paris: Éditions sociales, 1976.

Ambjörnsson, Ronny. *Ellen Key. En europeisk intellektuell*. Stockholm: Albert Bonniers förlag, 2012.

Ambrosius, Gerold and William H. Hubbard. *A Social and Economic History of Twentieth Century Europe*. Cambridge, Masschusetts: Harvard University Press, 1989.

Anderson, Benedict. *Imagined Communities. Reflections on the Origin and Spread of Nationalism*. London: Verso, 1983.

Andersson, Irene. "Kolleger! Det är dags att handla nu! Lärare för freds bildande och yrkesetikens betydelse, 1982–1984." In *En historiker korsar sitt spår: En vänbok till Roger Johansson om att lära sig av historien och lära ut historia*, edited by Katarina Blennow, Pål Brunnström, and David Örbring, 205–219. Malmö: Malmö university, 2019.

Arnfred, Signe, Litten Hansen, and Anne Houe. *Bladet Kvinder 1975–1984*. Copenhagen: Tiderne Skifter, 2015.

Arni-Kauttu, Meri. *Itäistä kelvottomuutta vastaan: Suomen ruotsinkielisten diskursiiviset mielikuvat suomalaisista 1896–1924*. Joensuu: Itä-Suomen yliopisto, 2020.

Åse, Cecilia. "Ship of Shame: Gender and Nation in Narratives of the 1981 Soviet Submarine Crisis in Sweden." *Journal of Cold War Studies* 18, no.1 (2016): 112–132.

Bailey, Michael. "Editor's Introduction." In *Narrating Media History*, edited by Michael Bailey, xx–xxii. London and New York: Routledge, 2009.

Ballaster, Ros, Margaret Beetham, Elizabeth Fraser, and Sandra Hebron, eds. *Women's Worlds: Ideology, Femininity and the Woman's Magazine*. Basingstoke: Macmillan, 1991.

Barker, Hannah, and Simon Burrows. "Introduction." In *Press, Politics and the Public Sphere in Europe and North America, 1760–1820,* edited by Hannah Barker and Simon Burrows, 1–22. Cambridge: Cambridge University Press, 2004.

Barker, Hannah. "England, 1760–1815." In *Press, Politics and the Public Sphere in Europe and North America, 1760–1820,* edited by Hannah Barker and Simon Burrows, 93–112. Cambridge: Cambridge University Press, 2004.

Barthes, Ronald. *Mythologies.* London: Paladin Books, 1973.

Bastiansen, Henrik G., and Hans Fredrik Dahl. *Norsk mediehistorie.* Oslo: Universitetsforlaget, 2003.

Bastiansen, Henrik G. "Da Berlinmuren falt: En komparativ studie av presse, radio og TV i 1989." *Mediehistorisk Tidsskrift* 15, no. 1 (2018): 34–90.

Bastiansen, Henrik G. "Reporting Glasnost: The Changing Soviet News in a Norwegian Daily, 1985–1988." In *Media and the Cold War in the 1980s: Between Star Wars and Glasnost,* edited by Henrik G. Bastiansen Martin Klimke Bastiansen, and Rolf Werenskjold, 235–262. Cham: Palgrave Macmillan, 2019.

Bastiansen, Henrik G. and Rolf Werenskjold, eds. *Nordic Media and the Cold War.* Gothenburg: Nordicom, 2015.

Bastiansen, Henrik G., and Rolf Werenskjold. "Mapping Nordic Media and the Cold War." In *Nordic Media and the Cold War,* edited by Henrik G. Bastiansen, and Rolf Werenskjold, 9–27. Gothenburg: Nordicom, 2015.

Bastiansen, Henrik G., Martin Klimke, and Rolf Werenskjold, eds. *Media and the Cold War in the 1980s.* New York/London: Palgrave, 2018.

Bastiansen, Henrik G., Martin Klimke, and Rolf Werenskjold. "Introduction: Mapping the Role of the Media in the Late Cold War Methodological and Transnational Perspectives." In *Media and the Cold War in the 1980s: Between Star Wars and Glasnost,* edited by Henrik G. Bastiansen, Martin Klimke, and Rolf Werenskjold, 1–17. Cham: Palgrave Macmillan, 2019.

Bazin, Victoria. "'A New Kind of Trade': Advertising Feminism in Spare Rib." In *Re-reading Spare Rib,* edited by Angela Smith, 197–212. Cham: Palgrave Macmillan, 2017.

Bazin, Victoria. "Miss-Represented? Mediating Miss World in *Shrew* Magazine." *Women: A Cultural Review* 27, no. 4 (2016): 412–431.

Bechmann Pedersen, Sune, Marie Cronqvist, and Ulrika Holgersson. "Introduction: Expanding media, expanding histories." In *Expanding media histories: Cultural and material perspectives,* edited by Sune Bechman Pedersen et al., 9–23. Lund: Kriterium, 2023.

Becker-Schaum, Christoph, Philipp Gassert, Martin Klimke, Wilfried Mausbach, and Marianne Zep. "Introduction: The Nuclear Crisis, NATO's Double-Track Decision, and the Peace Movement of the 1980s." In *The Nuclear Crisis: The Arms Race, Cold War Anxiety, and the German Peace Movement of the 1980s,* edited by Christoph Becker-Schaum, Philipp GassertMartin Klimke, Wilfried Mausbach, and Marianne Zep, 1–36. New York and Oxford: Berghahn Books, 2016.

Beetham, Margaret and Kay Boardman. *Victorian Women's Magazines. An anthology.* Manchester & New York: Manchester University Press, 2001.

Beetham, Margaret. *A Magazine of her own? Domesticity and Desire in the Woman's Magazine 1800–1914.* London: Routledge, 1996.

Berger, Peter, and Thomas Luckmann. *The Social Construction of Reality: A Treatise in the Sociology of Knowledge*. London: Penguin, 1991 [1966].

Bergman, Solveig. *The Politics of Feminism: Autonomous Feminist Movements in Finland and West Germany from the 1960s to the 1980s*. Turku: Åbo Akademi University Press, 2002.

Bergstrom, Andrea, "Women in Magazines: Feminist magazines," in *Encyclopedia of Gender in Media*, edited by Mary Kosut, 439–442. Thousand Oaks, Calif.: Sage, 2012.

Billig, Michael. *Banal Nationalism*. London: Sage, 1995.

Birgersson, Bengt Owe, Stig Hadenius, Björn Molin, and Hans Wieslander. *Sverige efter 1900: En modern politisk historia*. 10:e upplagan. Stockholm: Bonnier Fakta, 1984.

Bjerstedt, Åke. *"Peace Education" – "Friedenserzihung" – "Education de la Paix": Fredsorienterande aktiviteter i skolan i olika länder vid 1980-talet mitt*. Lund: Lund university, 1986.

Bjørgo, Tore, and Jacob Aasland Ravndal. *Extreme-Right Violence and Terrorism: Concepts, Patterns, and Responses*. The Hague: International Centre for Counter-Terrorism, 2019.

Björneberg, Anna-Lisa. "Internationella kvinnoförbundet för fred och frihet: Göteborgskretsen." In *"Så här kan vi inte ha det!": Fem kvinnoorganisationer i Göteborg: 100 års ideellt arbete, när samhället svek*, edited by Anna-Lisa Björneberg et al. Gothenburg: Göteborgskvinnor i rörelser, 2019.

Blair, Tony. *The Third Way. New Politics for the New Century*. London: Fabian Society, 1998

Bokholm, Sif. "Annie Åkerhielm." In *Svenskt kvinnobiografiskt lexikon* (https://skbl.se/en/article/AnnieAkerhielm).

Bondebjerg, Ib. "Scandinavian Media Histories. A Comparative Study. Institutions, Genres and Culture in a National and Global Perspective." *Nordicom Review* 23, no. 1–2 (2002): 61–79.

Borchorst, Anette, and Birte Siim. "Woman-friendly policies and state feminism: Theorizing Scandinavian gender equality." *Feminist Theory* 9, no. 2 (2008): 207–224.

Bracke, Maud Anne. *Women and the Reinvention of the Political: Feminism in Italy, 1968–1983*. New York and London: Routledge, 2014.

Bracke, Maud, Julia C. Bullock, Penelope Morris, and Kristina Schulz, eds. *Translating Feminism: Interdisciplinary Approaches to Text, Place and Agency (1945–2000)*. Cham: Palgrave, 2021.

Bradley, Patricia. *Mass Media and the Shaping of American Feminism, 1963–1975*. Mississippi: University of Mississippi Press, 2003.

Brake, Laurel. "Gendered space and the British Press." *Studies in Newspaper and Periodical History*, 3, no. 1–2 (1995): 99–110.

Branciforte, Laura. "The women's peace camp at Comiso, 1983: transnational feminism and the anti-nuclear movement." *Women's History Review* 31, no. 2 (2022): 316–343.

Bryn, Steinar. "The Americanization of the Global Village: A Case Study of Norway." In *Networks of Americanization. Aspects of the American Influence in Sweden*, edited by Rolf Lundén and Erik Åsard, 20–37. Uppsala: Uppsala University, 1992.

Carlsson, Holger. *Nazismen i Sverige: Ett varningsord.* Stockholm: Federativs, 1942.

Ceadel, Martin. "Pacifism and pacificism." In *The Cambridge History of Twentieth-Century Political Thought,* edited by Terence Ball, and Rickhard Bellamy, 473–492. Cambridge: Cambridge University Press, 2008.

Chetty, Naganna, and Sreejith Alathur. "Hate speech review in the context of online social networks." *Aggression and Violent Behavior* 40 (May-June 2018): 108–118.

Christians, Clifford G., Theodore L. Glasser, Denis McQuail, Kaarle Nordenstreng and Robert A. White. *Normative Theories of the Media. Journalism in Democratic Societies.* Urbana & Chicago, IL: University of Illinois Press, 2009.

Cooper, Alice Holmes. "Media framing and social movement mobilization: German peace protest against INF missiles, the Gulf War, and NATO peace enforcement in Bosnia." *European Journal of Political Research* 41 (2002): 37–80.

Copeland, David. "America, 1750–1820." In *Press, Politics and the Public Sphere in Europe and North America, 1760–1820,* edited by Hannah Barker and Simon Burrows, 140–158. Cambridge: Cambridge University Press, 2004.

Corbin, Juliet M., and Anselm L. Strauss. *Basics of Qualitative Research: Techniques and Procedures for Developing Grounded Theory.* 4th edition. Los Angeles: Sage, 2015.

Cronqvist, Marie and Christoph Hilgert. "Entangled Media Histories: The value of Transnational and Transmedial Approaches in Media Historiography." *Media History* 23, no. 1 (2017): 130–141.

Cronqvist, Marie, Patrik Lundell, and Pelle Snickars, eds. *Återkoplingar.* Mediehistoriskt arkiv nr. 28. Lund: Lunds Universitet, 2014.

Cronqvist, Marie. "From Socialist Hero to Capitalist Icon: The Cultural Transfer of the East German Children's Television Programme Unser-Sandmännchen to Sweden in the Early 1970s." *Historical Journal of Film, Radio and Television* 41, no. 2 (2021): 378–393.

Cronqvist, Marie. "Survival in the Welfare Cocoon: The Culture of Civil Defense in Cold War Sweden." In *Cold War Cultures: Perspectives on Eastern and Western European Societies,* edited by Annette Vowinckel et al., 191–210. New York: Berghahn Books, 2012.

Curtius, Ernst Robert. *European Literature and the Latin Middle Ages.* Translated by Willard R. Trask. London: Routledge & Kegan Paul, 1953.

Dahl, Hans Fredrik. "The Pursuit of Media History." *Media, Culture & Society* 16, no. 4 (1994): 551–563.

Dahlerup, Drude. *Rødstrømperne: Den danske Rødstrømpebevægelses udvikling, nytænkning og gennemslag 1970-1985, bind I & II.* Copenhagen: Gyldendal, 1998.

Danielsen, Hilde. *Da det personlige ble politisk. Den nye kvinne- og mannsbevegelsen på 1970-tallet.* Oslo: Scandinavian Academic Press, 2013.

Delap, Lucy and Maria DiCenzo. "Transatlantic Print Culture: The Anglo-American Feminist Press and Emerging 'Modernities.'" In *Transatlantic Print Culture, 1880–1940: Emerging Media, Emerging Modernisms,* edited by Ann Ardis, and Patrick Collier, 48–65. London: Palgrave Macmillan, 2008.

Delap, Lucy. "Feminist Bookshops, Reading Cultures and the Women's Liberation Movement in Great Britain, c. 1974–2000." *History Workshop Journal* 81 no. 1 (2016): 171–196.

Delap, Lucy. *The Feminist Avant-Garde. Transatlantic Encounters of the Early Twentieth Century.* Cambridge: Cambridge University Press, 2007.

Diamant, Lincoln. *Television's Classic Commercials: The Golden Years, 1948-58.* New York: Hastings House, 1971.

Doracic, Alen and Petter Edlund. "Armlängdsprincipen och Statens kulturråd: En fallstudie om maktfördelning i svensk kulturpolitik." Masters diss. Högskolan i Borås, 2005.

Duchen, Claire. *Feminism in France: From May '68 to Mitterrand.* London: Routledge, 1986.

Dyer, Gillian. *Advertising as Communication.* London: Methuen, 1982.

Edgar, Andrew, and Peter Sedgwick, eds. *Cultural Theory. The Key Concepts.* London & New York: Routledge, 2004.

Eide, Martin, and Christine Myrvang. *Alltid foran skjermen. Dagbladet og det digitale skiftet.* Oslo: Universitetsforlaget, 2018.

Ekberg, Henrik. *Führerns trogna följeslagare: Den finländska nazismen 1932–1941.* Helsingfors: Schildts, 1991.

El-Aswad, El-Sayed. "Images of Muslims in Western Scholarship and Media after 9/11." *Digest of Middle East Studies* 22, no. 1 (2013): 39–56.

Elgán, Elisabeth. *Att ge sig själv makt: Grupp 8 och 1970-talets feminism.* Gothenburg: Makadam Förlag, 2015.

Endres, Kathleen R. "Women's Magazines: Fashion." In *Encyclopedia of Gender in Media,* edited by Mary Kosut, 434–439. Thousand Oaks, Calif.: Sage, 2012.

Enli, Gunn, Trine Syvertsen, and Ole J. Mjøs, O. J. "The welfare state and the media system." *Scandinavian Journal of History* 43, No. 5, (2018): 609–612.

Entwistle, Joanne. *The Fashioned Body. Fashion, Dress and Modern Social Theory.* Cambridge: Polity, 2000.

Epitropoulus, Mike-Frank G. and Victor Roudometof, eds. *American Culture in Europe. Interdisciplinary Perspectives.* Westport, Connecticut: Praeger, 1998.

Erdman Farrell, Amy. *Yours is Sisterhood: Ms. Magazine and the Promise of Popular Feminism.* Chapel Hill: University of North Carolina Press, 1998.

Erickson, Bailee. "'Every Woman Needs Courage': Feminist Periodicals in 1970s West Germany." *The Graduate History Review* 2 (2010): 31–44.

Eriksson, Moa. "Pizza, beer and kittens: Negotiating cultural trauma discourses on Twitter in the wake of the 2017 Stockholm attack." *New media & society* 20, no. 11 (2018): 3980–3996.

Fagerholm, Andreas. "The radical right and the radical left in contemporary Europe: Two min–max definitions." *Journal of Contemporary European Studies* 26, no. 4 (2018): 411–424.

Fahlenbrach, Kathrin and, Laura Stapane. "Visual and Media Strategies of the Peace Movement." In *The Nuclear Crisis: The Arms Race, Cold War Anxiety, and the German Peace Movement of the 1980s,* edited by Christoph Becker-Schaum, Philipp Gassert Martin Klimke, Wilfried Mausbach, and Marianne Zep, 222–241. New York and Oxford: Berghahn Books, 2016.

Fahnestock, Jeanne and Marie Secor. "The rhetoric of literary criticism." In *Textual Dynamics of the Professions: Historical and Contemporary Studies of*

*Writing in Professional Communities*, edited by Charles Bazerman and James Paradis, 77–96. Madison: University of Wisconsin Press, 1991.

Fahy, Declan. "Objectivity, False Balance, and Advocacy in News Coverage of Climate Change." In *Oxford Research Encyclopedia of Climate Science*. Oxford: Oxford University Press, 2017.

Fairclough, Norman. *Language and Power*. London & New York: Longman 1989.

Farrell, Amy. "Attentive to Difference: Ms. Magazine, Coalition Building, and Sisterhood." In *Feminist Coalitions: Historical Perspectives on Second-Wave Feminism in the United States*, edited by Stephanie Gilmore, 48–62. Urbana: University of Illinois Press, 2008.

Fehrenbach, Heide and Uta G. Poiger, eds., *Transactions, Transgressions, Transformations: American Culture in Western Europe and Japan*. New York, Oxford: Bergham Books, 2000.

Felski, Rita. *Beyond Feminist Aesthetics: Feminist Literature and Social Change*. Cambridge: Harvard University Press, 1989.

Fischer, Gayle V(eronica). *Pantaloons and Power. A Nineteenth-Century Dress Reform in the United States*. Kent: The Kent State University Press, 2001.

Fonn, Birgitte Kjos, Harald Hornmoen, Nathalie Hyde-Clarke and Yngve Benestad Hågvar, eds. *Individual Exposure and Subjectivity in Journalism*. Oslo: Cappelen Damm Akademisk, 2017.

Fonn, Birgitte Kjos. "Denne gangen er det annerledes. En studie av børskrakket i 1987 i to norske aviser." In *Presse, profesjon og politikk. Festskrift til Paul Bjerke*, edited by Birgitte Kjos Fonn, Ellen Lexerød Hovlid, and Birgit Røe Mathisen. Oslo: Cappelen Damm Akademisk, 2022.

Fonn, Birgitte Kjos. "Nye måter å dekke Vesten på. En studie av internasjonalt stoff i to norske aviser 1975–2005." *Mediehistorisk Tidsskrift* 19, no. 1–2 (2022): 178–202.

Fonn, Birgitte Kjos. *Orientering. Rebellenes avis*. Oslo: Pax, 2011.

Forsman, Michael. "Media Literacy and the Emerging Media Citizen in the Nordic Media Welfare State." *Nordic Journal of Media Studies* 2 (2020): 59–70.

Forssell, Pia. "Från skrivande damer till yrkesförfattrinnor." In *Finlands svenska litteraturhistoria*, edited by Johan Wrede, 448–466. Helsingfors: Svenska Litteratursällskapet i Finland, 1999.

Forster, Laurel. "Spreading the Word: feminist print cultures and the Women's Liberation Movement." *Women's History Review* 25 no.5 (2016): 812–831.

Fox, Stephen R. *The Mirror Makers: A History of American Advertising and Its Creators*. 1st ed. New York: Morrow, 1984.

Fraser, Nancy. "Rethinking the Public Sphere: A Contribution to the Critique of Actually Existing Democracy." *Social Texts* 25/26 (1990): 56–80.

Friedberg, Anne. *Window Shopping: Cinema and the Postmodern*. London: University of California Press, 1994.

Galbraith, John Kenneth. *The Affluent Society*. London: Hamish Hamilton, 1958.

Galtung, Johan, and Mari Ruge. "The Structure of Foreign News: The Presentation of the Congo, Cuba and Cyprus Crises in Four Norwegian Newspapers." *Journal of International Peace Research*, no. 2 (1965): 64–90.

Gorp, Baldwin Van. "Culture and Protest in Media Frames." In *Media and Revolt. Strategies and Performances from the 1960s to the Present*, edited by

Kathrin Fahlenbrach, Erling Sivertsen and Rolf Werenskjold, 75–90. Oxford: Berghahn Books, 2014.

Gelber, Katharine. *Speech Matters: Getting Free Speech Right.* St Lucia, Queensland, Australia: University of Queensland Press, 2011.

Gelley, Alexander. "Ernst Robert Curtius: Topology and Critical Method," *MLN* 81, no. 5 (1966): 579–94.

Gellner, Ernest. *Nations and Nationalism.* Second Edition. Introduction by John Breuilly. Ithaca, NY: Cornell University Press, 2006.

Giddens, Anthony. *The Third Way: The Renewal of Social Democracy*.Cambridge: Polity Press, 1998.

Gitelman, Lisa. *Always Already New: Media, History, and the Data of Culture.* Cambridge, MA.: MIT Press, 2006.

Glaser, Barney, and Anselm Strauss. *The Discovery of Grounded Theory: Strategies for Qualitative Research.* Chicago: Aldine, 1967.

Goffman, Erving. *Frame Analysis: An Essay on the Organization of Experience.* Cambridge, Mass.: Harvard University Press, 1974.

Grepstad, Jon. "The Peace Movement in the Nordic Countries." *International Peace Research Newsletter,* no. 4 (1982): 10–15.

Haagerup, Niels Jorgen. "The Nordic Peace Movements." In *European Peace Movements and the Future of the Western Alliance,* edited by Walter Laqueur, and Robert Hunter, 144–165. New Brunswick, N.J.: Transaction, 1988.

Haasio, Ari, and Markku Mattila. *Suvaitsematon Suomi: Suvaitsemattomuuden historia.* Helsinki: Avain, 2021.

Haasio, Ari, Anu Ojaranta, and Markku Mattila. *Valheen jäljillä.* Helsinki: Avain, 2018.

Haasio, Ari, Markku Mattila, Anu Ojaranta, and Elisa Kannasto. "Terrori-isku tiedontarpeiden virittäjänä: Turun puukotusten aiheuttamat tiedontarpeet." *Informaatiotutkimus* 37, no. 2 (2018): 5–36.

Habermas, Jürgen. *The Structural Transformation of the Public Sphere: An Inquiry into a Category of Bourgeois Society.* Cambridge: MIT Press, 1991.

Habermas, Jürgen. *The Philosophical Discourse of Modernity: Twelve Lectures.* Cambridge: Polity Press, 1987.

Hagner, Minna, and Teija Försti. *Suffragettien sisaret.* Helsinki: Unioni naisasialiitto, 2006.

Hakulinen, Lauri. "Euren, Gustaf Erik." In *Kansallinen elämäkerrasto 1,* edited by Blomstedt, Kaarlo et al., 601–603. Porvoo: WSOY, 1927.

Hall, Stuart. "Culture, the media and the ideological effect." In *Mass Communication and Society,* edited by James Curran, Michael Gurevitch, and Janet Woollacott, 315–348. Beverly Hills: SAGE, 1979.

Hall, Stuart. "Ideology and Communication Theory." In *Rethinking Communication. Volume 1: Paradigm Issues,* edited by Brenda Dervin, 40–52. Newbury Park: Sage, 1989.

Hall, Stuart. "The Rediscovery of 'Ideology': Return of the Repressed in Media Studies." In *Culture, Society and the Media,* edited by Tony Gurevitch, Michael Bennet, James Curran, and Jane Woollacott. London: Methuen, 1982.

Hallin, Daniel C., and Paolo Mancini. *Comparing Media Systems. Three Models of Media and Politics. Communication, Society and Politics.* Cambridge: Cambridge University Press, 2004.

Hamilo, Marko. *Punavihreä kupla: Perussuomalaiset ja media.* Helsinki: Suomen Perusta, 2015.

Hankamäki, Jukka. *Totuus kiihottaa: Filosofinen tutkimus vasemmistopopulistisen valtamedian tieto- ja totuuskriisistä.* Helsinki: Suomen Perusta, 2020.

Hamilton, Peter. *Knowledge and Social Structure. An Introduction to the Classical Argument in the Sociology of Knowledge.* London: Routledge & Kegan Paul, 1974.

Hanitzsch, Thomas. "Deconstructing Journalism Culture: Toward a Universal Theory." *Communication Theory* 17, no. 4 (2007): 367–385.

Hannula, Risto, Kari J. Kettula, and Kari Vaijärvi. *Kulttuuri- ja mielipidelehdet.* Helsinki: Kirjastopalvelu Oy, 1981.

Hanski, Jari. *Juutalaisviha Suomessa 1918–1944.* Helsinki: Ajatus Kirjat, 2006.

Hanski, Pentti. *Pöllön siivin. MTV:n vuodet 1955–1984,* edited by Markku Onttonen. Helsinki: Otava, 2001.

Harcup, Tony, and Deirdre O'Neill. "What is News? Galtung and Ruge Revisited." *Journalism Studies* 2, no. 2 (2001): 261–280.

Harcup, Tony, and Deirdre O'Neill. "What is News? News values revisited (again)." *Journalism Studies,* 18, no. 12 (2017): 1470–1488.

Hartog, Francois. *Regimes of Historicity. Presentism and Experiences of Time.* New York: Columbia University Press, 2015.

Harvard, Jonas, and Peter Stadius. "A Communicative Perspective on the Formation of the North: Contexts, Channels and Concepts." In *Communicating the North: Media Structures and Images in the Making of the Nordic Region,* edited by Jonas Harvard and Peter Stadius, 1–24. London and New York: Routledge, 2016.

Haveman, Heather A. *Magazines and the Making of America: Modernization, Community, and Print Culture, 1741–1860.* Princeton: Princeton University Press, 2016.

Heggestad, Eva. "Anna Mathilda Roos." In *Svenskt kvinnobiografiskt lexikon* (https://skbl.se/en/article/MathildaRoos).

Heikkinen, Merja. "Government policy and definitions of art: The case of comics." *International Journal of Cultural Policy* 14, no. 1 (2008): 79–93.

Heinonen, Visa and Hannu Konttinen. *Nyt Uutta Suomessa. Suomalaisen mainonnan historia.* Helsinki: Mainostajien Liitto, 2001.

Heinonen, Visa and Mika Pantzar. "Little America: The Modernization of the Finnish Consumer Society in the 1950s and 1960s." In *Americanisation in 20th Century Europe: Business, Culture, Politics, Vol.2,* edited by Mathias Kipping and Nick Tiratsoo, 41–59. Centre d'Histoire de l'Europe du Nord-Ouest: Université Charles de Gaulle Lille 3, 2002.

Heinonen, Visa, Jukka Kortti, and Mika Pantzar. "How Lifestyle Products Became Rooted in the Finnish Consumer Market – Domestication of Jeans, Chewing Gum, Sunglasses and Cigarettes." In *National Consumer Research Centre working papers* 80. Helsinki: National Consumer Research Centre, 2003.

Heinonen, Visa. "Kolme 'mainosmestaria' ja modernin mainonnan alku Suomessa." In *Keulakuvia ja peränpitäjiä: Vanhan ja uuden yhteiskunnan rajalla*, toimittaneet Riitta Oittinen and Marjatta Rahikainen, 331–346. Helsinki: Suomen Historiallinen Seura, 2000.

Helminen, Minna. *Väkevää akkaväkeä: Naisten kulttuuriyhdistys 20* vuotta. Helsinki: Naisten kulttuuriyhdistys, 2002.

Helmut, Todd, Elizabeth Bodine-Baron, Andrew Radin, Madeline Magnuson, Joshua Mendelsohn, William Marcellino, Andriy Bega, and Zev Winkelman. *Russian Social Media Influence: Understanding Russian Propaganda in Eastern Europe.* Santa Monica, California: Rand Corporation, 2018.

Hepp, Andreas, and Nick Couldry. "What should comparative media research be comparing? Towards a transcultural approach to 'media cultures.'" In *Internationalizing Media Studies*, edited by Daya Kishan Thussu, 32–47. London: Routledge, 2009.

Herkman, Juha. "The Structural Transformation of The Democratic Corporatist Model: The Case of Finland." *Javnost – The Public: Journal of the European Institute for Communication and Culture* 16, no. 4 (2009): 73–90.

Hirvonen, Katrina. "Sweden: When hate becomes the norm." *Race & Class* 55, no. 1 (2013): 78–86.

Holappa, Henrik. *Minä perustin uusnatsijärjestön: Suomen Vastarintaliikkeen ex-johtajan muistelmat.* Helsinki: Into, 2016.

Holgersson, Ulrika. "Från tågresor till social medier. Rösträttens mediehistoria." In *Rösträttens århundrade. Kampen, utvecklingen och framtiden för demokratin i Sverige*, edited by Ulrika Holgersson, and Lena Wängnerud, 103–128. Stockholm: Makadam, 2018.

Hollows, Joanne. "*Spare Rib*, Second-Wave Feminism and the Politics of Consumption." *Feminist Media Studies* 13 no. 2 (2013): 268–287.

Holm, Hans Henrik. "The Effect of Globalization on Media Structures and Norms: Globalization and the Choice of foreign news." In *News in a Globalized Society*, edited by Stig Hjarvard, 113–147. Gothenburg: Nordicom, 2001.

Houe, Poul, and Sven Hakon Rossel, eds. *Images of America in Scandinavia.* Amsterdam: Atlanta, 1998.

Hovden, Jan Fredrik and Rolf Werenskjold. "The Cold War Reporters: The Norwegian Foreign-News Journalists and Foreign-News Correspondents, 1945–1995." In *Media and the Cold War in the 1980s: Between Star Wars and Glasnost*, edited by Henrik G. Bastiansen, Martin Klimke, and Rolf Werenskjold, 189–222. Cham: Palgrave Macmillan, 2019.

Huo, Jing Jing. *The Third Way Reforms: Social Democracy after the Golden Age.* New York: Cambridge University Press, 2009.

Hvid Kromann, Thomas. "Subpublications from a Basement in Snaregade 6, Copenhagen – Arena Sub-Pub (1969–1970)." In *A Cultural History of the Avant-Garde in the Nordic Countries 1950–1975*, edited by Tania Ørum and Jesper Olsson, 175–180. Leiden: Brill, 2016.

Hänninen, Reetta. *Tulisydän. Maissi Erkon kiihkeä elämä.* Helsinki: Otava, 2022.

Immonen, Kari. *Ryssästä saa puhua...: Neuvostoliitto suomalaisessa julkisuudessa ja kirjat julkisuuden muotona 1918–39.* Helsinki: Otava, 1987.

Iriye, Akira. *Global Community: The Role of International Organizations in the Making of the Contemporary World.* Berkeley: University of California Press, 2002.

Isaksson, Emma. *Kvinnokamp – Synen på underordning och motstånd i den nya kvinnorörelsen.* Stockholm: Atlas, 2007.

Isänmaallisen kansanliikkeen yleiset ohjelmaperusteet (Perusohjelma hyväksytty perustavassa kokouksessa Hämeenlinnassa 5.6.1932).https://www.fsd.tuni.fi/pohtiva/ohjelmalistat/IKL/291.

Jallinoja, Riitta. *Suomalaisen naisasialiikkeen taistelukaudet: Naisasialiike naisten elämäntilanteen muutoksen ja yhteiskunnallis-aatteellisen murroksen heijastajana.* Helsinki: WSOY, 1983.

Jensen, Helle Strandgaard. *From Superman to Social Realism: Children's media and Scandinavian childhood.* Amsterdam: John Benjamin's Publishing Company, 2017.

Jensen, Klaus Bruhn. *Dansk mediehistorie, 1–4.* Fredriksberg: Samfundslitteratur 1996–1998, 2016.

Johannisson, Jenny and Veronica Trépagny. "The (dis)location of cultural policy: two Swedish cases." Accessed July 10, 2022. http://neumann.hec.ca/iccpr/PDF_Texts/Johannisson_Trepagny.pdf.

Johanson, Katya. "Culture for or by the child? 'Children's culture' and cultural policy." *Poetics* 38 (2010): 386–401.

Jonsson, Karin. "Unifying Solidarity: The Concept of International Solidarity in Swedish Social Democracy 1972–1985." *Redescriptions: Political Thought, Conceptual History and Feminist Theory* 25 (1) (2022): 27–48.

Jordheim, Helge. "Against Periodization: Koselleck's Theory of Multiple Temporalities." *History and Theory* 51, no. 2 (2012): 151–171.

Juntunen, Tapio. "'We Just Got to Keep Harping On About It': Anti-Nuclearism and the Role of Sub-Regional Arms Control Initiatives in the Nordic Countries During the Second Cold War." In *The INF Treaty of 1987: A Reappraisal*, edited by Philipp Gassert, Tim Geiger, and Hermann Wentker, 215–236. Göttingen: Vandenhoeck & Ruprecht GmbH & Co., 2020.

Kalyadin, Aleksander N. "Role of Non-Governmental Organizations in UN Activities for Peace and Disarmament." *Bulletin of Peace Proposals* 18:3 (1987): 393–398.

Kammer, Aske. "A Welfare Perspective on Nordic Media Subsidies." *Journal of Media Business Studies* 13, no. 3 (2016): 140–152.

Karemaa, Outi. *Vihollisia, vainoojia, syöpäläisiä: Venäläisviha Suomessa 1917–1923.* Helsinki: SHS, 1998.

Karhu, Sirpa. "Ajan Suunnan juutalaiskuva 1932–1944." Master's thesis. University of Jyväskylä, 2014.

Kaukonen, Väinö. "Europaeuksen osa Kalevalan laadinnassa." In *D. E. D Europaeus. Suurmies vai kummajainen*, edited by Kuusi, Matti, Pekka Laaksonen and Senni Timonen, 65–81. Helsinki: SKS, 1988.

Kawamura, Yunuya. *Fashion-ology.* Oxford: Berg, 2005.

Keinonen, Heidi. "Early Commercial Television in Finland. Balancing between East and West." *Media History* 18, no 4 (2012): 177–189.

Kellner, Douglas. *Media culture. Cultural studies, Identity and Politics between the Modern and the Postmodern.* London and New York: Routledge, 1995.

Kilpiö, Kaarina. "The Use of Music in Early Finnish Cinema and TV Advertising." In *Advertising Research in the Nordic Countries*, edited by Lotte Yssing Hansen and Flemming Hansen, 68–76. Copenhagen: Samfundslitteratur, 2001.

Kinnunen, Tiina. "'Fighting Sisters': a comparative biography of Ellen Key (1849–1926) and Alexandra Gripenberg (1857–1913) in the contested field of European feminisms." In *Biography, Gender and History: Nordic Perspectives*, edited by Erla Hulda Halldórsdóttir, Tiina Kinnunen, Maarit Leskelä-Kärki, and Birgitta Possing, 143–164. Turku: k&h, 2016.

Kinnunen, Tiina. "Alexandra Gripenberg and Lost Faith in National Belonging." In *Nineteenth-Century Nationalisms and Emotions in the Baltic Sea Region. The Production of Loss*, edited by Anna Bohlin, Tiina Kinnunen, and Heidi Grönstrand, 344–369. Leiden, Boston: Brill, 2021.

Kinnunen, Tiina. "Alexandra Gripenberg's Feminist Christianity." In *Finnish Women Making Religion. Between Ancestors and Angels*, edited by Terhi Utriainen and Päivi Salmesvuori, 61–79. Basingstoke: Palgrave Macmillan, 2014.

Kinnunen, Tiina. "History as Argument – Alexandra Gripenberg, Ellen Key and the Notion of True Feminism." In *Gendering Historiography. Beyond National Canons*, edited by Angelika Epple, and Angelika Schaser, 181–207. Frankfurt, New York: Campus Verlag, 2009.

Kinnunen, Tiina. "The National and International in Making a Feminist: the Case of Alexandra Gripenberg." *Women's History Review* 25, no. 4 (2016): 652–670.

Kirchhof, Astrid Mignon. "Spanning the Globe: West-German Support for the Australian Anti-Nuclear Movement." *Historical Social Research* 39, no. 1 (2014): 254–273.

Kiros, Sara Loredana. *Hate Speech: A Comparative Study of the Rhetoric in the Official Documents of the Sweden Democrats and the Rhetoric in Samtiden, a News Site Owned by the Sweden Democrats*. Bachelor's thesis. Malmö University, 2019.

Kivikuru, Ullamaija, and Kaarle Nordenstreng. "National, global, regional – Where is the core of the Nordic communication research?" In *Norden och världen. Perspektiv från forskningen om medier och kommunikation: = The Nordic countries and the world: perspectives from research on media and communication: en bok tillägnad Ulla Carlsson*, edited by Thorbjörn Broddason. Göteborg: Göteborgs universitet, 2010): 105–124.

Kjær, Peter and Tore Slaatta, eds. *Mediating Business*. Copenhagen: Copenhagen Business School, 2007.

Klinge, Matti. *Keisarin Suomi*, Trans. Marketta Klinge. Helsinki: Schildts, 1997.

Klockmann, Jette Baagø. "Remembrance Diplomacy by the Mayors of Hiroshima and Nagasaki in the UN, 1976–2015." *The International History Review* 40, no. 3 (2018): 523–545.

Knoblauch, William M. "Selling 'Star Wars' in American Mass Media." In *Media and the Cold War in the 1980s: Between Star Wars and Glasnost*, edited by Henrik G. Bastiansen Martin Klimke, and Rolf Werenskjold, 19–42. Cham: Palgrave Macmillan, 2019.

Kodama, Katsuya. *Peace on the move: A sociological survey of the members of Swedish peace organizations*. Stockholm: Almqvist & Wiksell International, 1990.

Koivulaakso, Dan, Mikael Brunila, and Li Andersson. *Äärioikeisto Suomessa.* Helsinki: Into, 2012.

Kokko, Heikki and Minna Harjula. "Social History of Experiences: A Theoretical-Methodological Approach." In *Experiencing Society and the Lived Welfare State,* edited by Pertti Haapala, Minna Harjula, Heikki Kokko, 17–40. Cham: Palgrave Macmillan, 2023.

Kokko, Heikki. "Suomenkielisen julkisuuden nousu 1850-luvulla ja sen yhteiskunnallinen merkitys." *Historiallinen Aikakauskirja,* no.1 (2019): 5–21.

Kokko, Heikki. "Suomenkielisen lehdistön paikalliskirjekulttuuria tallentava digitaalinen Translocalis-tietokanta." *Ennen ja nyt. Historian tietosanomat* (2/2019). https://journal.fi/ennenjanyt/article/view/108930

Kokko, Heikki. "Temporalization of Experiencing. First-Hand Experience of the Nation in Mid-Nineteenth Century Finland." In *Lived Nation as the History of Experiences and Emotions in Finland, 1800–2000,* edited by Ville Kivimäki, Sami Suodenjoki, and Tanja Vahtikari, 109–133. London: Palgrave, 2021.

Kokko, Heikki. "Kotomaamme katveinen kuva: Suomenkielisen lehdistön paikalliskirjekulttuurin marginalisoituminen." In *Kaanon ja marginaali. Kulttuuriperinnön vaiennetut äänet.* Kalevalaseuran vuosikirja 101, edited by Niina Hämäläinen and Lotte Tarkka, 263–283, Helsinki: SKS, 2022.

Kokko, Heikki. "Sivistyksen surkea tila," in *Kansa kaikkivaltias: suurlakko Suomessa 1905,* edited by Pertti Haapala, Olli Löytty, Kukku Melkas and Marko Tikka, 307–312 . Helsinki: Teos, 2008.

Kokko, Heikki. "From Local to Translocal Experience. The Nationwide Culture of Letters to the Press in Mid-1800s Finland." *Media History* 28, no. 2 (2022), 181–198.

Kokko, Heikki. *Kuviteltu minuus. Ihmiskäsityksen murros suomenkielisen kansanosan kulttuurissa 1800-luvun puolivälissä.* Tampere: Tampere University Press, 2016.

Kortti, Jukka. "Generations and Media History." In *Broadband Society and Generational Changes Series: Participation in Broadband Society - Volume 5,* edited by Leopoldina Fortunati ja Fausto Colombo, 69–93. Frankfurt am Main: Peter Lang, 2011.

Kortti, Jukka. "Television Creating Finnish Consumer Mentality in the 1960s." In *Finnish Consumption. Emerging Consumer Society between East and West,* edited by Visa Heinonen & Matti Peltonen, 154–176. Helsinki: SKS 2013.

Kortti, Jukka. "Slow media under cross pressures: US educational diplomacy in the Nordic countries during the Cold War." In A *Nordic Model of Propaganda and Persuasion,* edited by Fredrik Norén, Emil Stjernholm and Claire Thomas, 181–200. London: Palgrave Macmillan, 2022.

Kortti, Jukka. "Temporalities and Theory in Media History." *Media History* 28, no. 3 (2022): 442–454.

Kortti, Jukka. *Mediahistoria. Viestinnän merkityksiä puheesta bitteihin.* Helsinki: SKS, 2016.

Kortti, Jukka. *Modernisaatiomurroksen kaupalliset merkit. 60-luvun suomalainen televisiomainonta.* Helsinki: SKS, 2003.

Kortti, Jukka. *Media in History. An Introduction to the Meanings and Transformations of Communication over Time*. London: Macmillan Red Globe Press, 2019.

Koselleck, Reinhart. *Futures Past: On the Semantics of Historical* Time. New York: Columbia University Press, 2004.

Kotonen, Tommi, and Daniel Sallamaa. "Pohjoismaisen Vastarintaliikkeen kieltäminen ja sen seuraukset." *Politiikassa*, 10 November 2020.

Krippendorf, Klaus. *Content Analysis: An Introduction to Its Methodology*. 2nd edition. Thousand Oaks, London, & New Delhi: Sage Publications, 2004.

Kroes, Rob. *If You've Seen One, You've Seen the Mall: Europeans and American Mass Culture*. Urbana and Chicago: University of Illinois Press, 1996.

Kurkela, Reijo. *Tupakka tupakkalain jälkeen*. Helsinki: Tilastokeskus, 1987.

Kurvinen, Heidi and Arja Turunen. "Radical sex role ideology and the Finnish gender role movement in the late 1960s." *Women's History Review* (2022).

Kurvinen, Heidi and Arja Turunen. "Toinen aalto uudelleen tarkasteltuna: Yhdistys 9:n rooli suomalaisen feminisminhistoriassa." *Sukupuolentutkimus– Genusforskning* 31, no. 3 (2018): 21–34.

Kurvinen, Heidi. "Adopting Public Relations-Like Strategies to Promote Labour Feminism in Finland, 1965–1975." *European History Quarterly* 53, no. 4 (2023), 664–684.

Kurvinen, Heidi. "Children and the Mediated Experiences of the Welfare State: The International Year of the Child (1979) in the Finnish Public Sphere." In *Experiencing Society and the Lived Welfare State*, edited by Pertti Haapala, Minna Harjula, and Heikki Kokko, 233–253. Cham: Palgrave Macmillan.

Kurvinen, Heidi. "Nordic Women Journalists." In *The International Encyclopaedia of Gender, Media, and Communication*, edited by Karen Ross et al. Wiley Blackwell, 2020.

Kuş, Oğuz. "Documenting and Categorizing Hate Speech: Investigating Islamophobia in User Comments on Social Networks." In *International Symposium of New Media from the Past to the Future (May 10, 2017, Istanbul, TURKEY) Proceedings* (E-Book).

Kuusi, Matti, and Senni Timonen. "Suurmies? Kummajainen? Uhrilammas? Keskustelua Europaeuksen elämästä ja työstä." In *D. E. D Europaeus. Suurmies vai kummajainen*, edited by Matti Kuusi, Pekka Laaksonen, and Senni Timonen, 23–50. SKS: Helsinki, 1988.

Lähteenmäki, Maria. *Vuosisadan naisliike. Naiset ja sosialidemokratia 1900-luvun Suomessa*. Helsinki: Sosialidemokraattiset naiset, 2002.

Laitinen, Kai. "Polén, Rietrikki." *Kansallisbiografia-verkkojulkaisu. Studia Biographica 4*. Helsinki: Suomalaisen Kirjallisuuden Seura, 1997. http://urn.fi/urn:nbn:fi:sks-kbg-002933

Landes, Richard, and Steven T. Katz. "Introduction: The Protocols in the Dawn of the 21st Century." In *The Paranoid Apocalypse: A Hundred-Year Retrospective on The Protocols of the Elders of Zion*, edited by Richard Landes and Steven T. Katz, 1–20. New York: New York University Press, 2012.

Landgren, Lars. "Kieli ja aate – politisoituva sanomalehdistö 1860–1889." In *Suomen lehdistön historia 1. Sanomalehdistön vaiheet vuoteen 1905*, edited by Päiviö Tommila, Lars Landgren, and Pirkko Leino-Kaukiainen, 267–420. Kuopio, Kustannuskiila, 1988.

Larsson, Lisbeth. "Trender i svensk veckopress." In *Veckopressbranschens struktur och ekonomi*, edited by Karl Erik Gustafsson, 19–34. Göteborg: Handelshögskolan vid Göteborgs universitet, 1991.

Larsson, Lisbeth. *En annan historia: Om kvinnors läsning och svensk veckopress.* Stockholm: Symposion, 1989.

Latham, Michael E. *Modernization as Ideology: American Social Science and "Nation Building" in the Kennedy Era.* Chapel Hill and London: The University of North Carolina Press, 2000.

Leerssen, Joseph Theodoor. *National Thought in Europe: A Cultural History.* Amsterdam: Amsterdam University Press, 2006.

Leino-Kaukiainen, Pirkko. "Kasvava sanomalehdistö sensuurin kahleissa 1890–1905." In *Suomen lehdistön historia I*, edited by Päiviö Tommila, 421–626. Kuopio: Kustannuskiila, 1988.

Leiss, William, Stephen Kline, and Sut Jhally, *Social Communication in Advertising: Persons, Products and Images of Well-Being.* London and New York: Routledge, 1997.

Lerner, Daniel. *The Passing of Traditional Society: Modernizing the Middle East.* New York: The Free Press, 1958.

Liedman, Sven-Eric, *Att se sig själv i andra: om solidaritet.* Stockholm: Bonnier, 1999

Liikanen, Ilkka. *Fennomania ja kansa. Joukkojärjestäytymisen läpimurto ja Suomalaisen puolueen synty.* Helsinki, SHS, 1995.

Lindblom, Louise. *Ellen Key & Selma Lagerlöf – Breven.* Stockholm: Blue Publishing, 2022.

Lindholm-Narváez, Elena. "The Valkyrie in a Bikini: The Nordic Woman as Progressive Media Icon in Spain, 1891–1975." In *Communicating the North: Media Structures and Images in the Making of the Nordic Region*, edited by Jonas Harvard, and Peter Stadius, 197–218. London: Routledge, 2016.

Litmanen, Tapio. "International Anti-Nuclear Movements in Finland, France and the United States." *Peace Research* 30, no. 4 (1998): 1–19.

Ljunggren, Jens. *Den uppskjutna vreden: socialdemokratisk känslopolitik från 1880- till 1980-talet.* Lund: Nordic Academic Press, 2015.

Lodenius, Anna-Lena, and Mats Wingborg. *Slaget om svenskheten: Ta debatten med Sverigedemokraterna.* Stockholm: Premiss förlag, 2009.

Lodenius, Anna-Lena, and Stieg Larsson. *Extremhögern.* Stockholm: Tidens Förlag, 1994.

Löfgren, Orva. "Medierna i nationsbygget: Hur press, radio och TV gjorde Sverige svenskt." In *Medier och kulturer*, ed. Ulf Hannerz. Stockholm: Carlssons, 1990.

Lööw, Heléne. *Hakkorset och Wasakärven: En studie av nationalsocialismen i Sverige 1924–1950.* Göteborg: Historiska institutionen i Göteborg Universitet, 1990.

Louhivuori, O. W. *Suometar. 1. Perustaminen ja ensimmäiset vaiheet 1847–1852.* Helsinki: Oy Uusi Suomi, 1940.

Loukkola, Pekka. "Kansanedustaja Sebastian Tynkkysen tuomio kiihottamisesta kansanryhmää vastaan pysyi hovissa – aikoo valittaa Euroopan ihmisoikeustuomioistuimeen." *YLE Uutiset*, 2 July 2020.

Löyttyniemi, Leena, "Harmaja, Laura (1881–1954)." In *Kansallisbiografia. Studia Biographica 4*. Helsinki: Suomalaisen Kirjallisuuden Seura, 2000. Accessed February 26, 2016. http://urn.fi/urn:nbn:fi:sks-kbg-008346

Luhtala, Johanna, Markus Manninen and Sari Schulman. "Hanasaari: rakennushistoriaselvitys." https://www.senaatti.fi/app/uploads/2017/05/31 702013_Schulman_Espoo_Hanasaari_RHS.pdf. Accessed August 1, 2022.

Lundén, Rolf and Erik Åsard, eds. *Networks of Americanization. Aspects of the American Influence in Sweden*. Uppsala: Uppsala Univestiry, 1992.

Malmberg, Raili. "Naisten ja kotien lehdet aikansa kuvastimina." In *Suomen lehdistön historia 8. Aikakauslehdistön historia*, edited by Päiviö Tommila, 193–291. Kuopio: Kustannuskiila oy, 1991.

Mannheim, Karl. *Ideology and Utopia. An Introduction to the Sociology of Knowledge*. London: Routledge & Kegan Paul, 1936.

Manns, Ulla. *Den sanna frigörelsen. Fredrika-Bremer-förbundet 1884–1921*. Stockholm: Brutus Östlings Bokförlag Symposion, 1997.

Marjomaa, Ulpu. "Hannula, Mandi (1880–1952)." In *Kansallisbiografia. Studia Biographica 4*. Helsinki: Suomalaisen Kirjallisuuden Seura, 2004. Accessed February 26, 2016. http://urn.fi/urn:nbn:fi:sks-kbg-007562.

Marklund, Carl. "The Social Laboratory, the Middle Way and the Swedish Model: Three frames for the image of Sweden." *Scandinavian Journal of History* 34, no. 3 (2009): 264–285.

Marx, Karl, and Friedrich Engels. *The German Ideology*. Moscow: Progress, 1976.

Matheson, Donald. *Media Discourses: Analysing Media Texts*. Maidenhead: Open University Press, 2005.

Mattila, Markku, and Ari Haasio. "Fake News, Fake Media and Hate Speech in Finnish MV-Magazine—How Can Libraries Fight Against the Lies?" In *New Trends and Challenges in Information Science and Information Seeking Behaviour*, edited by Octavia-Luciana Madge, 75–87. Cham, Switzerland: Springer, 2021.

Mattila, Markku, Ari Haasio, and Anu Ojaranta. "Vihapuhetta valemediassa." *Tiede ja Edistys* 44, no. 1 (2019): 29–49.

Mattila, Markku. "Förlåten faller ... Nimimerkki S. ja Siionin viisaitten pöytäkirjojen tulo Suomeen." Master's thesis. University of Tampere, 1991.

Mattoni, Alice and Emiliano Treré. "Media Practices, Mediation Processes, and Mediatization in the Study of Social Movements." *Communication Theory* 24 no.3 (2014): 252–271.

Mattoni, Alice. *Media Practices and Protest Politics: How Precarious Workers Mobilise*. London: Routledge, 2016.

Mattoni, Alice. *Media Practices and Protest Politics: How Precarious Workers Mobilise*. Farnham: Ashgate, 2012.

Mattsson, Christer. *Nordiska motståndsrörelsens ideologi, propaganda och livsåskådning*. Göteborg: Göteborgs universitet, Segerstedtinstitutet, 2018.

McCombs, Maxwell. *Setting the Agenda: The Mass Media and Public Opinion*. Cambridge: Polity, 2004.

McCracken, Ellen. *Decoding Women's Magazines: From Mademoiselle to Miss*. Basingstoke: Macmillan, 1993.

McMillian, John. *Smoking Typewriters. The Sixties Underground Press and the Rise of Alternative Media in America.* New York: Oxford University Press, 2011.

Mikkola, Kati. *Tulevaisuutta vastaan. Uutuuksien vastustus, kansatiedon keruu ja kansakunnan rakentaminen.* Helsinki: Suomalaisen Kirjallisuuden Seura, 2009.

Mitsui, Hideko. "Uses of Finland in Japan's Social Imaginary." In *Reflections on Imagination: Human Capacity and Ethnographic Method,* edited by Mark Harris and Nigel Rapport, 161–162. Farnham & Burlington: Ashgate, 2015.

Morgan, Sue, ed. *Women, Religion and Feminism in Britain, 1750–1900.* Basingstoke: Palgrave Macmillan, 2002.

Mosco, Vincent. "The Two Marxes. Bridging the Political Economy/Technology and Culture Divide." In *The International Encyclopaedia of Media Studies, Volume I: Media History and the Foundations of Media Studies,* edited by John Nerone, 59–87. General Editor Angharad N. Valdivia. Malden, MA: Wiley Blackwell, 2013.

Mouffe, Chantal. "Hegemony and Ideology in Gramsci." In *Culture, Ideology and Social Process. A Reader,* eds., Tony Bennet, Graham Martin, Colin Mercer & Janet Woollacott London: The Open University Press 1985.

Mourlon-Druol, Emmanuel. "'Managing from the Top': Globalisation and the Rise of Regular Summitry, Mid-1970s–early 1980s." *Diplomacy & Statecraft* 23, no. 4 (2012): 679–703.

Moyn, Samuel. *Not Enough: Human Rights in an Unequal World.* Cambridge, MA: Belknap Press of Harvard University Press, 2018.

Moyn, Samuel. *The Last Utopia: Human Rights in History.* Cambridge, MA: Belknap Press of Harvard University Press, 2010.

Munck, Pirjo. *Valistajista ammattimiehiksi: Toimittajien ammattilaistumisen pitkä tie 1771–1921.* Helsinki: Helsingin yliopisto, 2016.

Murray, Simone. *Mixed Media: Feminist Presses and Publishing Politics.* London: Pluto Press, 2004.

Nerone, John. *The Media and Public Life: A History.* Cambridge & Malden: Polity, 2015.

Nevala-Nurmi, Seija-Leena. *Perhe maanpuolustajana: Sukupuoli ja sukupolvi Lotta Svärd- ja suojeluskuntajärjestöissä 1918–1944.* Tampere: Tampere University Press, 2012.

Newell, Jay, Charles T. Salmon, and Susan Chang. "The Hidden History of Product Placement." *Journal of Broadcasting & Electronic Media* 50, no. 4 (2006): 575–594.

Nilus, S.[ergei]. *Förlåten faller... Det tillkommande världssjälvhärskardömet enligt "Sions vises hemliga protokoll."* Översättning från det ryska originalets fjärde upplaga av S. Helsingfors: Enskilt förlag, 1919.

Nilsson, Mikael. *The Battle for Hearts and Minds in the High North.* New York: Brill, 2016.

Nolan, Mary. "America in the German imaginations." In *Transactions, Transgressions, Transformations: American Culture in Western Europe and Japan,* edited by Heide Ferenbach and Uta G. Poiger, 3–25. New York: Bergham Books, 2000.

Nord, Lars, "Comparing Nordic Media Systems: North between West and East?" *Central European Journal of Communication* 1, no. 1 (2008): 95–110.

Nordenstam, Anna, ed. *Nya Röster: Svenska kvinnotidskrifter under 150 år.* Möklinta: Gidlunds förlag, 2021.

Nygaard, Bertel. "Mediating Rock and Roll: Tommy Steele in Denmark, 1957-8." *Cultural History* 11 no. 1, (2022): 27–48.

Oates, Sarah. "Russian Media in the Digital Age: Propaganda Rewired." *Russian Politics*, 1, no. 4 (2016): 398–417.

O'Dell, Tom. *Culture Unbound. Americanization and Everyday Life in Sweden.* Lund: Nordic Academic Press, 1997.

Offen, Karen. *European Feminisms, 1700–1950: A Political History.* Stanford: Stanford University Press, 2000.

Ohtonen, Tanja. *Oikeuden, laillisuuden ja ihmisyyden hengessä: Suomalainen naisliitto vuosina 1907–1939.* Helsinki: Suomalainen naisliitto, 2007.

Olcott, Jocelyn. "Empires of Information: Media Strategies for the 1975 International Women's Year." *Journal of Women's History* 24 no. 4 (Winter 2012): 24–48.

Ollila, Anne, "Women's voluntary associations in Finland during the 1920s and 1930s." *Scandinavian Journal of History* 20, no. 2 (1995), 97–107.

Ollila, Anne. *Suomen kotien päivä valkenee... Marttajärjestö suomalaisessa yhteiskunnassa vuoteen 1939.* Helsinki: Suomen Historiallinen Seura, 1993.

Olsson, Pia. *Eteen vapahan valkean Suomen.* Helsinki: Suomen muinais-muistoyhdistys, 1999.

Orlov, Janina. "'Var glad som sparven kvittrar' – barnlitteraturen." In *Finlands svenska litteraturhistoria*, edited by Johan Wrede, 339–350. Helsingfors: Svenska Litteratursällskapet i Finland, 1999.

Östberg, Kjell. "Sweden and the long '1968': Break or Continuity? *Scandinavian Journal of History* 33 (2008: 4), 339–352.

Ousidhoum, Nedjma, Zizheng Lin, Hongming Zhang, Yangqiu Song, and Dit-Yan Yeung. "Multilingual and multi-aspect hate speech analysis." *arXiv preprint arXiv:1908.11049.*

Outshoorn, Joyce, and Johanna Kantola. *Changing State Feminism.* Basingstoke and New York: Palgrave Macmillan, 2007.

Paqvalén, Rita. *Queera minnen. Essäer om tystnad, längtan och motstånd.* Helsingfors: Schildts & Söderströms, 2021.

Parekh Bhikhu. "Is There a Case for Banning Hate Speech?" In *The Content and Concept of Hate Speech: Rethinking Regulation and Responses*, edited by Michael Herz and Peter Molnar. 37–56. New York: Cambridge University Press, 2012.

Parsons, Wayne. *The power of the financial press. Journalism and economic opinion in Britain and America.* Cheltenham: Edward Elgar, 1989.

Pasti, Svetlana, Mikhail Chernysh, and Luiza Svitich. "Russian Journalist and Their Profession." In *The Global Journalist in the 21st Century*, edited by David H. Weaver and Lars Willnat, 267–268. New York and Abingdon: Routledge, 2012.

Railo, Erkka and Paavo Oinonen, eds. *Media historiassa.* Turku: Turun Historiallinen Yhdistys ry., 2012.

Railo, Erkka. "Women's Magazines, the Female Body, and Political Participation." *NORA: Nordic Journal of Women's Studies* 22, no. 1 (2014): 48–62.

Rainio-Niemi, Johanna. *The Ideological Cold War: The Politics of Neutrality in Austria and Finland* London and New York: Routledge, 2014.

Ranstorp, Magnus, Filip Ahlin, and Magnus Normark. "Nordiska motstånds-rörelsen – den samlande kraften inom den nationalsocialistiska miljön i Norden." In *Från Nordiska motståndsrörelsen till alternativhögern: En studie om den svenska radikalnationalistiska miljön*, edited by Magnus Ranstorp and Filip Ahlin, 146–238. Stockholm: Försvarshögskolan, 2020.

Räsänen, Joona. *Liberaalin dilemma: Monikulttuurisuus ja vapaa yhteiskunta.* Helsinki: Suomen Perusta, 2015.

Raundalen, Jon. "The End of the World Revisited: Nuclear War Films and their Reception in Norwegian Media." In *The Nordic Media and the Cold War*, edited by Henrik G. Bastiansen and Rolf Werenksjold, 347–364. Gothenburg: Nordicom, 2015.

Rehmann, Jan. *Theories of Ideology. The Powers of Alienation and Subjection.* Leiden: Brill, 2013.

Richter, Melvin and Michaela Richter. "Introduction: Translation of Reinhart Koselleck's Krise. In Geschichtliche Grundbegriffe." *Journal of the History of Ideas*, no. 67, 2006.

Ridenhour, Michael, Arunkumar Bagavathi, Elaheh Raisi, and Siddharth Krishnan. "Detecting Online Hate Speech: Approaches Using Weak Supervision and Network Embedding Models." In *Social, Cultural, and Behavioral Modeling*, edited by Robert Thomson, Halil Bisgin, Christopher Dancy, Ayaz Hyder, and Muhammad Hussain, 202–212. Cham, Switzerland: Springer, 2020.

Ritchie, Rachel, Sue Hawkins, Nicola Phillips, and Jay S. Kleinberg. "Introduction." In *Women in Magazines: Research, Representation, Production and Consumption*, edited by Rachel Ritchie, Sue Hawkins, Nicola Phillips, and Jay S. Kleinberg, 1–22. London: Routledge, 2016.

Roberts, Mary Louise. *Civilization without Sexes: Reconstructing Gender in Postwar France, 1917–1927.* Chicago: The University of Chicago Press, 1994.

Rosa, Hartmut. *Acceleration, modernitet och identitet: tre essäer.* Göteborg: Daidalos, 2014.

Roseneil, Sasha. "The Global Common: The Global, Local and Personal; Dynamics of the Women's Peace Movement of the 1980s." In *The Limits of Globalization*, edited by Alan Scott, 55–71. Second edition London and New York: Routledge, 2003.

Rosengren, Emma. *Gendering Nuclear Disarmament: Identity and Disarmament in Sweden during the Cold War.* Stockholm: Stockholm University, 2020.

Ross, Kristin. *Fast Cars, Clean Bodies: Decolonization and the Reordering of French Culture.* Cambridge: The MIT Press, 1997.

Rutherford, Paul. *The New Icons? The Art of Television Advertising.* Toronto: Toronto University Press, 1994.

Rønlev, Rasmus. "Aktivistisk journalistik med måde: Når journalister hyldes for at tilskrive sociale bevægelser retorisk handlekraft." *Rhetorica Scandinavica* 27, no. 86 (2023): 122–140.

Saarela, Tauno. *Suomalainen kommunismi ja vallankumous 1923–1930.* Helsinki: Suomen Kirjallisuuden Seura, 2008.

Saarenmaa, Laura. "Interviewing the Enemy and Other Cold War Players: US Foreign Policy as Seen Through Playboy During the Reagan Years." In *Media and the Cold War in the 1980s: Between Star Wars and Glasnost*, edited by Henrik G. Bastiansen, Martin Klimke, and Rolf Werenskjold, 45–62. Cham: Palgrave Macmillan, 2019.

Saarenmaa, Laura. "Political Nonconformity in Finnish Men's Magazines during the Cold War." In *The Nordic Media and the Cold War*, edited by Henrik G. Bastiansen and Rolf Werenskjold, 101–114. Gothenburg: Nordicon, 2015.

Saarimäki, Pasi. "Bourgeois Women and The Question of Divorce in Finland in The Late 19th and Early 20th Centuries." *Scandinavian Journal of History* 43, no. 1 (2018), 64–90.

Saksholm, Juho. *Reform, Revolution, Riot? Transnational Nordic Sixties in the Radical Press, c. 1958–1968*. Jyväskylä: University of Jyväskylä, 2020, http://urn.fi/URN:ISBN:978-951-39-8374-1

Salmi, Hannu, Jukka Sarjala, and Heli Rantala. "Embryonic Modernity: Infectious Dynamics in Early Nineteenth-Century Finnish Culture." *International Journal for History, Culture and Modernity* 8, no. 2 (2020): 105–127.

Salmi, Hannu. *What is Digital History?* Cambridge and Medford: Polity Press, 2021.

Salokangas, Raimo. "The Finnish Broadcasting Company and the Changing Finnish Society, 1949–1966." In *Yleisradio 1926–1996: A History of Broadcasting in Finland*, edited by Rauno Endén, 107–228. Helsinki: SKS 1996.

Salokangas, Raimo. "The Shadow of the Bear: Finnish Broadcasting, National Interest and Self-censorship during the Cold War." In *Nordic Media and the Cold War*, edited by Henrik G. Bastiansen and Rolf Werenksjold, 67–82. Gothenburg: Nordicom, 2015.

Salokangas, Raimo. "Mediahistorian tutkimuskohdetta etsimässä. Aatehistorian materiaalista kohti viestintähistoriaa." *Historiallinen aikakauskirja* 103, no. 4 (2005): 483–492.

Salokangas, Raimo. "Puoluepolitiikkaa ja uutisjournalismia muuttuvilla lehtimarkkinoilla." In *Sanomalehdistö suurlakosta talvisotaan*, Suomen lehdistön historia, 2, 169–443. Kuopio: Kustannuskiila, 1987.

Salokangas, Raimo. "Tekstit, kontekstit ja poikittaiskatse mediahistorian kohtauspaikalla." In *Media historiassa*, edited by Erkka Railo and Paavo Oinonen, 25–46. Historia Mirabilis 9. Turku: Turun historiallinen yhdistys ry 2012.

Salomon, Kim. "The Peace Movement – An Anti-Establishment Movement." *Journal of Peace Research* 23, no. 2 (1986): 115–127.

Samuel, Lawrence R. *Brought to You By: Postwar Television and the American Dream*. Austin: University of Texas Press, 2001.

Samuelsson, Lina. "Dagny. En tidskrift för den nya dagens kvinna." In *Nya Röster: Svenska kvinnotidskrifter under 150 år*, edited by Anna Nordenstam, 19–27. Möklinta: Gidlunds förlag, 2021.

Schmitz, Eva. "Den nya kvinnorörelsens uppkomst i Sverige från 1968." In *Kvinnorörelsen och '68: aspekter och vittnesbörd*, edited by Elisabeth Elgán, 4–48. Huddinge: Samtidshistoriska institutet, 2001.

Scholz, Sally J., *Political Solidarity*. University Park. Pa.: Penn State University Press, 2008.

Schudson, Michael. *Advertising, the Uneasy Persuasion: Its Dubious Impact on American Society.* New York: Basic Books, 1984.

Schulz, Kristina. "The Women's Movement." In *1968 in Europe: A History of Protest and Activism, 1956–1977*, edited by Martin Klimke and Joachim Scharloth, 281–293. Basingstoke: Palgrave MacMillan, 2008.

Schwarzmantel, John. *The Age of Ideology. Political ideologies from the American Revolution to Post-Modern Times.* Basingstoke: Palgrave Macmillan, 1998.

Senghaas, Dieter. *The European Experience. A Historical Critique of Development Theory.* Leamington Spa/Dover, New Hampshire: Berg Publishers, 1985.

Severinsson, Emma. *Moderna kvinnor: Modernitet, femininitet och svenskhet i svensk veckopress 1920–1933.* Lund: Historiska institutionen, Lunds universitet, 2018.

Shaw, Eric H. and Alan Stuart. "Cigarettes." In *The Advertising Age: Encyclopedia of Advertising. Vol 1*, edited by John McDonough and Karen Egolf, 310–318. New York, London: Fitzroy Dearborn, 2003.

Shaw, Tony. *Hollywood's Cold War.* Edinburgh: Edinburgh University Press, 2007.

Shah, Dhavan V., Douglas M. McLeod, Melissa R. Gotlieb, and Nam-Jin Lee. "Framing and Agenda Setting." In *The Sage Handbook of Media Processes and Effects*, edited by Robin L. Nabi and Mary Beth Oliver, 83–98. London: Sage, 2009.

Shevelow, Kathryn. *Women and Print Culture. The Construction of Femininity in the Early Periodical.* London: Routledge, 1989.

Siebert, Fred, Theodore Peterson, and Wilbur Schramm. *Four Theories of the Press. The Authoritarian, Libertarian, Social Responsibility and Soviet Communist Concepts of What the Press Should be and do.* Urbana: University of Illinois Press, 1956.

Siltala, Juha. *Lapuan liike ja kyyditykset 1930.* Helsingissä: Otava,1985.

Silvennoinen, Oula, Marko Tikka, and Aapo Roselius. 2016. *Suomalaiset fasistit: Mustan sarastuksen airuet.* Helsinki: WSOY, 2016.

Simpson, Christopher, eds. *Universities and Empire. Money and Politics in the Social Sciences during the Cold War.* New York: The New Press, 1998.

Skarsbø Lindtner, Synnøve . "Over disk som varmt hvetebrød – *Sirene* og den norske populærfeminismen." In *Da det personlige ble politisk. Den nye kvinne- og mannsbevegelsen på 1970-tallet*, edited by Hilde Danielsen, 103–151. Oslo: Scandinavian Academic Press, 2013.

Skogerbø, Eli. "The Press Subsidy System in Norway: Controversial Past – Unpredictable Future?" *Europepan Journal of Communication* 12, no. 1 (1999): 99–118.

Skovsgaard, Morten, Erik Albæk, Peter Bro, and Claes de Vreese. "Media Professionals or Organizational Marionettes? Professional Values and Constraints of Danish Journalists." In *The Global Journalist in the 21st Century*, edited by David H. Weaver and Lars Willnat. New York and Abingdon: Routledge, 2012.

Soland, Birgitte. *Becoming modern: Young Women and the Reconstruction of Womanhood in the 1920s.* Princeton: Princeton University Press, 2000.

Sorensen, Nils Arne and Klaus Petersen. "Ameri-Dames and Pro-American Anti-Americanism in Denmark after 1945." In *The Americanization of Europe.*

*Culture, Diplomacy, and Anti-Americanism after 1945*, edited by Alexander Stephan, 115–146. New York and Oxford: Berghahn Books 2007.

Sovey, Mark and Hamilton Cravens, eds. *Cold War Social Science. Knowledge Production, Liberal Democracy, and Human Nature*. New York: Palgrave Macmillan, 2012.

Stål, Margareta. "För quinnans framåtskridande.' Idun – de första 25 åren." In *Nya Röster: Svenska kvinnotidskrifter under 150 år*, edited by Anna Nordenstam, 89–106. Möklinta: Gidlunds förlag, 2021.

Stål, Margareta. "Kvinnorna i det offentliga samtalet. Om hur pennskaften blev reportrar." *Kvinnovetenskaplig tidskrift* 24, no. 2 (2003): 69–79.

Stark, Laura. "Sanomalehtien maaseutukirjeet. Itseilmaisun into ja lehdistön portinvartijat. " In *Kynällä kyntäjät. Kansan kirjallistuminen 1800-luvun Suomessa*, edited by Laitinen Lea and Kati Mikkola. Helsinki: SKS, 2013.

Stark, Laura. "Toimittajien ja itseoppineiden maaseutukirjeenvaihtajien suhde osana suomenkielisen lehdistön nousua 1847–1865." *Historiallinen Aikakauskirja* (1/2013): 28– 42.

Stark, Laura. *The Limits of Patriarchy. How Female Networks of Pilfering and Gossip Sparked the First Debates on Rural Gender Rights in the 19th-Century Finnish-Language Press*. Helsinki: SKS, 2011.

*Statistik årsbok för Sverige, år 2000*. Stockholm: Statistiska centralbyrån, 2001.

Steene, Birgitta. "The Swedish Image of America." In *Images of America in Scandinavia*, edited by Poul Houe and Sven Hakon Rossel, 145–191. Amsterdam: Atlanta, 1998.

Ştefăniţă, Oana, and Diana-Maria Buf. "Hate Speech in Social Media and Its Effects on the LGBT Community: A Review of the Current Research." *Romanian Journal of Communication and Public Relations 23*, no. 1 (2021): 47–55.

Steiner, Linda. "Nineteenth-Century Suffrage Journals. Inventing and Defending New Women." In *Front Pages, Front Lines: Media and the Fight for Women's Suffrage*, edited by Linda Steiner, Carolyn Kitch, and Brooke Kroeger, 42–60. Urbana, Chicago: Illinois University Press, 2020.

Steinmetz, Willibald, and Freeden, Michael. "Introduction." In *Conceptual History in the European Space*, edited by Willibald Steinmetz, Michael Freeden and Javier Fernández-Sebastián. New York: Berghahn Books, 2017.

Stenberg, Lisbeth. "En 'lifsmakt för kvinnan' – Toini Topelius, Alexandra Gripenberg och Maria Cedeschiöld." In *Den kvinnliga tvåsamhetens frirum. Kvinnopar i kvinnorörelsen 1890–1960*, edited by Eva Borgström, and Hanna Markusson Winkvist, 95–103. Stockholm: Appell förlag, 2018.

Stenberg, Lisbeth. "Tidskriften Framåt. Två åsiktsriktningar möts i unika debatter." In *Nya Röster: Svenska kvinnotidskrifter under 150 år*, edited by Anna Nordenstam, 49–67. Möklinta: Gidlunds förlag, 2021.

Steorn, Patrick. "Konstnärligt antimode. Svensk Reformdräkt kring sekelsskiftet 1900." In *Mode – en introduktion. En tvärvetenskaplig betraktelse*, edited by Dirk Gindt and Louise Wallenberg, 225–249. Stockholm: Raster Förlag, 2009.

Stephan, Alexander. *The Americanization of Europe. Culture, Diplomacy, and Anti-Americanism after 1945*. New York: Berghahn Books, 2006.

Stevenson, Nick. *Understanding Media Cultures. Social Theory and Mass Communication* London: Sage 1995.

Stjernø, Steinar. *Solidarity in Europe: The History of an Idea.* Cambridge: Cambridge University Press, 2005.

Stones, Sharon D. "The Peace Movement and Toronto Newspapers." *Canadian Journal of Communication* 14, no. 1 (1989): 57–69.

Strath, Bo. "Neutralitet som självförstålse." In *Den svenska framgångssagan?*, edited by Kurt Almqvist, and Kaj Glans. Stockholm: Bokforlaget Fisher, 2001.

Strauss, Jonathan. "The Australian Nuclear Disarmament Movement in the 1980s." In *Issues on War & Peace: Proceedings of the 14th Biennial Labour History Conference*, edited by Phillip Deery, and Julie Kimber, 39–50. Melbourne: Australian Society for the Study of Labour History, 2015.

Strömbäck, Jesper, Lars Nord, and Adam Shehata. "Swedish Journalists: Between Professionalization and Commersialization." In David H. Weaver & Lars Willnat (eds.) *The Global Journalist in the 21st Century.* New York and Abingdon: Routledge, 2012.

Styrkársdóttir, Auður. "From Social movement to political party: the new women's movement in Iceland." In *The New Women's Movement: Feminism and Political Power in Europe and the USA*, edited by Drude Dahlerup, 141–157. London: Sage, 1986.

Sulkunen, Irma. *Naisen kutsumus. Miina Sillanpää ja sukupuolten maailmojen erkaantuminen.* Helsinki: Hanki ja jää, 1989.

Sulkunen, Irma. *Suomalaisen Kirjallisuuden Seura 1831–1892.* Helsinki: SKS, 2004.

Sulkunen, Irma. "Suffrage, Nation and Citizenship – The Finnish Case in an International Context." In *Suffrage, Gender and Citizenship: International Perspectives on Parliamentary Reforms*, edited by Irma Sulkunen, Seija-Leena Nevala-Nurmi, and Pirjo Markkola, 83–105. Newcastle upon Tyne: Cambridge Scholars Publishing, 2009.

Suolahti, Gunnar. *Y. S. Yrjö-Koskisen elämä. 1, Nuori Yrjö Koskinen.* Otava: Helsinki, 1974.

Sysiharju, Anna-Liisa. "Gebhard, Hedvig (1867–1961)." In *Kansallisbiografia. Studia Biographica 4.* Helsinki: Suomalaisen Kirjallisuuden Seura, 2007. Accessed February 26, 2016. http://urn.fi/urn:nbn:fi:sks-kbg-004644

Syvertsen, Trine, Gunn Enli, Ole J. Mjøs, and Hallvard Moe. *The Media Welfare State: Nordic Media In The Digital Era.* Michigan: University of Michigan Press, 2014.

Taylor, Anthea. *Celebrity and the Feminist Blockbuster.* London: Palgrave Macmillan, 2016.

Teperi, Jouko. *Vanhan Suomen suomalaisuusliike I: kehityspiirteitä ja edustajia 1830-luvulta 1850-luvun alkuun.* Helsinki: Suomen Historiallinen Seura, 1965.

Thelin, Bengt. "Early tendencies of peace education in Sweden." *Peabody Journal of Education* 71, no. 3 (1996): 95–110.

Thompson, John B. *Ideology and Modern Culture. Critical Social Theory in the Era of Mass Communication.* Cambridge: Polity Press, 1990.

Thompson, John B. *The Media and Modernity: A Social Theory of the Media.* Cambridge: Polity Press, 1995.

Thörn, Håkan. "Nya sociala rörelser, globalisering och den sociologiska eurocentrismen." *Sociologisk Forskning,* no. 2 (2003): 3–9.

Thorslund, Tove. *Do You Have a TV? Negotiating Swedish Public Service through 1950s Programming, "Americanization," and Domesticity.* Stockholm: Stockholm University, 2018.

Tommila, Päiviö. "Yhdestä lehdestä sanomalehdistöksi 1809–1859." In *Suomen lehdistön historia 1. Sanomalehdistön vaiheet vuoteen 1905,* edited by Tommila, Päiviö Lars Landgren and Pirkko Leino-Kaukiainen, 77–266. Kuopio: Kustannuskiila, 1988.

Tommila, Päiviö. *Suomen lehdistön levikki ennen vuotta 1860.* Helsinki: WSOY, 1963.

Töyry, Maija. "Gender Contract and Localization in Early Women's Magazines in Finland Since 1782." *Media History* 22, no. 1 (2016): 13–26.

Töyry, Maija. *Varhaiset naistenlehdet ja naisten elämän ristiriidat. Neuvotteluja lukijasopimuksesta.* Helsinki: Helsingin yliopisto, 2005.

Trappel, Josef, and Hannu Nieminen. "Media and Democracy: A Couple Walking Hand in Hand?" In *Comparative Media Policy, Regulation and Governance in Europe,* edited by Leen d'Haenens, Helena Sousa and Josef Trappel, 187–206. Bristol: Intellect, 2018.

Turunen, Arja. "Naistenlehdet Suomessa 1880-luvulta 1930-luvulle." *Media ja viestintä* 37, no. 2 (2014): 38–56.

Turunen, Arja. "Nykyaikaista naista luomassa. Kotilieden, Emäntälehden ja Toverittaren pukeutumisohjeet kansalaiskasvatuksena 1920–1930-luvuilla." *Kasvatus ja Aika* 13, no. 4 (2019), 4–25.

Turunen, Arja. "Kapinaa ja ahtaita raameja: Suomalaisten feministien muistoja 1970- ja 1980-lukujen yhteiskunnallisesta toimintakulttuurista." *Sukupuoolentutkimus– Genusforskning* 31, no.3 (2018): 37–50.

Turunen, Arja. *Hame, housut, hamehousut! Vai mikä on tulevaisuutemme? Naisten päällyshousujen käyttöä koskevat pukeutumisohjeet ja niissä rakentuvat naiseuden ihanteet suomalaisissa naistenlehdissä 1889–1945.* Helsinki: Suomen muinaismuistoyhdistys, 2011.

Tuulio, Tyyni. *Aleksandra Gripenberg: Kirjailija, taistelija, ihminen.* Porvoo, Helsinki: Werner Söderström Osakeyhtiö, 1959.

Ulvros, Eva Helen. "Sophie Elkan och Selma Lagerlöf – kärlek och kvinnorörelse." In *Den kvinnliga tvåsamhetens frirum. Kvinnopar i kvinnorörelsen 1890–1960,* edited by Eva Borgström, and Hanna Markusson Winkvist, 33–75. Stockholm: Appell förlag, 2018.

Uusitalo, Kari. "Suomalainen elokuvatuotanto 1948–1952. Taustaa ja tosiasioita." In *Suomen kansallisfilmografia 1948–1952, osa 4,* chief edited by Kari Uusitalo, 19–31. Helsinki: Edita & Suomen elokuva-arkisto, 1992.

Van Sas, Nicolaas. "The Netherlands, 1750–1813." In *Press, Politics and the Public Sphere in Europe and North America, 1760–1820,* edited by Hannah Barker and Simon Burrows, 48–68. Cambridge: Cambridge University Press, 2004.

Vares, Vesa and Uino, Ari. *Suomalaiskansallinen Kokoomus. Kansallisen Kokoomuspuolueen historia 1929–1944.* Helsinki: Edita, 2007.

Vehkalahti, Kaisa. "Jazz-tyttö ja naistenlehtien siveä katse." In *Modernin lumo ja pelko. Kymmenen kirjoitusta 1800–1900-lukujen vaihteen sukupuolisuudesta,* edited by Kari Immonen, Ritva Hapuli, Maarit Leskelä, and Kaisa Vehkalahti. Helsinki: Suomalaisen Kirjallisuuden Seura, 2000.

Verkuyten, Maykel. "Discourses about ethnic group (de-)essentialism: Oppressive and progressive aspects." *British Journal of Social Psychology* 42, no. 3 (2003): 371–391.

Virtanen, Anna-Maija. "Gobineaun rotuoppi ja germaanien ihannointi." In *Mongoleja vai germaaneja? – rotuteorioiden suomalaiset,* edited by Hietala, Marjatta, Aira Kemiläinen and Pekka Suvanto, 53–68. Helsinki: SHS, 1985.

Vowinckel, Annette, Marcus Payk, and Thomas Lindenberger. "European Cold War Culture(s)? An Introduction." In *Cold War Cultures: Perspectives on Eastern and Western European Societies,* edited by Annette Vowinckel et al., 1–22. New York: Berghahn Books, 2012.

Vuorinen, Marja, ed. *Vihapuheen, viholliskuvien ja disinformaation historiaa: Vallan ja vastarinnan välineitä.* Turku: Turun Historiallinen Yhdistys, 2021.

Wagnleitner, Reinhold. *Coca-Colonization and the Cold War. The Cultural Mission of the United States in Austria after the Second War.* Translated by Diana M. Wolf. Chapel Hill & London: The University of North Carolina Press, 1994.

Wärenstam, Eric. *Fascismen och nazismen i Sverige.* Stockholm: Almqvist & Wiksell, 1972.

Warner, Michael. *Publics and Counterpublics.* New York: Zone Books, 2002.

Warren, Michelle R. "Introduction: Relating philology, practicing humanism." *PMLA/Publications of the Modern Language Association of America* 125, no. 2 (2010): 283–288.

Werenskjold, Rolf. *That's The Way It Is? Medienes rolle i proteståret 1968.* PhD thesis in media studies, University of Oslo, 2011.

Westerståhl, Jörgen, and Folke Johansson, "News Ideologies as Moulders of Domestic News." *European Journal of Communication* 1, no. 2 (1986): 133–149.

Wikander, Ulla, Alice Kessler-Harris, and Jane Lewis ed. *Protecting Women. Labor Legislation in Europe, the United States, and Australia, 1880–1920.* Urbana, Chicago: University of Illinois Press, 1995.

Williamson, Judith. *Decoding Advertisements. Ideology and Meaning in Advertisements.* London: Boyers, 1998 (1978).

Withers, D. M. "Enterprising Women: Independence, Finance and Virago Press, c.1976–93." *Twentieth Century British History* 31 no. 4 (2019): 1–24.

Witt-Brattström, Ebba. *Å alla kära systrar!: historien om mitt sjuttiotalet.* Stockholm: Nordstedt, 2010.

Wittner, Lawrence S. "The Forgotten Years of the World Nuclear Disarmament Movement, 1975–78." *Journal of Peace Research* 40, no. 4 (2003): 435–456.

Wonders, Bec. "Mapping second wave feminist periodicals: Networks of conflict and counterpublics, 1970–1990." *Arts Libraries Journal* 45 no. 3 (2020): 106–113.

Yoken, Hannah. "Nordic Transnational Feminist Activism: The New Women's Movements in Finland, Sweden and Denmark, 1960s–1990s." PhD diss., University of Glasgow, 2020.

Yoken, Hannah. "Transnational Transfers and Mainstream Mappings: Women's Liberation Calendars of the 1970s and 1980s." In *Translating Feminism: Interdisciplinary Approaches to Text, Place and Agency (1945–2000),* edited by

Maud Bracke, Julia C. Bullock, Penelope Morris, and Kristina Schulz, 117–146. Cham: Palgrave, 2021.

Zilliacus-Tikkanen, Henrika. *När Könet började skriva. Kvinnor i finländsk press 1771–1900*. Helsingfors: Finska Vetenskaps-Societeten, 2005.

Öhman, Anton. "Peace Actions and Mainstream Media: Framing Nuclear Disarmament Protests in Welfare Sweden." In *Social Movements in 1980s Sweden*, edited by Helena Hill, and Andrés Brink Pinto, 165–181. Cham: Palgrave Macmillan, 2023.

# List of contributors

**Jukka Kortti.** Dr. Jukka Kortti is a social science historian, who has made several comprehensive studies on media history and intellectual history. As a media historian he has published textbooks and theoretical articles and studied the history of television, advertising, journalism and documentary film. As a social historian, he has been interested in intellectual history, historical culture, university history, culture and student activism, the history of everyday life, the history of consumption and modernization processes. Currently, he directs two research projects at University of Helsinki. He is the chair of Nordic Media History Network (NOMEH).

**Heidi Kurvinen.** Dr. Heidi Kurvinen is a media historian who has specialized in the gendered history of professional journalism in the Nordic region as well as the encounters between social movements and mainstream media. Currently, she works as a Collegium Researcher at the Turku Institute for Advanced Studies (TIAS) in University of Turku, Finland. She is the secretary of Nordic Media History Network (NOMEH).

**Heikki Kokko.** Dr. Heikki Kokko is a Senior Research Fellow at the Tampere University, Finland. His research has focused on history of society in 19th century Finland and theory and methodology of history of experiences.

**Ari Haasio.** PhD (information sciences), MA (history) Ari Haasio is a Principal Lecturer at the Seinäjoki University of Applied Sciences, Finland. His main research interests are internet crimes, hate speech, information behavior and social history.

**Markku Mattila.** Dr. Markku Mattila is senior research fellow at the Migration Institute of Finland (Seinäjoki Unit). His research has focused on Social History, History of Science and Ideas, and Migration (and related topics).

**Karin Jonsson.** Dr. Karin Jonsson is a historian and senior lecturer at Historical and Contemporary Studies at Södertörn University, Sweden. Her research has focused on the conceptual history of the labor movement in Sweden and Germany with special attention given to the concepts of revolution and solidarity.

**Tiina Kinnunen.** Tiina Kinnunen works as a Professor of Finnish and Northern European History at the University of Oulu, Finland. Her research focuses on the history of feminisms, social and cultural history of war, as well as history cultures and the history of historiography.

**Arja Turunen.** Dr. Arja Turunen is a senior research fellow in the University of Jyväskylä. Her research has focused on history of women's magazines, history of dress and history of feminist activism.

**Hannah Yoken.** Dr. Hannah Kaarina Yoken is an Academy of Finland postdoctoral researcher at the University of Jyväskylä, Finland. Her research focuses on gender history and the history of emotions in the Nordic countries, especially Finland.

**Birgitte Kjos Fonn.** Birgitte Kjos Fonn is a Professor of Journalism at the Department of Journalism and Media Studies at the Oslo Metropolitan University, Norway. Her research has among other things focused on media history and economic journalism.

# Index

Milton Keynes UK
Ingram Content Group UK Ltd.
UKHW052218140424
440909UK00011B/62/J